Blockchain Applications in Cybersecurity Solutions

Edited By

R. Agrawal
Faculty of Computer Applications
Manav Rachna International Institute of Research and Studies
Faridabad
India

&

N. Gupta
Faculty of Computer Applications
Manav Rachna International Institute of Research and Studies
Faridabad
India

Blockchain Applications in Cybersecurity Solutions

Editors: R.Agrawal and N.Gupta

ISBN (Online): 978-981-5080-59-9

ISBN (Print): 978-981-5080-60-5

ISBN (Paperback): 978-981-5080-61-2

First published in 2023.

need for a court order if at any point you breach any terms of this License Agreement. In no event will any delay or failure by Bentham Science Publishers in enforcing your compliance with this License Agreement constitute a waiver of any of its rights.

3. You acknowledge that you have read this License Agreement, and agree to be bound by its terms and conditions. To the extent that any other terms and conditions presented on any website of Bentham Science Publishers conflict with, or are inconsistent with, the terms and conditions set out in this License Agreement, you acknowledge that the terms and conditions set out in this License Agreement shall prevail.

Bentham Science Publishers Pte. Ltd.
80 Robinson Road #02-00
Singapore 068898
Singapore
Email: subscriptions@benthamscience.net

BENTHAM SCIENCE

CONTENTS

FOREWORD i

PREFACE ii

LIST OF CONTRIBUTORS v

CHAPTER 1 INTRODUCTION TO BLOCKCHAIN TECHNOLOGY 1
N. Devi, P.L. Rani and *A.R.G. Gokul*
INTRODUCTION 1
Block 2
Distributed Ledger 5
Smart Contract 5
Blockchain Protocol Stack 6
Tamper Resistant 7
CONSENSUS PROTOCOL 8
Proof of Work (PoW) 9
Proof of Stake (PoS) 10
Delegated Proof of Stake (DPoS) 10
Practical Byzantine Fault Tolerance (pBFT) 10
Proof-of-Burn (PoB) 11
Proof of Elapsed Time (PoET) 12
Proof of Identity (PoId) 12
Proof of Authority (PoAu) 12
IMPLEMENTATION OF BLOCKCHAIN 12
Creation of new Block 13
Generation of Blockchain 14
Testing 15
Verify the Integrity of the Blockchain 15
Implementation of proof-of-work 16
CHALLENGES IN BLOCKCHAIN TECHNOLOGY 19
Scalability 19
Network Interoperability 19
Consumption of Energy 20
Talent Deficit 20
Standardization 20
Cross Chain Technology 20
Blockchain Consequences 20
RESEARCH PERSPECTIVES 22
CONCLUSION 22
CONSENT FOR PUBLICATION 22
CONFLICT OF INTEREST 23
ACKNOWLEDGEMENT 23
REFERENCES 23

CHAPTER 2 CYBERSECURITY AND BLOCKCHAIN 26
H. Saini and *V. Garg*
INTRODUCTION 26
BLOCKCHAIN TECHNOLOGY IS SECURE OR NOT? 29
ROLE OF BLOCKCHAIN IN CYBERSECURITY 33
INDUSTRIES USING BLOCKCHAIN IN CYBERSECURITY 34
How Crypto Currencies Using Blockchain in Cyber Security 34

Mobilecoin ... 35
Coinbase ... 35
Javvy ... 35
How Healthcare Industries using Blockchain in Cybersecurity ... 35
How the Government Using Blockchain in Cybersecurity? ... 36
How Military and Defense Using Blockchain in Cybersecurity ... 37
How Banking Systems Use Blockchain in Cybersecurity ... 37
FUTURE BENEFITS OF BLOCKCHAIN TO STRENGTHEN CYBERSECURITY ... 38
IoT (Internet of Things) Security ... 38
Cyber-Physical Infrastructure's Verification ... 38
Reducing Human Safety Adversity by Cyber-Attacks ... 38
The Origin of Computer Software ... 39
Private Message Security ... 39
Securing Domain Name System (DNS) and Distributed Denial of Services (DDoS) ... 39
Medium Storage Decentralization ... 40
Data Transfer Protection ... 40
MAJOR PROS AND CONS OF BLOCKCHAIN FOR CYBERSECURITY ... 40
ADVANTAGES AND DISADVANTAGES OF BLOCKCHAIN ... 41
Advantages of Blockchain ... 42
Disadvantages of Blockchain ... 43
CHALLENGES WITH BLOCKCHAIN ... 43
Regulations ... 43
Privacy of Data ... 43
Interoperability ... 44
Scalability ... 44
Risks Associated with Technology ... 44
CONCLUSION ... 45
CONSENT FOR PUBLICATION ... 45
CONFLICT OF INTEREST ... 45
ACKNOWLEDGEMENTS ... 45
REFERENCES ... 46

CHAPTER 3 APPLICATIONS OF BLOCKCHAIN IN CYBER SECURITY INDUSTRY ... 48
N. Gupta and *R. Agrawal*
INTRODUCTION ... 48
Objectives of the Study ... 49
Research Methodology ... 49
ROLE OF BLOCKCHAIN IN CYBER SECURITY ... 49
ELIMINATING HUMAN FACTOR FROM AUTHENTICATION ... 50
Decentralized Storage ... 50
Traceability ... 50
HOW DOES BLOCKCHAIN PROVIDE CYBER SECURITY? ... 52
USES OF BLOCKCHAIN TECHNOLOGY IN CYBER SECURITY ... 54
FUTURE OF BLOCKCHAIN TECHNOLOGY: PREDICTIONS FOR 2030 ... 56
Blockchain will be Leveraged for a Majority of the World Trade ... 56
Frictionless Flows And Digital Assets ... 57
Blockchain Identity for All ... 57
Considerable Improvements in the Global Standard of Living ... 58
FINDINGS AND SUGGESTIONS ... 58
CONCLUSION ... 59
CONSENT FOR PUBLICATION ... 60

CONFLICT OF INTEREST 60
ACKNOWLEDGEMENT 60
REFERENCES 60

CHAPTER 4 OVERVIEW OF ATTACK SURFACES IN BLOCKCHAIN 62
S. Zalte, H. Bhatia, R. Deshmukh, N. Gupta and *R. Kamat*
INTRODUCTION 63
BLOCKCHAIN SECURITY ISSUES 64
Transaction Malleability 64
Network Security 65
Privacy 65
Redundancy 66
Regulatory Compliance 66
Criminal Activity 66
TAXONOMY OF ATTACK SURFACES 66
a. Blockchain Network Attacks 67
Transaction Malleability Attack 67
Timejacking 68
DDOS Attack 68
Routing Attacks 68
Sybil Attack 69
Eclipse Attacks 69
Long-range Attacks 69
b. User Wallet Attacks 70
Phishing 70
Dictionary Attacks 70
Vulnerable Signatures 70
Flawed Key Generation 71
Attacks on Cold Wallets 71
Attacks on Hot Wallets 71
c. Smart Contract Attacks 71
Vulnerabilities in Contract Source Code 72
Vulnerabilities in Virtual Machines 72
d. Transaction Verification Mechanism Attacks 73
Double Spending Attack 73
Finney Attacks 73
Race Attacks 73
Vector76 73
Alternative history attacks 74
51% or Majority Attacks 74
e. Mining Pool Attacks 75
Selfish Mining 75
Fork After Withholding 75
MEANS OF PROTECTION AGAINST CYBER ATTACK INTERFACE 75
CONCLUSION 76
CONSENT FOR PUBLICATION 77
CONFLICT OF INTEREST 77
ACKNOWLEDGEMENT 77
REFERENCES 77

CHAPTER 5 REVIEW OF ANTI-COUNTERFEIT SOLUTIONS IN BLOCKCHAIN 81
H. Bhatia, S. Zalte, I. Chatterjee and *D. Mantri*

INTRODUCTION 81
COUNTERFEIT SOLUTIONS FOR ATTACK SURFACES 82
Countermeasure against Blockchain Network Attacks 82
Countermeasures against Distributed Denial of Service Attack 82
Countermeasures against Transaction Malleability Attack- 83
Countermeasures against Timejacking 84
Countermeasures against Routing Attacks 84
Countermeasures against Sybil Attacks 84
Countermeasures against Eclipse Attacks 85
Random Node Selection: 85
Deterministic Node Selection: 85
Increased Node Connections: 85
Restrictions on New Nodes: 86
Countermeasures against Long-Range Attacks on Proof of Stake Networks 86
Defence Mechanism against User Wallet Attacks 86
Countermeasures against Phishing 86
Countermeasures against Dictionary Attacks 86
Countermeasures against Vulnerable Signatures 87
Countermeasures against Flawed key generation 87
Countermeasures against Cold Wallets and Hot Wallets Attacks 87
Mechanism against Smart Contract Attacks 88
Defense Mechanism against Transaction Verification Mechanism Attacks 88
Countermeasures against Finney Attacks 88
Countermeasures against Race Attacks 88
Countermeasures against Vector76 89
Countermeasures against Alternative History Attacks 89
Countermeasures for 51% Or Majority Attacks 89
Defense Mechanism Mining Pool Attacks 91
Countermeasures against Selfish Mining 91
Countermeasures against fork after withholding (FAW) Attack- 92
CONCLUSION 93
CONSENT FOR PUBLICATION 94
CONFLICT OF INTEREST 94
ACKNOWLEDGEMENT 94
REFERENCES 94

CHAPTER 6 PRESERVING THE PRIVACY OF WEARABLE IOT DEVICE DATA USING BLOCKCHAIN 97
K.K. Sowjanya, K.P.B. Madavi and *G. Thahniyath*
INTRODUCTION 97
IOT ARCHITECTURE 98
IOT FITBIT INTRODUCTION 99
Fitbit Architecture 100
Challenges of IoT Devices 101
INTRODUCTION TO BLOCKCHAIN 102
Characteristics of the Blockchain 102
BLOCKCHAIN ARCHITECTURE 103
Components of Blockchain 104
SECURITY USING BLOCKCHAIN 104
Authentication of IoT device 105
Verification of the sender 107

Proof of Work 107
Smart Contract 107
RELATED WORKS 108
PROPOSED METHOD 109
Chain Validation 111
RESULTS 112
CONCLUSION & FUTURE WORKS 114
CONSENT FOR PUBLICATION 114
CONFLICT OF INTEREST 114
ACKNOWLEDGEMENT 115
REFERENCES 115

CHAPTER 7 BLOCKCHAIN BASED ACCESS CONTROL SYSTEMS 117
R. Agrawal and *N. Gupta*
INTRODUCTION 117
BACKGROUND 119
BLOCKCHAIN-BASED ACCESS CONTROL FOR IOT 121
CONCLUSION & FUTURE SCOPE 124
CONSENT FOR PUBLICATION 125
CONFLICT OF INTEREST 125
ACKNOWLEDGEMENT 125
REFERENCES 125

CHAPTER 8 MULTI-CHAIN DEPLOYMENT OVER SMART CONTRACTS TO ENHANCE SECURITY 127
N. Gupta and *R. Agrawal*
INTRODUCTION 128
BLOCKCHAIN AND SMART CONTRACTS 128
Implementation Techniques for Blockchains 128
Blockchain Clients for Participants 129
Application Development Environments for Blockchains 130
Blockchains for Supply Chains with Smart Contracts 130
SECURITY ATTACKS ON SMART CONTRACTS 131
MULTI-CHAIN AND SMART CONTRACTS 132
The Objectives of Multichain 133
The Hand-Shaking Process 133
The Process of Mining in Multichain Technology 133
The efficacy of block is verifiable by performing the following: 133
How Smart Contracts in Multichain Redefine Value Exchange 134
The following are some of the advantages of smart contracts: 134
Some of the example that shows the value exchanges due to Smart contracts are given below: 135
a). Freelance Work Exchanges 135
b). Digital Rights and Intellectual Property 136
MULTIPLE BLOCKCHAIN AND SMART CONTRACTS TRANSFOR- MING CONTRACT MANAGEMENT IN RECENT TIMES 136
Blockchain and Distributed Ledger Technology 136
Through the use of smart contracts, a business will become faster and more flexible in 2020 and beyond by: 137
EtherCore: 137
A Multi-Chain Decentralized Application and Smart Contract Platform 137
EtherCore Features: 137

Fast 137
Stable 138
How Contract Vendors Benefit Forward-Thinking Organizations: 138
Tools for Smart Contract Deployment in Multichain Environment 138
b). eb3 on TestRPC 139
CONCLUSION AND FUTURE SCOPE 139
CONSENT FOR PUBLICATION 140
CONFLICT OF INTEREST 140
ACKNOWLEDGEMENT 140
REFERENCES 140

CHAPTER 9 BLOCKCHAIN FOR DECENTRALIZED SERVICES: ON IMPROVING SECURITY AND PERFORMANCE OF DISTRIBUTED IPFS-BASED WEB APPLICATIONS 142
V. Le, R. Moazeni, M. Moh, R. Agrawal and *N. Gupta*
INTRODUCTION 142
BACKGROUND AND RELATED WORK 144
Background of Blockchain Technology 144
Types of Blockchain 146
Open 146
Private 146
Smart Contracts 146
Interplanetary File System 147
Distributed Hash Table 147
RELATED WORK 147
APPLICATION DESIGN 148
IMPLEMENTATION 150
a. Encryption and Decryption 150
b. Access Control using Smart Contracts 150
c. Migration of the Application to Remote IPFS 151
Key-Value Memory Cache 151
Method Get File Node from Path 151
Method find ProvidersAsync 152
PERFORMANCE AND SECURITY ANALYSIS 154
Security Analysis 154
Performance Analysis 154
TRADEOFF BETWEEN PERFORMANCE AND SECURITY 157
CONCLUSION AND FUTURE WORK 158
DISCLOSURE 159
CONSENT FOR PUBLICATION 159
CONFLICT OF INTEREST 159
ACKNOWLEDGEMENT 159
REFERENCES 159

SUBJECT INDEX 162

FOREWORD

Currently, there is an increase in the number of social media platforms that we use, and most of them have so-called weak and unreliable passwords. During social media interactions, large quantities of metadata are collected, and hackers can take advantage of this and create havoc. In contrast to end-to-end encryption, blockchain technology can be used to develop a standard security protocol. As part of a unified API framework, it can also be used to enable cross-messaging capabilities by securing private messaging.

Even though the blockchain is not infallible, it has evolved to become one of the most foolproof means of transacting in the world of digital networks. Since the technology is designed and intended to ensure information integrity, it has been praised for its effectiveness. There are many sectors that can benefit from it if it is used properly. As blockchain has the potential to be practical for many utilisations, it can be implemented for many uses in a variety of ways. The most practical use of this kind of system would be to use its integrity assurance to build cybersecurity solutions for many other technologies as well. This book is a good step in that direction.

The book "**Applications of Blockchain in Cybersecurity Solutions,**" edited by Dr. Rashmi Agrawal and Dr. Neha Gupta, is a comprehensive book on Blockchain Technologies. The authors have tried their best to present the concepts and techniques to every extent. Practical applications of blockchain in cybersecurity are also well presented in some chapters.

Abhishek Kumar
Associate Professor
Chitkara University,
India

PREFACE

The concept of a blockchain can be defined as a linked set of records maintained in a decentralized environment. The records in the blockchain are publicly accessible but cryptographically protected. An interesting property of the blockchain is that once some information has been recorded, it is impossible to alter the information after it was recorded. An example of a blockchain can be seen as a chain of blocks containing time-stamped digital documents in such a way that they cannot be backdated or modified in any way. The time-stamped digital documents are kept as a collection of records and are grouped into a set of blocks, which are chronologically linked by date and time.

Each time the blockchain needs to be updated; a new block is created and appended to the existing blockchain. Each block in the blockchain contains a hash of the previous block, a collection of records of its own, and the hashed value records, also known as Merkle trees, that correspond to the block before it. Depending on the nature of the blockchain, the information inside each block differs. For instance, when it comes to bitcoin, the blockchain is supposed to store the complete details about a transaction, namely the sender, the receiver and the number of coins, whereas a blockchain used for medical records is supposed to store the complete health history of a patient over time. As blockchains are distributed, efficient hashing techniques are used to ensure their integrity and robustness. Eleven chapters of this book are devoted to demonstrating the benefits and applications of blockchain.

"Introduction to Blockchain Technology", in the first chapter, briefly explains what blockchain technology is all about. The chapter focuses on the nuances of blockchain technology, the protocol stack, and the most common consensus mechanisms used. Additionally, recent advances, challenges, and future trends of blockchain are discussed in this chapter.

The second chapter discusses the relationship between cybersecurity and blockchain. Blockchain technology plays a crucial role in strengthening cybersecurity in various industries due to its decentralized nature. Through this chapter, the readers will get to know how blockchain technology is helping in providing cybersecurity to the different sectors of industries with its advantages and disadvantages of blockchain. The author also explores the role of blockchain in cybersecurity and the future benefits of blockchain technology to strengthen cybersecurity.

A majority of specialists are working on the acceptance of blockchain to safeguard IoT (Internet of Things) devices, systems, and information. Chapter 3 will examine the methods proposed by previous analysts through which blockchain can carry the expense of security. The chapter will illustrate the subjective investigation of supporting information to assess the relevance of Blockchain innovation in the present cybersecurity industry.

Chapter 4 is on "Attack Surfaces in Blockchain". Attacks are believed to be caused by the blockchain cryptographic architecture, the bottom-line architecture, and the substance in which they are applied. Progressive defense research is believed to be the primary threat. Current research suggests that other attacks on the blockchain can be launched without being able to withstand traditional defenses, a few of which may be used to deliver other attacks. Delineating these attacks and examining their countermeasures reveal the direction of new research that should be pursued to foster safer and more competent use of blockchains.

Blockchain technology offers a data format that has built-in security. It is built on cryptography, decentralisation, and consensus concepts to ensure trust in transactions. Decentralization is enabled by blockchain technology, which allows members to participate in a distributed network. Since all transactions are transparent and visible to all users on the network, a single user cannot alter the transaction. However, blockchain differs significantly from other systems in terms of security. The blockchain is vulnerable to so many attacks nowadays. The purpose of Chapter 5, "Review of Anti Counterfeit Solutions in Block Chains", is to examine the effective anti-counterfeit measures taken by blockchain technology or the patches for and related vulnerabilities offered by researchers to reduce the impact of these attacks.

Due to the increasing number of connections, the popularity of cloud services, and advances in the Internet of Things (IoT), a decentralized approach to trust is becoming more common. In the research community, blockchain technology is receiving considerable attention because it provides a distributed ledger. This technology, however, does not provide cybersecurity in its entirety. Thus, the objective of this chapter is to provide a comprehensive overview of the proposed methods and factors for achieving cybersecurity in blockchain-based systems.

The objective of the Sixth chapter, "Preserving the Privacy of Wearable IoT Device Data Using Blockchain," is to provide the solution for the above-mentioned problems using Blockchain technology.

The cloud environment is a way to use faraway servers accommodated on the internet for data storage, data control, and information processing, more readily than a private computer or native server. There are still many challenges in the cloud environment, including authenticity, confidentiality, and integrity.

Chapter 7 discusses Blockchain-Based Access Control Systems. The need for secure and distributed access control architecture to overcome the single point of failure problem of a centralized entity becomes a big challenge when coupled with scalability and lightweight features. It is possible to achieve this through the use of Blockchain technology, which has recently been used to provide access control services. IoT device management would be used to manage distribution, heterogeneity, scalability, the ability to tolerate failure, security and privacy aspects of IoT devices at scale in the near future as it is useful.

"Multi-chain Deployment over Smart Contracts" is covered in Chapter 8. As the greatest enabling technology for blockchains, smart contracts are considered to be the best. As a result, blockchain ecosystems become self-governing, transparent, consent-based, and credible. Blockchains can operate without human intervention due to a compilation of smart contracts. These smart contracts are set up so they can be deployed at the predefined blockchain nodes. This can be done through the callbacks either from the blockchain system, the other smart contracts, or even the participants' information systems. As smart contracts, both the operations on the blockchain and the rules that govern the applications can usually be predetermined. While the use cases and real-world functions of this technology differ from one another, some principles remain the same: immutability, transparency, redundancy, and security.

The title of Chapter 9 is "Blockchain for Decentralized Services: On Improving Security and Performance of Distributed IPFS-based Web Applications". Blockchain technology, with its associated decentralization, is used to develop decentralized application platforms. The Interplanetary File System (IPFS) is built on top of a distributed system consisting of a group of nodes that shares the data and takes advantage of blockchain to permanently store the data. The IPFS is very useful in transferring remote data. This work focuses on applying blockchain technology to the IPFS to improve its security and performance

R. Agrawal
Manav Rachna International Institute of Research & Studies,
Faridabad
India

&

N. Gupta
Manav Rachna International Institute of Research & Studies
Faridabad
India

List of Contributors

AR.G. Gokul	Department of Information Technology, Sri Venkateswara College of Engineering, Sriperumbudu, India
B.K.P. Madavi	GITAM University, Bangalore
D. Mantri	Sinhgad Institute of Engineering, Lonavala, Pune
G. Thahniyath	Dayananda Sagar University, Bangalore
H. Saini	Research Schola, IBM, GLA University, Mathura, Uttar Pradesh, India
H. Bhatia	School of Computer Scienc, Engineering and Applications, D Y Patil International University, Pune, India
I. Chatterjee	Department of Computer Engineering, Tongmyong University, Busan, South Korea
K.K. Sowjanya	CMR Institute of Technology, Bangalore
M. Moh	San Jose State University, San Jose, CA 95192-0249, USA
N. Devi	Department of Information Technology, Sri Venkateswara College of Engineering, Sriperumbudu, India
N. Gupta	Manav Rachna International Institute of Research and Studies, Faridabad, Haryana
P.L. Rani	Department of Information Technology, Sri Venkateswara College of Engineering, Sriperumbudu, India
R. Agrawal	Manav Rachna International Institute of Research and Studies, Faridabad, Haryana
R. Deshmukh	Department of Computer Scienc, Shivaji University, Kolhapur, India
R. Kamat	Department of Computer Scienc, Shivaji University, Kolhapur, India
R. Moazeni	San Jose State University, San Jose, CA 95192-0249, USA
S. Zalte	Department of Computer Science, Shivaji University, Kolhapur, India
V. Garg	Amity UniversityUttar Pradesh, India
V. Le	San Jose State University, San Jose, CA 95192-0249, USA

CHAPTER 1

Introduction to Blockchain Technology

N. Devi[1,*], **P.L. Rani**[1] and **A.R.G. Gokul**[1]

[1] *Department of Information Technology, Sri Venkateswara College of Engineering, Sriperumbudur, India*

Abstract: A blockchain is a linked set of records maintained in a decentralized environment. The records in blockchain are publicly available but cryptographically secured. The interesting property exhibited by blockchain is that once some information is recorded, it is infeasible to modify the information. Blockchain is generated as a chain of blocks that contains time-stamped digital documents so that it is infeasible to back date them or tamper the documents. These time-stamped digital documents are stored as a collection of records and grouped as a set of blocks, chronologically linked in order of time.

A new block is created and appended to the existing blockchain, whenever there is a need for updating the blockchain. Every block in the blockchain comprises of a hash of the preceding block, collections of records of its own, and the hashed value records known as merkle tree. The information inside the blocks varies depending on the nature of blockchain. For example, when the nature of blockchain is bitcoin, they are supposed to store the details about a transaction *viz.*, sender, receiver and amount of coins where as blockchain used for medical records stores the complete health history of a patient over time. Since blockchain is stored in a distributed way, efficient hashing techniques are used to ensure the integrity and robustness of blockchain. This chapter describes the nuances of blockchain technology along with the protocol stack and the most common consensus mechanisms. Furthermore, recent advances, challenges and future trends of blockchain are discussed.

Keywords: Bitcoin, Blockchain, Cryptography, Distributed, Decentralized, Hash, Merkle Tree, Robustness, Time Stamp, Transaction.

INTRODUCTION

A blockchain [1] is a decentralized distributed ledger of records that is cryptographically secured and accessible unlimitedly to all. It possesses a fascinating characteristic: when an information is stored inside a blockchain, it is infeasible to modify the recorded information. The blockchain is generated as a

* **Corresponding author N. Devi:** Sri Venkateswara College of Engineering, Pennalur, Sriperumbudur, Kancheepuram, Tamil Nadu, India; E-mail: leela@svce.ac.in

chain of blocks that contains time-stamped digital documents.. These time-stamped digital documents are stored as a collection of records and grouped as a set of blocks. These blocks are then linked together in chronological order of time in a continuous line. To update, a new block is created and appended to the existing blockchain, thus, providing blockchain, a non-destructive way to track data changes over time. Every block in the blockchain comprises hash of the preceding block, collections of records of its own, and the hashed value records known as Merkle tree. The information stored inside the blockchain depends on the type of blockchain. For example, the blockchain used in bitcoin records the information of a transaction *viz.*, number of coins, contributor and receiver whereas the blockchain used for medical records stores the complete health history of a patient over time. Since blockchain is stored in a distributed way, efficient hashing techniques are used to ensure the integrity and robustness of the blockchain. The main characteristics of blockchain are depicted in Fig. (**1**). This section describes the nuances of blockchain technology.

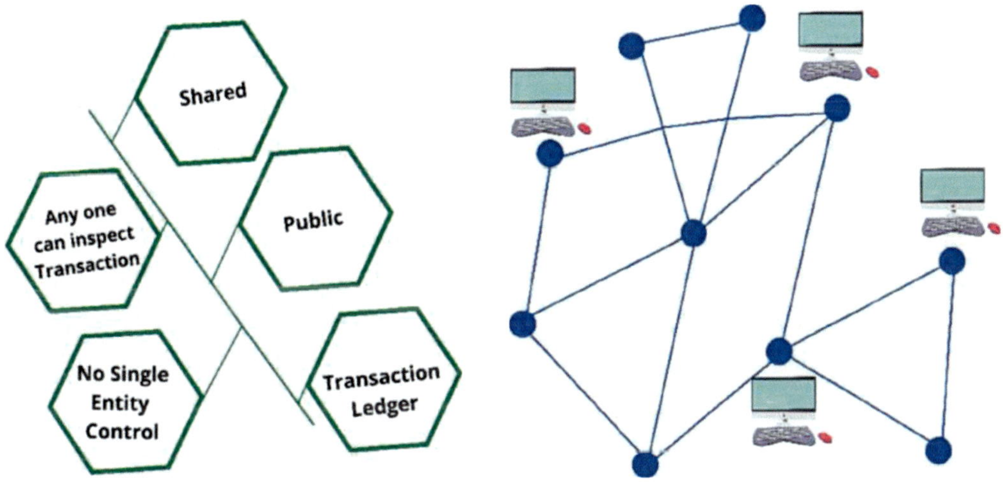

Fig. (1). Different Aspects of Blockchain.

Block

A block in a blockchain is a collection of various items such as the hash of its preceding block, the Merkle root and its own records as shown in Fig. (**2**). A Merkle tree for a block is formed by placing the hash of the individual records of that block as the leaf nodes and the non-leaf nodes are the combined hash of their own children. Using hash ensures data integrity and also helps in ensuring the correctness of the data at any given time. A hash function accepts an input of any length and converts it into a fixed length. The hash function may produce a 32-bit or 64-bit or 128-bit or 256-bit fixed length called a hash. Hash functions protects the data integrity. If a trusted hash of the data is provided, it is possible to compute the hash of the data and verify the two values. If they match, then the data has not been changed since the original hash is formed.

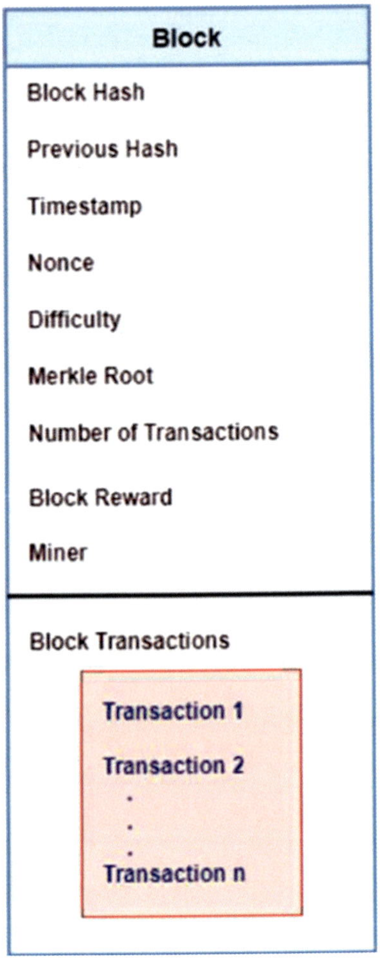

Fig. (2). Block in a Blockchain.

The first block is called a genesis block and is created at the beginning with the set of records and its Merkle root.

Merkle trees are the basic blocks of blockchain technology. It is a structure that permits verification of the consistency of content in a secure and efficient way. Bitcoin and Ethereum use Merkle trees. A Merkle tree produces a fingerprint of the summary of all the transactions in a block. It enables a user to verify whether a transaction is part of a block. Repeated hashing of pairs of nodes is performed from the bottom up, until only one hash is left as depicted in Fig. (**3**). This hash is referred to as the Merkle Root, or the Root Hash. The hashes of individual transactions, Transaction IDs are considered as leaf nodes for the construction of Merkle Tree. The hash of the previous hashes forms the non leaf nodes in the Merkle Tree. The trees are binary and hence, it is mandatory to have an even number of leaf nodes. In case of odd transaction numbers, the last hash will be replicated once to form an even number of leaves.

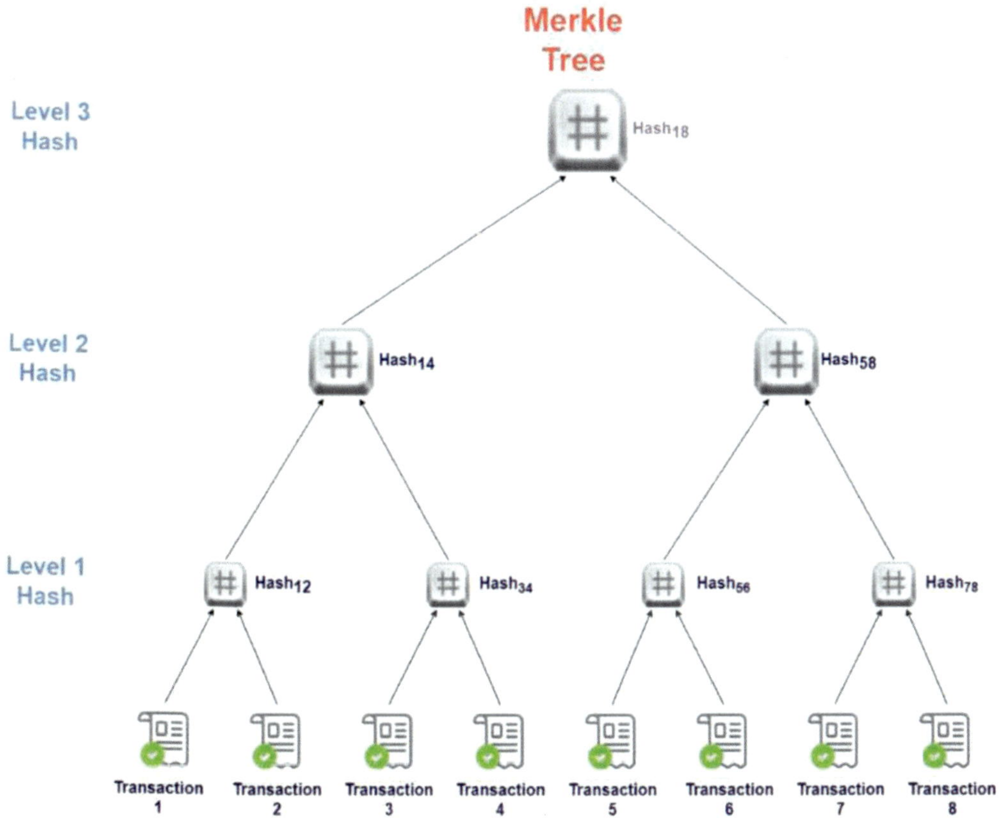

Fig. (3). Sample Merkle Tree.

In blockchain, once the block is created, it is computationally infeasible to change the record in that block as the hash of this block is stored in the succeeding block with its hash value stored in the next block and so on. This dependency between the new and the old blocks in the blockchain ensures data integrity and also ensures that there is no possibility for unauthorized data modification. If one wants to change an information recorded in a particular block *x,* then the change is recorded in a new block showing that *x* is changed to *y* at a particular date and time. This helps to keep track of the data that changes over time.

Distributed Ledger

A blockchain is analogous to a financial ledger that can be programmed to record and track anything of value from financial transactions to medical records or even land titles [2]. Storing only the hash values of the block in the consecutive block is not enough to ensure data security. In order to improve data security, blockchain is designed to be decentralised and distributed among all the peers connected in the network. This decentralisation reduces the ability for data tampering, thus creating trust. A Peer-To-Peer (P2P) network of computing resources is used to run this ledger. Each peer in the network has a copy of the blockchain and creates a consensus by regularly performing Proof-o--Work(PoW). PoW is a mechanism which is used to ensure genuineness of transactions and to append new blocks to the chain. So the security of the blockchain depends on the complex hashing technique and PoW.

Any distributed consensus for validating transaction works by utilising the mechanisms from game theory, cryptography and P2P networks as depicted in Fig. (**4**) [3]. This distributed consensus bypasses the necessity of the trusted third party for validation process. This safe P2P transaction concept came into light in October 2008 as one of the important functionalities in implementing bitcoins for cashless financial transactions. The details about all the transactions are recorded in the blockchain. This can be viewed as analogous to Google docs where each person holds the latest copy of the document and when one person wants to update the document, he has to reach a common agreement with all other persons. In Google docs, the file is kept in a central place and all are allowed to access and view it, whereas in a distributed ledger, each person in the network owns a copy of the blockchain.

Smart Contract

A smart contract is a defined set of rules agreed upon by two nodes to perform a transaction [4]. These sets of rules are implemented as a tiny computer program stored inside the blockchain. This allows a decentralised control of the transaction. The transaction cannot be completed without satisfying all the set of rules defined in the smart contract. Any association of a third party in the blockchain is removed by the implementation of a smart contract and they are consequently activated when a transaction is being done. Smart contracts are immutable ensuring that no one can intrude the transaction. They are also distributed so that the output of the transactions can be verified by all the peers in the network. Ethereum is the biggest blockchain that uses smart contracts. Smart contracts are written using the solidity programming language.

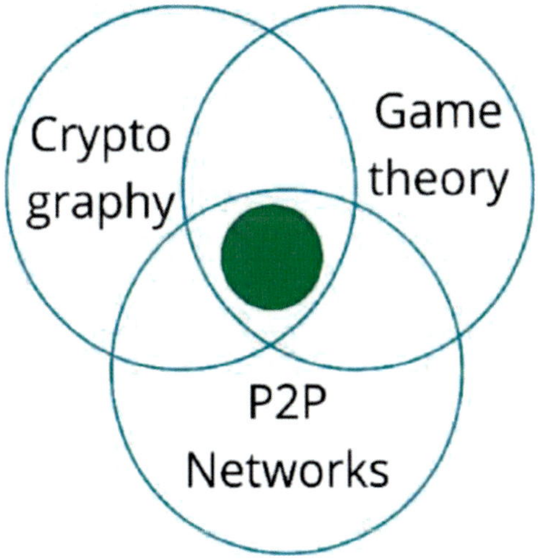

Fig. (4). Distributed Consensus.

Blockchain Protocol Stack

The blockchain protocol stack [5] presented in Fig. (**5**) contains blockchain at the bottom level and on top of it, lies the smart contract and other overlay networks followed by protocols and API's to interact with the application. Digital assets are managed using blockchain based on smart contracts. A smart contract defines a set of rules for mutual agreement among peers. This is entirely different from a legal contract in the way that the smart contract will execute the transaction only when all the peers satisfy the rule mentioned in the contract. This is much superior to the contract laws in providing more secure transactions with minimum coordination costs during the transaction.

Smart contracts are deployed in many scenarios from simple financial transactions like fund transfer from A to B, to more complex transactions involving registration for land ownership, patented rights in IP, handling smart applications. One significant complex smart contract is the Decentralized Autonomous Organizations (DAOs), where smart contracts are deployed for performing a transaction involving a cluster of single-minded persons with common aims and ideas. Today's digital world embeds contracts into many types of code *viz.*, bar code, QR code, where these codes are kept in public and transparent databases . The databases are protected from any kind of tampering with the help of smart contracts and blockchains. It transits the world into a new era where each process, event, agreement, and task, are recorded digitally and the signature present in the records can be validated easily. Individuals, governments, industries, and automated systems can now liberally communicate and transact with each other without any intermediaries with minimal transaction cost.

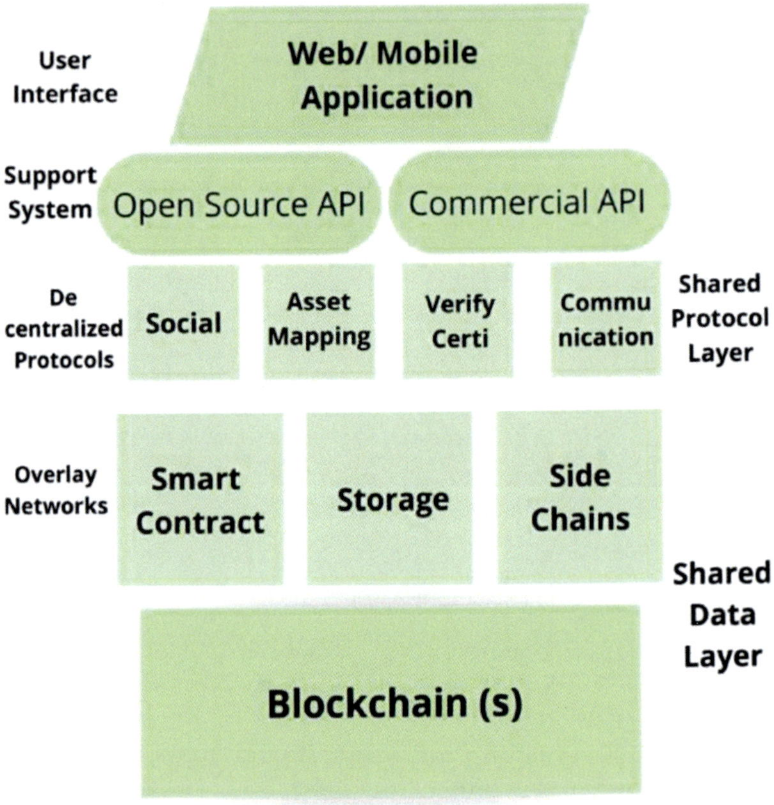

Fig. (5). Blockchain Protocol Stack.

Tamper Resistant

The blockchain protocol running on the nodes of a P2P network performs the validation process of a transaction as depicted in Fig. (**6**) without involving third-party agents [6]. The validation process is done by majority vote consensus. This protocol is responsible for administering all the nodes to participate in validating the transaction through a set of pre-defined governance rules.

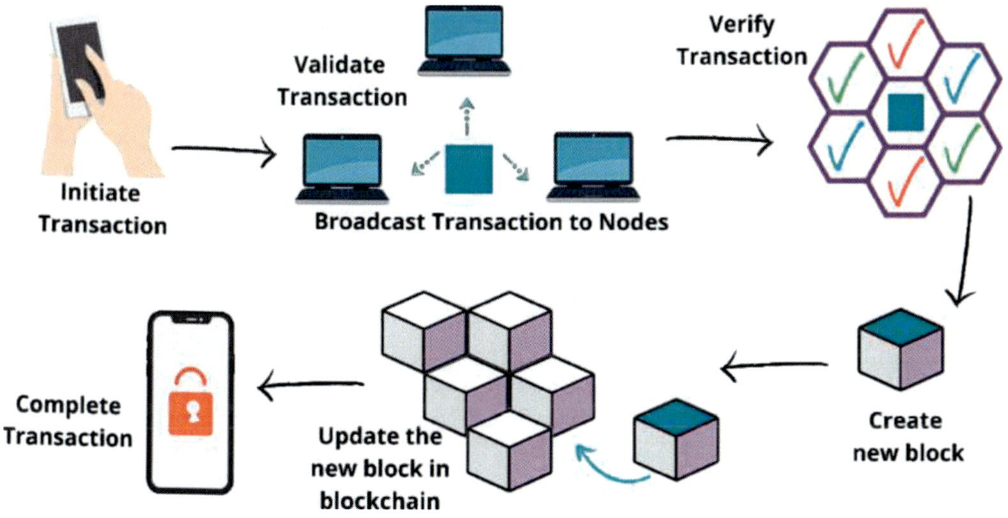

Fig. (6). Validation Process of a transaction that uses blockchain.

The pre-defined governance rules of the network oversee how the nodes in the P2P network cooperate with one another to validate the transaction. These rules elucidate

- The criteria based on which the transaction is said to be valid.
- The cost incurred during the transaction.
- Validating the transaction using game theory and cryptographic techniques.
- Procedures to update the predefined rules as and when necessary.

Consider a bitcoin scenario; the financial transactions are validated through a majority vote with the help of bitcoin protocols instead of validating manually through ledgers stored in servers in a traditional banking application.

CONSENSUS PROTOCOL

A consensus mechanism in a blockchain is a robust mechanism to achieve common agreement on a specific state among the nodes in a P2P network. This mechanism involves a set of predefined rules for synchronizing the nodes during transactions that are trusted and recorded in the blockchain. The purpose of these rules is to assure the validity and legitimacy of the transactions. Some of the widely used consensus mechanisms [7] *viz.*, PoW, PoS, DPoS, pBFT, PoC, PoA, PoR, PoI, PoB, PoET, PoId and PoAu are described in this section.

Proof of Work (PoW)

The process of mining is termed PoW. The nodes denote the miners [8]. Complex mathematical puzzles are decrypted by the miners. This requires extensive computing resources. Various mining techniques *viz.*, ASIC mining, FPGA mining, CPU mining, GPU mining, and mining pools are adopted by miners to decipher the puzzles in a short time. When the miner is the first one to solve the puzzle, he is rewarded with a block as an incentive for decoding the puzzle. Moreover, some miners decrypt the puzzles through experimentation as shown in Fig. (**7**). Each transaction will have puzzles with varying difficulty levels to validate it and as a result, blocks are mined with different paces. This leads to the requirement of extensive and varying computational resources for solving the puzzles rapidly. When more number of blocks need to be included in the blockchain within a specific time, then it necessitates more complex and hard to solve puzzles to make it fault-tolerant. PoW is adopted by many popular cryptocurrencies such as Bitcoin to strengthen their robustness. Nevertheless, the PoW consensus mechanism uses resources at an unbelievable rate. As per external sources, the present anticipated yearly power consumption of bitcoin is 51.13 TWh. Therefore, this PoW approach is quite overpriced.

Fig. (7). Puzzles for Proof of Work.

Proof of Stake (PoS)

PoS employs a randomized procedure to find out who has the likelihood to produce the subsequent block [9]. Blockchain users can hold their tokens for a certain duration to become a validator. The nodes are not only involved in validating process as a validator, but sometimes generate a new block and become a contributor. The nodes that act as validators are changed from time to time depending on their active involvement in rendering the blockchain. The probability at which the nodes generate new blocks depends on the number of coins or stakes they possess. The validator node involved in the validating process of a transaction gets a reward amount depending on their level of involvement in forming the block. On the other hand, due to inflation, validators may get a particular amount of coins. These rewards allow retaining the validators in the blockchain network. PoS is more efficient in conserving energy compared to any other consensus mechanisms.

Delegated Proof of Stake (DPoS)

DPoS allows the users to gamble with their stakes to cast votes to different representatives in a transaction [10]. Each user's vote has a different weightage in the transaction depending on how much stake they have used for casting the vote to a delegate. The vote of user 'X' had more weightage than the vote of user 'Y', when user 'X' used his 100 stakes for casting the vote whereas user 'Y' uses only 25. The representatives who secured more votes are given the right to generate a new block. The representatives receive a reward of a certain amount of stakes as transaction fee as in other consensus mechanisms. DPoS is faster and deals with more number of transactions. This mechanism is considered provide digital democracy as it follows a voting system based on stake-weighted votes.

Practical Byzantine Fault Tolerance (pBFT)

In P2P networks, undisputed concurrences among trustworthy and non-faulty nodes help in accomplishing consensus. The basis of BFT is observable in a situation where all nodes reiterate an incoming message [11]. If a node keeps repeating the incoming message, then it evidently signifies that it does not have any fault. Alternatively, if the receivers replicate the incoming message, the network could effortlessly rule out the prospect of Byzantine nodes. Byzantine node denotes the traitor nodes which lie or mislead other nodes in the network deliberately. The byzantine node could also lie to the nodes that are concerned with the consensus protocol. An absolutely functional blockchain network would make sure that Byzantine Fault Tolerance in blockchain assists it in dealing with failures. Byzantine node or malicious node leads to pitfalls recognized as Byzantine failures. Users could encounter two different types of Byzantine failures, among which, the first one is entirely technical in nature. A slight technical error in the node could influence its functionality, and in certain cases, it might discontinue reacting or working in general. The other type of Byzantine failure is related to random node failure. In case of a random node failure, a node might exhibit the following traits:

- Failure to return an end result
- Replying with erroneous results
- Replying with intentionally ambiguous results for queries
- Replying to a single query with various results to various constituent parts of the system

BFT helps to overcome all these problems efficiently by decreasing the impact of harmful nodes. It can guard the network from risky failures and make sure the network is functioning ideally. Fundamentally, the sincere nodes and malicious nodes can do their own work without any effect on the performance of the network. Extensive investigation into the Byzantine General's Problem and optimization has served as the stepping stone to introduce many improvements over the traditional BFT.

Proof-of-Burn (PoB)

PoB also expends minimum energy when compared to other consensus mechanisms [16]. PoB is a decentralized mechanism that involves removing the stakes from exchange to indicate that miners already reached an agreement. This removal process is referred to as burning. This serves to reduce inflation. PoB-based blockchain is used to authenticate transactions. PoB employs virtual mining rigs to authenticate transactions. PoB miners begin coin burning to display their contribution in the network and are permitted to mine. The number of coins burnt by a miner exhibits his virtual mining capacity. Higher mining power enhances the speed of determining new blocks. As a result, the miner is rewarded more. In PoB networks, the coins are addressed to a randomized eater address. This address is openly verifiable but unreachable. PoB is analogous to PoS in terms of using stakes for network protection. The main issue that needs to be considered is that the burned stakes are removed logically and not eternally which permits users to misuse them by peddling them to another one as the processor can still access them. PoB results in a scarcity of coins. PoB is a new consensus algorithm that is not tried on larger networks. However, PoB is sustainable and its mining is greatly decentralized.

Proof of Elapsed Time (PoET)

In PoET, each user is assigned a random waiting time [17]. The user who waits for a longer time with earlier finish time will get a chance to generate the new block. PoET relies on the random waiting time assigned to the users and it has to ensure waiting time is assigned purely in a random fashion.

Proof of Identity (PoId)

In PoId, the user's private key is compared with a qualified identity [18]. This ensures that all transactions are embedded with the private key of the user involved in that transaction. In this way, every certified user is allowed to generate a new block and circulate it to all other users in the network. This helps to maintain the authenticity and integrity of the blocks. . PoId is widely used in smart cities to authenticate the citizen's identity.

Proof of Authority (PoAu)

PoS is customized in such a way that the identities of validators are at stake [19]. The validator's identity associates credentials of individual with the organisation and then the combined credentials serve as the validator's identity to authenticate the transactions. In this way, the reputation of validators is at stake in the network. PoAu allows only the validators to generate new blocks. Also, validators are responsible for maintaining and protecting the blockchain network. The number of validators is usually limited to less than 25.

The industries using blockchain use different consensus mechanisms in its business transaction, as a single mechanism will not satisfy all the stipulated specifications of the blockchain technology. As the specification of blockchain gets changed frequently in today's digital world, any particular consensus mechanism is accommodated for an extended time duration. Consensus mechanism which is more efficient today, will not help much in the future. Hence the organisations that employ blockchain technology in their business must upgrade their consensus mechanism from time to time.

IMPLEMENTATION OF BLOCKCHAIN

This section presents the implementation of blockchain using python in order to understand the working of blockchain in practical scenarios [20]. The blockchain created using the code is similar to the one in Fig. (**8**).

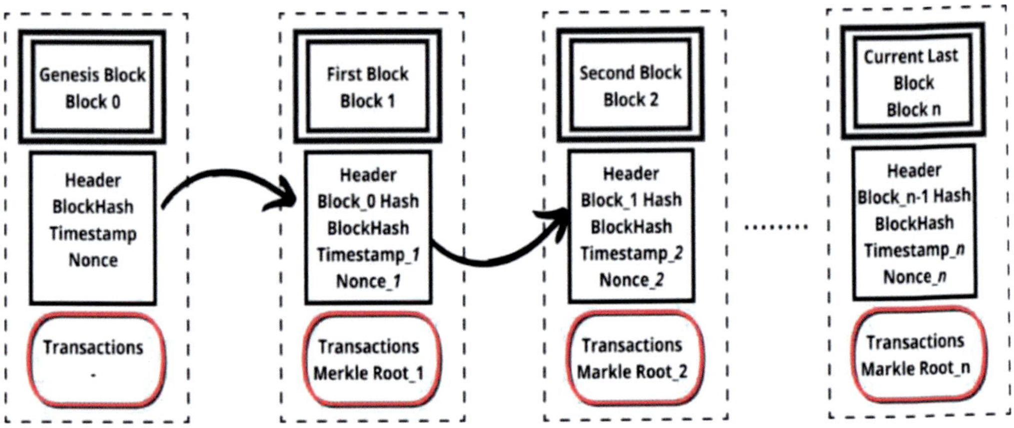

Fig. (8). Sample Blockchain with 4 blocks.

Creation of new Block

A Block class is defined with a constructor that accepts a timestamp, some data and the hash of the previous block. A block class used to represent a block is given below:

```
class Blockchain:

    def __init__(self,ts,record,prevHash):

        self.pHash = prevHash

        self.record = record

        self.ts = ts

        self.hash = self.compute_Hash()
```

In the above code fragment, the parameter ts represents the timestamp that is used to store the time at which the block is created, the parameter record represents the information or transaction details that are stored inside the block and the parameter pHash represents the string that contains the hash of the previous block.

Intuitively, a hash represents the fingerprint of the main document. Each block consists of a unique hash value. The hash value of a particular block is computed by applying the hash function to all the contents of the block. The compute_Hash method is used for computing the hash of the newly generated block. This method uses the SHA256 hash function which is available in the hashlib library and imported as given below:

```
import hashlib

strHash = compute_Hash(mes)

def compute_Hash(str):

sHash = hashlib.sha256(mes.encode())

return(sHash.hexdigest())
```

Generation of Blockchain

A blockchain is generated using the Blockchain class as given below:

```
import time

class Blockchain:

    def__init__(self):

        self.unconfirmed_transactions = []

        self.chain = []

        self.create_genesis_block()

    def create_genesis_block(self):

        genesis_block = Block(0,[],time.time(),"0")

        genesis_block.hash=
genesis_block.compute_Hash()

        self.chain.append(genesis_block)

    @property

    def recent_block(self):

        return self.chain[-1]
```

The Blockchain class is instantiated as a simple and manageable object with chain as its property. The property chain is an array and its main purpose is to store all the blocks in the blockchain. Genesis block is created for the first block in the chain using the method create_genesis_block(). The recent_block() method returns the last element on the chain array. The add_new_block() method is used to add a new block into the chain, This includes assigning the hash value of previous block through prevHash property and the hash value of the newly generated block is also computed and assigned into the property hash.

Testing

An instance of Blockchain with three blocks is created for testing based on the following methodologies.

Verify the Integrity of the Blockchain

Blockchains are great because once a new block is included in the chain, it is computationally difficult to alter its content without invalidating the remaining blocks present in the chain. The integrity of the blocks is validated using new method is_chain_valid() which is included in the Blockchain class. This method returns a true value when the blocks present in the chain are untampered otherwise it returns false value. The code for is_chain_valid() method is given below:

```
def is_chain_valid(self, blockchain):

        previous_block = blockchain[0]

        block_index =1

        while block_index<len(blockchain):

            block =blockchain [block_index]

            if block['previous_hash']
!=self.hash(previous_block):

                return False

            previous_proof =previous_block['proof']

            proof =block['proof']

            hash_operation =hashlib.sha256(

                str(proof**2-
previous_proof**2).encode()).hexdigest()

            if hash_operation[:4] !='00000':

                return False

            previous_block =block

            block_index +=1

        return True
```

Consider a scenario of tampering the chain using the following statements:

```
bc.chain[1].record = { amount: 50 };

bc.chain[1].hash = bc.chain[1].computeHash():
```

Here the data is changed and hash is recalculated, still it will notify as the chain has tampered. The above code implements a simple blockchain with the generation of new blocks and validation.

Implementation of proof-of-work

The section 3.3.1 described the implementation process of creating a simple blockchain. It also included the processes involved in detecting tampered content in the chain. Computers have much more faster and efficient processors that easily add numerous blocks within a short span of time. This leads to spamming of blocks in the chain. Also efficient computing resources make the tampering process easier, where the hacker modifies the data stored inside a block and the hashes of all the succeeding blocks are recalculated. In this case, the data tampering goes unnoticed, because it shows a valid chain during the validation process. These problems need to be addressed while implementing simple blockchain. These issues are solved by the consensus mechanism described in section 2. This section explains how PoW is implemented using the process called mining. Mining increases the usage of computing resources, thereby, increasing the time taken to create a new block. In PoW, the mining process starts with generating random data continuously until enough number of zeroes are prefixed to the hash of the block. The number of zeroes prefixed in the hash is referred to as the difficulty level of the mining process. The random number, nonce, is included as part of the block along with the user's data. The main objective of bitcoin is to create a new block every 10 minutes. It is possible because of the availability of faster computing resources. This necessitates more complex and difficult mining process. This is achieved by increasing the difficulty level.

Steps for implementing the mining process in the blockchain

Step 1: Add a nonce to the Block class:

```
class Block:

      def __init__(self,ts,record,prevHash):

            self.pHash = prevHash

            self.record = record

            self.ts = ts

            self.hash = self.compute_Hash()

self.nonce = 0;
```

Step 2: Create a proof_of_work() method that receives block as a parameter and the required difficulty is set as a value and iteratively generates the hash value until the hash value prefixes with enough number of zeros.

```
diff = 3

def proof_of_work(self, block):

        block.nonce =

        calculated_Hash = block.compute_Hash()

       while not calculated-Hash.startswith('0' *
Blockchain.diff):

            block.nonce += 1

            calculated_Hash = block.compute_Hash()

        return calculated_Hash
```

Step 3: Incorporate nonce into the calculate hash function.

```
def calculateHash:

new-hash = self.index+ self.previousHash+ self.tmstmp+
str(data)+ self.nonce

      return hashlib.sha256(new_hash).hexdigest()
```

Step 4: The difficulty level is assigned inside the constructor of Blockchain class.

```
def __init__(self,chain):

        self.chain = [self.create_genesis_block()];

        self.diff = 3;
```

Step 5: Update the add_new_block() method so that mining process takes place before inserting the block onto the chain.

```
def add_new_block(self, block, block_proof):

          prev_hash = self.recent_block.hash

          if prev_hash!= block. prev_hash:

                 return False

           if not self.is_valid_proof(block, block_proof):

                 return False

           block.hash = block_proof

           self.chain.append(block)

           return True

 def is_valid_proof(self, block, new_block_hash):

                 return   (new_block_hash.startswith('0'   *
 Blockchain.diff) and

                  new_block_hash == block.compute_Hash())

 def add_new_transaction(self, new_transaction):

       self.transactions-
 to_confirm.append(new_transaction)
```

Step 6: Creating instance for Blockchain and add two blocks onto the chain to understand working of PoW

```
bc = Blockchain()

bc.add-new-block(21/08/2020,{amount:15},
bc.chain[1].computeHash())

bc.add-new-block(22/08/2020,{amount:5},
bc.chain[2].computeHash())
```

While executing the above fragment of code, it is observed that now it takes more time to generate new blocks than the one presented in 3.3.1. This is due to the mining process where the difficulty is configured as 3 which requires the hash value to start with three zeroes. When the difficulty level is increased, the algorithm takes more time to produce the blocks.

Thus the PoW mechanism enables blockchain network to control the number of blocks inserted in the chain within a stipulated time.

CHALLENGES IN BLOCKCHAIN TECHNOLOGY

Many organizations and business persons are willing to take up this technology. However, there are challenges that hinder the adoption of blockchain technology [21]. The critical problems related to this technology are presented here.

Scalability

Scalability is the main factor that hinders the process of adoption of blockchain. It is a well known fact that this technology can process thousands of transactions per second, however, in Bitcoin and in Ethereum, the transaction speeds are 3 to 7 transactions and 15 to 20 transactions per second respectively. This property of slow processing of the transactions renders blockchain unsuitable for large applications. Bitcoin lightening network and Ethereum plasma are considered as solutions for offering spontaneity in transactions with nominal fees.

Network Interoperability

Most blockchains do not communicate with peer networks as they lack this feature. To address this second big concern, Ark uses Smart Bridges architecture to bridge the gap of communication between the networks. This project offers global interoperability.

Consumption of Energy

Blockchain technology uses PoW mechanism for transaction validation and to insert to the network. This needs computational power to decipher difficult mathematical puzzles to process, authenticate, and, secure the network. To address this issue, instead of PoW, PoS was advocated. In PoS, contestants are not forced to decipher complex puzzles and this results in the reduction of energy consumption.

Talent Deficit

Even though there is a huge demand for blockchain professionals, first-class talents are main concern in the blockchain adoption. The demand for blockchain engineers across the globe is predicted to be above 517% more than the demand in 2019. Blockchain is still considered a developing technology worldwide. Despite remarkable demand, deficit of blockchain experts is a noteworthy apprehension for all businesses. The deficiency of proficiently skilled and experienced developers for managing the complexity of networks has resulted in slow development.

Standardization

There is no universally accepted standard available for blockchain. This leads to problems such as amplified costs, interoperability, and complex mechanisms, which renders mass adoption an impractical task. Lack of standardization is a hurdle for the new engineers and investors.

Cross Chain Technology

The cross-chain assists in interoperability between different blockchain networks and facilitates the data exchange between various networks. However, Blockchain must support interoperability on its platform and adoption in various segments. The need for interoperability through cross chain technology also needs secure transfer of confidential data.

Blockchain Consequences

In addition to the above mentioned challenges, Table **1** lists the characteristics of the blockchain as mentioned in various available literatures and its consequences [22 - 24].

Table 1. Characteristics of the blockchain with associated consequences.

Properties	Consequences	
	Positive	Negative
Immutable	Internet of Value, Traceable	Inflexible
Transparent	Efficiency of data retrieval	Privacy, Information Leakage
Programmable	Execution in a deterministic manner	Unchangeable source code
Decentralized	Disintermediate	Disintermediate
Consensus	Minimize necessary trust	Energy Consumption, Centralized power
Distributed Trust	Establish	No personal relationship

Actual implementation of blockchain needs to be integrated with complicated social, economic, legislative, organizational and physical systems [25]. This integration poses plethora of problems, few of which are tabulated in Table **2**.

Table 2. Problems faced while implementing blockchain.

Challenge	Description
Throughput	Number of transactions being processed within a specific period of time.
Latency	Amount of time before a transaction is processed.
Size and bandwidth	The blockchain grows over time as new blocks are constantly added. This also consumes considerable bandwidth for downloading data.
Wasted resources	Blockchain-intrinsic inefficiencies such as redundant data transmission, storage and energy-consuming consensus protocols.
Usability	Users interactions with Blockchain applications.
Versioning, hard forks, multiple chains	A multitude of Blockchain versions and forks facilitate attacks and hamper cross-transactions.
Privacy	The right to control access to (personal) information as well as to delete it.
Evidentiary quality, Trustworthiness of records	Questions pertaining to the truthfulness of content on the Blockchain.
Lack of Standards	No standards have emerged yet for access rights, data structures and allowable transactions.
Regulations	Legislation is lagging behind technological development.
Shared governance	Blockchain solution call for new structures that might disrupt existing governance.
Viable ecosystem	The attraction of a critical mass of adopters.
Attack Surface	The Blockchain is a target of potential attacks.

RESEARCH PERSPECTIVES

There are various security challenges of blockchain applications in the industry. The blockchain enabled devices must be designed so as to construct an improved user centric data empowerment. Prospective research is still needed in many areas [26 - 32], not limited to:

- Specific blockchain-associated issues and attacks like withholding a block attack and mining incentives.
- Scalability issues in blockchain-enabled industry like healthcare. As healthcare is a rising industry, as more and more people are getting aged, blockchain-enabled healthcare applications will turn into an exponentially difficult task, as the application might not run properly, with the increase in the number of patients.
- The necessity to deploy open source real-world datasets to enable researchers to perform research and get their results verified to disseminate their findings and observations.
- Issues related to security and key management to effortlessly restore compromised keys.
- Challenges in identity authentication.
- Need for proper blockchain testing methods.
- Challenges in controlling AI-based misbehaviours on blockchain.

CONCLUSION

Blockchain is gaining popularity due to its peer-to-peer, decentralised infrastructure. Nevertheless, many researchers have already discussed a lot about blockchain technology but are limited to Bitcoin. However blockchain is applicable to various other fields as well. Blockchain has transformed the conventional industry with its features namely, auditability, decentralisation, anonymity and persistency. In this chapter, a brief introduction about blockchain is presented. A summary of the blockchain technologies including architecture and characteristics is presented. The consensus algorithm available for use in blockchain is described next. The process of block creation and mining is also explained. The issues that would disrupt the development of blockchain and few research perspectives are also discussed.

CONSENT FOR PUBLICATION

Not applicable.

CONFLICT OF INTEREST

The author declares no conflict of interest, financial or otherwise.

ACKNOWLEDGEMENT

Declared none.

REFERENCES

[1] Swan Melanie, “Blockchain: Blueprint for a new economy”, 1st ed., O'Reilly Media, Inc., 2015.

[2] D. Burkhardt, M. Werling, and H. Lasi, *“Distributed Ledger.” IEEE International Conference on Engineering, Technology and Innovation.* ICE/ITMC, 2018, pp. 1-9. https://blockchainhub.net/blockchain-intro/

[3] L.W. Cong, and Z. He, "Blockchain disruption and smart contracts", *Rev. Financ. Stud.,* vol. 32, no. 5, pp. 1754-1797, 2019. [http://dx.doi.org/10.1093/rfs/hhz007]

[4] Nelson, J. Scott, David Henderson, Glenn Jones, Micha Roon, Michael Zargham, Aleksandr Bulkin, Jake Brukhman, Kenny Rowe, Alex Felix, and Christian Crowley. "A blockchain-based protocol stack for global commerce and supply chains." Sweetbridge White Paper (2017).

[5] D. Ichikawa, M. Kashiyama, and T. Ueno, "Tamper-resistant mobile health using blockchain technology", *JMIR Mhealth Uhealth,* vol. 5, no. 7, 2017.e111 [http://dx.doi.org/10.2196/mhealth.7938] [PMID: 28747296]

[6] Sankar, Lakshmi Siva, M. Sindhu, and M. Sethumadhavan, "Survey of consensus protocols on blockchain applications.", 4th International Conference on Advanced Computing and Communication Systems (ICACCS), IEEE, pp. 1-5, 2017.

[7] Amitai Porat, "Blockchain Consensus: An analysis of Proof-of-Work and its applications", 2017.

[8] A. Barhanpure, P. Belandor, and B. Das, "Proof of stack consensus for blockchain networks", In: *International Symposium on Security in Computing and Communication* Springer: Singapore, 2018, pp. 104-116.

[9] S.M.S. Saad, and R.Z.R.M. Radzi, "Comparative Review of the Blockchain Consensus Algorithm Between Proof of Stake (POS) and Delegated Proof of Stake (DPOS)", *Int. J. Innov. Comput.,* vol. 10, no. 2, 2020.

[10] I. Abraham, "Revisiting fast practical byzantine fault tolerance", *arXiv preprint arXiv:1712.01367,* 2017.

[11] P. Racsko, "Blockchain and Democracy", *Soc. Econ.,* vol. 41, no. 3, pp. 353-369, 2019. [http://dx.doi.org/10.1556/204.2019.007]

[12] I. Bentov, C. Lee, A. Mizrahi, and M. Rosenfeld, "Proof of Activity", *Perform. Eval. Rev.,* vol. 42, no. 3, pp. 34-37, 2014. [http://dx.doi.org/10.1145/2695533.2695545]

[13] C.B. Tan, M.H.A. Hijazi, Y. Lim, and A. Gani, "A survey on Proof of Retrievability for cloud data integrity and availability: Cloud storage state-of-the-art, issues, solutions and future trends", *J. Netw. Comput. Appl.,* vol. 110, pp. 75-86, 2018. [http://dx.doi.org/10.1016/j.jnca.2018.03.017]

[14] H.T.M. Gamage, H.D. Weerasinghe, and N.G.J. Dias, "A survey on blockchain technology concepts, applications, and issues", *SN Computer Science,* vol. 1, no. 2, p. 114, 2020. [http://dx.doi.org/10.1007/s42979-020-00123-0]

[15] K. Karantias, A. Kiayias, and D. Zindros, "Proof-of-burn", In: *International Conference on Financial Cryptography and Data Security* Springer: Cham, 2020, pp. 523-540. [http://dx.doi.org/10.1007/978-3-030-51280-4_28]

[16] L. Chen, "On security analysis of proof-of-elapsed-time (poet)", In: *International Symposium on Stabilization, Safety, and Security of Distributed Systems* Springer: Cham, 2017, pp. 282-297.

[17] G. Chen, B. Xu, M. Lu, and N-S. Chen, "Exploring blockchain technology and its potential applications for education", *Smart Learning Environments,* vol. 5, no. 1, pp. 1-10, 2018. [http://dx.doi.org/10.1186/s40561-017-0050-x]

[18] K. Toyoda, K. Machi, Y. Ohtake, and A.N. Zhang, "Function-level bottleneck analysis of private proof-of-authority ethereum blockchain", *IEEE Access,* vol. 8, pp. 141611-141621, 2020. [http://dx.doi.org/10.1109/ACCESS.2020.3011876]

[19] https://www.codementor.io/@savjee/how-to-build-a-blockchain-with-javascript-part-1-k7d373dtk

[20] Z. Zheng, S. Xie, H. Dai, X. Chen, and H. Wang, An overview of blockchain technology: Architecture, consensus, and future trends.*IEEE international congress on big data (BigData congress).* IEEE, 2017, pp. 557-564. [http://dx.doi.org/10.1109/BigDataCongress.2017.85]

[21] Aleksandr Vasilievich Babkin, "Automation digitalization blockchain: trends and implementation problems." International Journal of Engineering and Technology (UAE), vol. 7, no. 3.14, pp. 254-260, 2018.

[22] David B. Meijer, "Consequences of the implementation of blockchain technology", 2017.

[23] S.V. Akram, P.K. Malik, R. Singh, G. Anita, and S. Tanwar, "Adoption of blockchain technology in various realms: Opportunities and challenges", *Secur. Priv.,* vol. 3, no. 5, 2020.e109 [http://dx.doi.org/10.1002/spy2.109]

[24] M.C. Lacity, "Addressing key challenges to making enterprise blockchain applications a reality", *MIS Q. Exec.,* vol. 17, no. 3, pp. 201-222, 2018.

[25] Y. Lu, "The blockchain: State-of-the-art and research challenges", *J. Ind. Inf. Integr.,* vol. 15, pp. 80-90, 2019.

[26] K. Salah, M.H.U. Rehman, N. Nizamuddin, and A. Al-Fuqaha, "Blockchain for AI: Review and open research challenges", *IEEE Access,* vol. 7, pp. 10127-10149, 2019. [http://dx.doi.org/10.1109/ACCESS.2018.2890507]

[27] S. Wang, L. Ouyang, Y. Yuan, X. Ni, X. Han, and F.Y. Wang, "Blockchain-enabled smart contracts: architecture, applications, and future trends", *IEEE Trans. Syst. Man Cybern. Syst.,* vol. 49, no. 11, pp. 2266-2277, 2019. [http://dx.doi.org/10.1109/TSMC.2019.2895123]

[28] M. Andoni, V. Robu, and D. Flynn, *et al.* "Blockchain technology in the energy sector: A systematic review of challenges and opportunities", Renew. Sustain. Energy Rev., vol. 100, pp. 143-174, 2019. [http://dx.doi.org/10.1016/j.rser.2018.10.014]

[29] P. Treleaven, R. Gendal Brown, and D. Yang, "Blockchain technology in finance", *Computer,* vol. 50, no. 9, pp. 14-17, 2017. [http://dx.doi.org/10.1109/MC.2017.3571047]

[30] O. Ali, A. Jaradat, A. Kulakli, and A. Abuhalimeh, "A comparative study: Blockchain technology utilization benefits, challenges and functionalities", *IEEE Access,* vol. 9, pp. 12730-12749, 2021. [http://dx.doi.org/10.1109/ACCESS.2021.3050241]

[31] A. Upadhyay, S. Mukhuty, V. Kumar, and Y. Kazancoglu, "Blockchain technology and the circular economy: Implications for sustainability and social responsibility", *J. Clean. Prod.,* vol. 293, 2021.126130 [http://dx.doi.org/10.1016/j.jclepro.2021.126130]

[32] M.K. Lim, Y. Li, C. Wang, and M.L. Tseng, "A literature review of blockchain technology applications in supply chains: A comprehensive analysis of themes, methodologies and industries", *Comput. Ind. Eng.*, vol. 154, 2021.107133 [http://dx.doi.org/10.1016/j.cie.2021.107133]

CHAPTER 2

Cybersecurity and Blockchain

H. Saini[1,*] and **V. Garg**[2]

[1] *Research Scholar, IBM, GLA University, Mathura, Uttar Pradesh, India*

[2] *Amity University, Uttar Pradesh, India*

Abstract: Blockchain technology provides unprecedented security to sensitive data to both businesses and individuals; it has become one of the most famous methods for securing data through a decentralized system. Cybercrime is a serious threat to enterprises as hackers are devising new techniques and implementing them to execute cybercrime. Blockchain technology has the potential to give higher security, which has no limit to keeping important and sensitive information and records. Blockchain is the technology that could go a long way in fighting this and keeping digital information safe and secured. Blockchain technology strengthens cyber security for different areas of industries and plays a vital role in making data more secure with its decentralized technology. Through this chapter, the authors will get to know how blockchain technology helps in providing cyber security to the different sectors of industries with its advantages and disadvantages of blockchain. The author also explores the role of blockchain in cybersecurity and the future benefits of blockchain technology to strengthen cybersecurity.

Keywords: Bitcoin, Blockchain, Blockchain in industries, Challenges with Blockchain, Crypto currencies, Cyber-attack, Cyber security, Data security, Decentralized, Internet of things (IoT).

INTRODUCTION

Blockchain is a database that is different from the usual database storing systems. Blockchain stores the data like a normal database system but it stores the data electronically in the form of groups in the computer system. The information saved through blockchain technology is saved in a set of groups that are also known as blocks that are later chained altogether into chronological order. Once the data is filled in the current block, new data will be stored in the new block automatically, and once data will be stored in new block, it will again be automatically added to the next block which becomes a chain of the trailing blocks. The most common use of the blockchain system is in ledger transactions.

* **Corresponding author H. Saini:** Research Scholar, IBM, GLA University, Mathura, Uttar Pradesh, India; E-mail: vgarg@gn.amity.edu

This record-keeping technology also works behind the Bitcoin network. In the case of bitcoin, decentralized blockchains are used so that any individual or group cannot control it. It also keeps records of all the data permanently that can be viewed later as per the need [1].

Daily, 2020 [2] stated that blockchain's instinctively decentralized nature makes it a perfectly suitable technology for cybersecurity. Blockchain technology is used as a new weapon in cybersecurity. CEO of IBM Ginni Rometty said that to every profession, industry, and company present in the world, cybercrime is the greatest threat for them. Cybercrime is very extensive and expanding very quickly in the industries of the world.

In an article published by Consolidated Technologies Inc., it has been said that blockchain gives cybersecurity to businesses by protecting their critical and sensitive data, and can also protect cryptocurrency and other smart assets of the entrepreneurs. Blockchain keeps the information safe by tracking and checking every single change that occurs in a database, backing up the data in numerous locations, identifying and pointing out the attacks and errors, and preventing identity theft by authenticating the data and keeping hackers out [3].

The amount of data generated by industries, businesses, and individuals is increasing day by day without any end to it. To the current demand of each sector, developing more sophisticated technologies to ensure the security of the stored data and information from hackers has become mandatory to put a stop to cybercrimes. There are strong culminating points of damning that affect cybersecurity: human error-caused data breaches, malware delivered by emails, fake invoices for malware distribution, *etc.* In the future with 5G networks, superfast download speeds will encourage huge cybercrimes as the number of globally connected devices through the IoT (Internet of Things) devices will also increase to the amount to 13.8 billion devices in 2021. Here is the situation where blockchain needs to strengthen cyber security [4]. Security experts have found blockchain as a solution for increasing cybercriminals that have been continuously evolving. Blockchain applies to almost all sectors of industries but its role in cybersecurity is more transformative [5]. The popularity of blockchain has increased worldwide, and apart from being a popular technology it also has successfully made its impact on the world. And now industries across the world are grasping the new technology that gives assurance of safety to the data and security with blockchain cybersecurity technology that is now leading the way. Blockchain technology has been commercially adopted and companies are queuing up to accept the largest cryptocurrency [6]. The distinctive characteristics of blockchain technology make its application different and attractive for many business ideas such as banking and there are majorly five areas of the banking industry that are affected the most. The affected areas of banking are Clearing and Settlement, Payment, Trade Finance, Identity, and Syndicate Loans [7]. However, industries are applying the core concept of blockchain technology to their existing business processes most importantly for cybersecurity solutions, and guardtime federal is dedicatedly providing cyber-security solutions to the Department of Defence (United States), the Intelligence community of the U.S., and other departments of the U.S. government [8]. All these solutions offer confidentially and authenticated services.

Rijmenam, 2016 has stated that organizations are exploring this revolutionary technology of blockchain systems and finding how it can be beneficial for their businesses. It has also been observed that there is a possibility that blockchain will be used in almost all industries with some sort of transaction and many of them will face job losses as intermediaries' jobs will not be needed or needed a lot less. Blockchain is a technology that can give a well-built cybersecurity solution to information and data security issues and a high-level privacy protection tool for confidential information [9]. Furthermore, the protection given by multi-signature (multi-sig) or to authorize a transaction by more than one key, will improve security and privacy more efficiently.

Blockchain is a technology that is behind bitcoin also, and it is an open distributor ledger that records the data of transactions securely, permanently, and safely in a very efficient manner. Transferring the share stock used to take a week but with blockchain, it can be done in seconds. Blockchain has cut down the cost of transitions and eliminated the intermediary involvement of bankers and lawyers. It will take years to adopt blockchain technology like other internet technologies took years in their adoption [10]. Those companies that are into financial services are already doing well in adopting blockchain technology, and there is a strong possibility that it will affect all kinds of businesses and industries. Hsieh (2017) [11] stated in an article that blockchain security issues are critical in terms of cybersecurity. Before implementing it to the system, security experts need to go through and understand its impact, scope, and challenges carefully.

It has been expected that by 2027, identity theft will increase 25% and will cause a loss of 40.62 billion dollars [12]. The impact of cybercrime that results in payment fraud is depicted in Fig. (**1**). which describes the statistics of payment fraud, cybersecurity education is essential in the fight against hackers [13].

The CIA (Confidentiality, Integrity and Availability) triad model is used as a baseline and a standard for cybersecurity evaluation of any organization's cybersecurity strategy. Confidentiality, Integrity, and Availability are the trio that needs to be secured and Blockchain technology allows users to secure these three applications by its decentralized method. Confidentiality allows only specific selected access to those who are authorized to access the data. Blockchain encryption ensures that data will not be accessed by unauthorized parties. Data integrity can be maintained by utilizing blockchain-unique features that ensure the security of data. The most frequent cyberattack is Distributed Denial of Services (DDoS), the aim of the attack is to impact the availability of the technical service. However, it is expensive in a blockchain-based system as an attacker can overpower the network with a lot of small transactions [14].

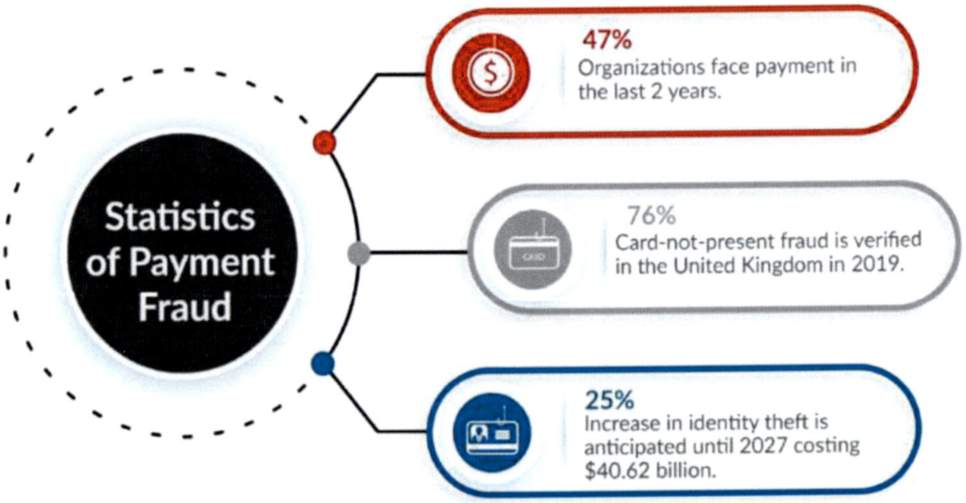

Fig. (1). Statistics of Payment Fraud. (Source: https://www.mdpi.com/applsci/applsci-11-07880/article_deploy/html/images/applsci-11-07880-g001.png).

New technologies that promise to enhance online safety are in progress to work upon and blockchain cybersecurity is leading the way. Unique features of blockchain can give benefits to the cybersecurity industry, which can create a virtually impassable wall between user information and hackers. Transparency of the ledger allows users an entry without passwords, use of biometrics including fingerprint scans and retina scans allows unbreakable single-source entry into the user's private data. To inhibit the information and data from hacking, decentralized storage makes sure that each block contains only a little information. This is a system of keeping records publicly. Blockchain's data manipulation is not easy, it will expose the cybercrime attempts in real-time.

BLOCKCHAIN TECHNOLOGY IS SECURE OR NOT?

The applications used by the industries are now based on remote communication that involves intermediate devices and numerous domains. The data and information related to users are linked to cyberspace and vulnerable to many attacks. Like in a healthcare system, a patient's data can result in serious consequences, which might threaten them. IoT platforms might have the same threats for their users, so it is important to provide security for the information and data shared by the network [15], and blockchain technology is the most appropriate solution to this problem. Blockchain technology keeps the data safe and secured like no other technology can do.

The ultimate goal of blockchain technology is to allow the storage of digital information that needs to be recorded and distributed but it doesn't allow editing of the recorded information, once the data is recorded it is very difficult to alter the stored content. If someone will try to change the information, the hash code will automatically change. The hash code is a small part of digital information in a form of numbers and letters, which is created by the math function. The change in the hash code can be found easily by others having the same information about the code.

Cybersecurity is a new approach that offers greater security with blockchain technology. This approach minimizes the risks and provides strong encryption. This approach has the expertise to verify data ownership and can remove the need for weak passwords that can be attacked by hackers easily. Blockchain uses a distributed ledger and it is the basic advantage of blockchain. Transactions on the distributed ledgers are recorded on every node and make it difficult for hackers to steal or attack the data. A distributive ledger can use the public key infrastructure for securing communication and validating changes in the configuration [16].

Blockchain will give nightmares to cybercriminals, data manipulators, and others whose intentions are to mishandle the personal data of any user. Blockchain seems a promising technology in which industries can foresee a safe and secure future by addressing multiple aspects of security and privacy. Challenges associated with the cloud can be directed and addressed by blockchain's decentralized and autonomous capabilities. Especially the decentralized structures provide a more secure approach while an increase in network size. The governments and the private sectors are overspreading in developing new and transformative technology such as blockchain. To encourage and support the private sector, the government should provide the necessary and required funding to those that are directed and working in the blockchain-based solution development and strengthen cybersecurity to protect privacy. While comparing the cloud and blockchain from a privacy and security perspective, various mechanisms have been mentioned to strengthen cybersecurity. In the cloud system, data is completely encrypted and creates a risk-free zone by monitoring suspicious activity constantly with a real-time response [17]. In addition, the data of blockchain technology is fully encrypted with cryptographic hash functions and the Private and Public-key cryptography ensures that the data is transferred between the intended users.

Serious consequences can occur for the users if an Internet of Things (IoT) device got hacked. It may result in the loss of personal data of users that can be used in any unlawful way. 20% of the resident's people of California (a state of the US) use smart water meters in their homes. Risks associated with cybersecurity should be considered with the dispersal of smart water meter as it collects the data and sends alerts on water leakage. Blockchain can be the most appropriate and promising tool to deal with the issue of privacy and security linked with these kinds of devices. It has been also noted that blockchain technology can give military-level security to IoT devices [18] and that can be considered a potential initiative contributing to strengthening the security and privacy of IoT devices.

New increasing demands on privacy protection and security are becoming a requirement for all with an increase in the popularity of blockchain technology. Various attacks have emerged with the increased usage of blockchain technology during the initial stage of its rapid development. Security risks may occur due to external entry attacks or by internal participants. According to the statistics report of the BCSEC economic losses, it's 2.1 billion dollars, which has occurred due to blockchain security incidents in 2018. Blockchain has layers of security that are divided into the top to bottom security levels. The blockchain structure is divided into six layers; Application, Smart Contract, Incentive, Consensus, Network, and Data layer [19].

The Application layer of the blockchain structure has the Mining Machine System, where the cyber security awareness of mining device manufacturers is irregular and the security code cannot be checked by the public due to its closed source system. The top layer of security is the Application layer - Which covers the security and privacy issues of centralized nodes that involve the transactions of a large amount of funds exchange. It provides security from unauthorized or unwanted access to an exchange server, as exchanges of large amounts of transactions are easy to target for hackers. Cybersecurity issues are serious and can give serious losses [20], blockchain seems a good fit to deal with issues related to cybersecurity.

The characteristics of blockchain technology offer promising cyber security and it gives security option to various fields of enterprises as well as startups. The sectors that are benefitted most from applying blockchain for cyber security include Finance, Real estate, Healthcare, Governance, and Supply chain [21]. There is no doubt that blockchain technology gives opportunities to maintain high-level data through data encryption, scalability, and network resilience. Switching to a blockchain-based system is more beneficial for almost all industries rather than sticking to the traditional system. Each technology came with challenges and drawbacks associated with it. So, organizations need to be ready and prepare themselves to deal with the complications while adopting blockchain technology [22]

It has been found by Peck, 2017 [17] that some areas of blockchain in cybersecurity need further investigation, based on a survey result and observations, the Blockchain for the Internet of Things (IoT) network is an utmost priority need of the industry that needs to be improved. The security of Internet of Things (IoT) systems may revive if they get support from blockchain technology. Furthermore, in the modern computing system, the data captured by different sources can be effectively secured by Artificial Intelligence (AI) technology. But intentionally or unintentionally, the data can be integrated by a malicious third party that could be based on adversarial inputs. As a popular ledger technology Blockchain has the potential to be leveraged in different areas of cyberspace and reduce the attempts of financial fraud. It has also been observed by Hasanova [23] that blockchain is a technology that brings an exorbitant array of possible solutions for finance, logistics, healthcare, and cyber security.

Traditional weaknesses like destructive actions and positive false errors can be eliminated and watched out through the blockchain's consensus algorithm without any interference from the central authority. Authentication and record management cannot be fooled by hackers attack [24]. However, Blockchain has many non-traditional features also, and it takes the advantage of its important cybersecurity tool which is encryption. A blockchain system can give a shield to many vulnerable devices like security cameras, *etc.* It has been found in a Palo Alto Network report that 98% of IoT devices traffic were unencrypted.

New challenges have been arising to improve cybersecurity with the development of the smart grid. With cutting-edge technologies, the smart grid is also emerging with other services of the smart cities like transportation, water/gas supply, *etc.* Several ways have been proposed to make the smart grid flexible against cyber-attacks and among the several methods, blockchain is the method that gives hope to protect the smart grid cybersecurity. It has also been found that blockchain can improve cybersecurity for data collection and other executions in the smart grid as blockchain is the most promising solution for the improvement of cybersecurity for the smart grid.

Blockchain adoption is the most visible in finance, cloud services, and supply chain management, these industries are more into storing huge data, managing the user's identity, and managing or creating smart contracts. And these are the applications where blockchain technology can be used fully. The development of blockchain technology is related to cybersecurity. The group of three pillars for any network is availability, confidentiality, and integrity. Blockchain provides integrity through its decentralized network validation and availability by showing transactions in blocks publicly that are not a means of satisfying confidentiality. There are a few vendors that are providing blockchain-powered cybersecurity, namely Block Armour, Hyland Credentials, Hacken, and Chronicled.

I. Block Armour offers a platform for unifying network access for Internet of Things (IoT) devices as well as for enterprises. This platform offers cybersecurity and using identity-based blockchain, it defends against internal threats.
II. Hyland credentials have grown into a leader that provides blockchain-secured digital records to private and public enterprises on a universal level. The company can manage the identity and activity that occurs in the system on a real-time secure blockchain.
III. Hacken was founded in 2017 and gives solutions in blockchain security, security assessment, and penetration testing.
IV. Chronicled started deploying its platform in 2014, it helps industries such as commodities, pharma, and metal to track their supply chain activities with their blockchain-enabled Internet of Things (IoT) devices.

ROLE OF BLOCKCHAIN IN CYBERSECURITY

Cybersecurity is an activity to protect, through which we can protect our systems and network from any kind of online hacking, attack, or threat that tries to edit, alter, delete, or tries to view any sensitive confidential data. With the increased reliance on technology, it has become necessary to check security systems that can protect data, as blockchain is one of the promising technologies for cybersecurity, its role has been discussed.

- To develop a standard security protocol, Blockchain technology can be used as it has end-to-end encryption and can also be used in private messaging to enable cross-messenger communication.
- By decentralized administration, blockchain technology can be used to secure the systems or individual devices.
- Blockchain technology can also assist in preventing the Distributed Denial of Services (DDoS) attacks by decentralizing Domain Name System (DNS) entries.
- Verifying the activities like firmware updates, patches, installers, *etc.* can be verified by blockchain technology.

- The data can get protection from unauthorized access while it is transformed by utilizing encryption and blockchain technology.
- Blockchain ensures its security feature that the information will be owned by only those people, who are in the network. Third-party interactions will not be needed.
- Security systems based on Blockchain authenticate devices as well as users through public key infrastructure. According to Remme's founder and CEO, Alex Momot, Blockchain makes authentication without a password, and it is possible through a combination of strong eliminating and authentication possibilities for a single point of attack.
- As social media is the center of today's generation, the end-to-end encryption provided by blockchain technology is being used by the obsidian app. This messenger app makes safeguards chats and also allows safe and secure exchange of data and files. Additionally, there is no need to link personal details with the Obsidian app, this app protects the user's privacy.

The major feature of blockchain is to secure the data and storage systems. The role of blockchain in cybersecurity has been discussed above which conclude that the use of these different ways of blockchain secures standard need of security for any organization as it provides the end-to-end encryption for private messages, secures systems, prevents the assaults, verifies the activities, provides a shield to that data from any kind of unauthorized access, and also protects the user's privacy. Blockchain has also been considered as an innovation for cybersecurity that will ensure and maintain confidentiality and data integrity. However, the implementation of blockchain technology may be challenging as its adoption for industries is a bit expensive.

INDUSTRIES USING BLOCKCHAIN IN CYBERSECURITY

Industries are using blockchain as a new weapon in cybersecurity to protect their sensitive information. The potential of blockchain technology with higher security has no limit to keeping important and sensitive information records. There are companies using blockchain in cybersecurity to intercede the most sensitive information. It also provides a variety of solutions to grow the business and industries have also started to realize the benefits and potential of blockchain technology in businesses.

How Crypto Currencies Using Blockchain in Cyber Security

The crypto currency was the first operational network that has been implemented behind Bitcoin. And now, blockchain has been used in thousands of different cryptocurrencies. Distributed Ledger Technology (DLT) gives protection to the crypto through encryption methods as well as public information sharing.

Encryption helps to control the cryptocurrencies amount being created. There are companies using blockchain as cybersecurity in cryptocurrency.

Mobilecoin

To handle the ledger information securely, the Mobile coin is working on developing a cryptocurrency that can be used easily for resource-constrained businesses. It will keep all transaction data encrypted that has been done between two parties. I will replace the third-party involvement in transactions and help to boost up security by keeping transparent records. To make an impact on industries, mobile coin is making their product to be easily integrated with Facebook Messenger, Signal, and WhatsApp.

Coinbase

Coinbase works as a mediating platform that allows users and buyers to exchange digital currency. Trading of Bitcoins, Litecoins, or Ethereum can be done on the company's secured platform blockchain. The system of coin base is entirely supported by encryption security. To ensure the users, the company saves the database of wallets and passwords with high security. The impact of coinbase on industries has been expended over 20 million coinbase users and more than 150 billion dollars has been processed in trades.

Javvy

A universal wallet has been built by Javvy, that trades and stores tokens and cryptocurrencies. Javvy uses Artificial Intelligence to detect fraudulent activities. The application of the company is fully based on blockchain decentralized technology with biometric logins. This application allows users to manage their cryptocurrencies more securely. On Nov 01, 2018, Javvy'stoken sale was launched and the funds were used to enhance cryptocurrency wallet technology.

How Healthcare Industries using Blockchain in Cybersecurity

The healthcare industry also experiences huge cyber-attacks as any other industry. Healthcare industries experience a doubling in the number of phishing emails and malware attacks. Patient information is important for cyber criminals so that more money can be demanded on the black market, so not only healthcare companies but hospitals, doctors, and clinic stores patients' data related to the bank need to be secured [25]. Card details of the patients are stolen constantly but now modern technologies resolve the issues quickly. Hackers can threaten or blackmail to release confidential information as they have already taken millions of dollars from hospitals and will continue to do the same unless more secure technologies will be implemented. In this situation, blockchain can be a badly needed solution. Distributed Ledger Technology (DLT) decentralized technology allows individuals to have a limited amount of information that would comprise a patient's full health information. There are some healthcare industries using blockchain cybersecurity technology to measure the attacks.

- Hashed Health: Hashed health is an innovation for healthcare industries that are working dedicatedly to implement blockchain technology. Hashed Health's system involves a blockchain healthcare community with hashed labs, hashed collective, and hashed enterprise, other than that company is also experimenting with the other ledger technologies. Hashed health also worked with other healthcare companies to secure patients' confidential information and protect the communication channels that work internally in the companies through blockchain networks. Hospitals and healthcare systems in the U.S. hold a value-based working group of hashed to improve payment efficiency and quality.
- Like hashed health, there are healthcare industries that are working on patient data security by using blockchain technology. Health Linkage (California) is working on making transparent data governance through blockchain technology and Philip healthcare (part of Philips research firm, Massachusetts) is using Artificial Intelligence with blockchain to create a new healthcare ecosystem. In partnership with hospitals, Artificial Intelligence is being used to analyze the administrative, medical, and operational data, and blockchain is being implemented to secure the huge amount of collected data.

How the Government Using Blockchain in Cybersecurity?

The government of many countries uses blockchain to protect their data and secure records storage. United States government has claimed that only 27% of the agencies had the potential to find out the large data, 38% of the companies from almost 31 thousand successful companies never find out the attacker as well as their methods, and 84% of all government agencies were failed to achieve basic encryption goals, the report on the same published by Office of Management and Budget (OMB). The issues faced by the United State government can be improved with blockchain technology because its system runs on encryption and puts a barrier for hackers. The features of blockchain-like decentralized information storage, encrypted data, and visible ledgers can be suitable solutions to implant the priorities of government cybersecurity.

In May 2018, The Colorado Senate also passed a bill to ask the government for considering blockchain in cybersecurity to protect important data and secure data storage. It has been stated in a report that Colorado experienced millions of attack attempts each day, so implementing the blockchain's technology encryption method is important.

Malta and Australian governments are those who are implementing blockchain and prioritizing the development of cybersecurity networks.

How Military and Defense Using Blockchain in Cybersecurity

The defense and military of the countries share important data and information with dispersed groups all over the world. Great innovative technological changes have been made in the defense sector in the past years and blockchain in cybersecurity can become the next breakthrough technology in the defense and military sector. It has been found by Accenture that 86% of the companies are planning to adopt blockchain, especially in cybersecurity in the coming years. Blockchain can safeguards and maximize the privacy of the confidential data and sensitive information of aerospace, defense, and military.

The technology branch of the United States Army is majorly interested in blockchain encryption and secure data transfer. Engineers are also working on creating a messaging system based on blockchain technology for the U.S. military. That can be used by military personnel to share information without worrying about hackers.

The Chinese military also thinks that blockchain encryption is a perfect tool to improve efficiency and it can defend against the attacker's attempt. China's government is looking at blockchain cybersecurity to protect their communication, data, and information from intelligence.

How Banking Systems Use Blockchain in Cybersecurity

"Banks are looking at blockchain for solutions to cybersecurity issues", said Jamie Dimon (Chairman and CEO of JP Morgan). Trillions of transactions and cash flow make banks an easy target for hackers and fraud. Outdated cybersecurity protocols of traditional banking make it easier for hackers and due to this many multinational banks experienced many cyber-attacks. An an annual report of the United States Office of the Comptroller of the Currency (OCC) suggests that multi-layered secured decentralized technological tools exactly like blockchain can provide safety to the banks.

Some banks have adopted blockchain technology like Santander, which was the first bank in the United Kingdom that has adopted blockchain to secure payments for their international-level transactions. Blockchain technology allows its users to pay between the accounts in Europe and South America securely.

J.P. Morgan is the largest financial institution in the United States and it has also developed a version of Ethereum called Quorum, which uses blockchain technology for processing private transactions.

FUTURE BENEFITS OF BLOCKCHAIN TO STRENGTHEN CYBERSECURITY

Businesses that use digital network platforms have the biggest challenge to save themselves from cyber-attacks. Cyber-attacks and breaches of online activities may result in huge damage. Although blockchain has become the trustable form of transaction in digital platforms, its design is also intended for its information integrity assurance. Blockchain has the potential to be implemented in multiple areas and one of the best uses can be assuring and building cybersecurity solutions. The key feature of blockchain technology is decentralization, which stops unauthorized activities and prevents cyber-attacks by providing cyber security through blockchain technology. There are some cases of future beneficial use of Blockchain in strengthening cybersecurity.

IoT (Internet of Things) Security

IoT devices have been used by the hackers and they are easy to target for them like through routers they gain access to the overall system very quickly. Artificial Intelligence obsession makes it easier for hackers to get access to the entire system by home automation as the edge devices have the smart switches option, and most of the IoT devices have this feature. In such cases, the devices can be secured by the blockchain's decentralized technology by using it in their administration. It will make the device capable of taking auto security decisions and securing it by detecting suspected activity from unknown networks. Hackers target the central administration of the device to get full control over it and by decentralized technology such device authority will not get harmed and blockchain ensures that this kind of attack will not be executed.

Cyber-Physical Infrastructure's Verification

The capability of blockchain technology in verifications and information integrity might be used in the authentication of the status of any cyber-physical infrastructure. Unknown and unwanted access to data or system misconfiguration affects the integrity of cyber-physical generated information. So, the data and information generated through blockchain can give more assurance completely.

Reducing Human Safety Adversity by Cyber-Attacks

The innovative technological devices, automated vehicles, and weapons facilitate the data transfer from sensors to remote-control databases. Automated military equipment and public transportation are examples of innovative technological advancements. Car Area Network (CAN) gives complete control access to hackers by only tapping, hackers have been continuously working on such activities to break and gain access to the networks. These kinds of activities impact human safety, but through data verification, many adversities can be stopped. Data verification conducted on the blockchain can save from such activities.

The Origin of Computer Software

The MD5 hashes can be utilized and blockchain can be applied to verify the integrity of downloaded software to prevent foreign intrusion. For the firmware updates, installers, and patchers, MD5 can be utilized to stop the entry of malicious software into the computer system. New software identity compared to hashes available on the vendor website. The method of the MD5 scenario is not completely infallible as the hashes can be already compromised. Although, in the case of blockchain technology, the hashes are permanently recorded and the recorded information is not changeable. So blockchain might be more efficient to verify the software integrity by comparing the hashes.

Private Message Security

Social applications are popular platforms and a source of collecting huge amounts of data through the interactions that occur between the users on social media platforms. As the internet is reaching every place, the world is shrinking into a global village, with an increase in social apps more people have now started joining social media. To protect their privacy, most social media platform users use weak and unreliable passwords. With the change in time and for user privacy, most messaging companies are now preparing to use blockchain technology as it gives end-to-end encryption. To form an integrated API framework, blockchain can be used to enable cross-messenger communication capabilities, as it creates a standard security protocol.

There are records of several attacks that have been executed against social platforms like some famous social media platforms such as Facebook and Twitter. If blockchain technology will be implemented well in social media apps or other messaging systems, it may prevent cyber-attacks in the future.

Securing Domain Name System (DNS) and Distributed Denial of Services (DDoS)

Attacks like DNS and Distributed Denial of Services (DDoS) happen when targeted user resources like networks, servers, or websites are denied the service or access. These kinds of attacks may result in slowing down the system or shutting it down. Domain Name System (DNS) has a centralized technology that makes it an easy target for hackers, who want to invade the connections between the website name and IP address. Blockchain's decentralized solutions can decrease the attacks by decentralizing the entries of the Domain Name System (DNS), and it can also remove the risky points that can be easily targeted by hackers.

Medium Storage Decentralization

Organizations now have primary concerns related to business data hacks and theft, most companies use a centralized form of storage which can be simply exploited by hackers. To get access to entire business data stored in the system, hackers can get it by finding a single weak point. These kinds of cyberattacks may give a huge loss of sensitive data related to business such as financial data records, *etc.* Blockchain can protect sensitive data by ensuring a decentralized storage form. This method will make it impossible for the hackers to get into the systems and attack the storage. Storage companies are now adopting the ways of blockchain to protect their data from hacker attacks. For example, Apollo Currency Team has already adopted blockchain technology to their systems as The Apollo Data Cloud.

Data Transfer Protection

The encryption feature of blockchain technology can be used in the future to stop unauthorized access of anyone during data transmission. It makes the transmission process secure and can lead to an increase in confidence in transferring data through blockchain technology [17].

MAJOR PROS AND CONS OF BLOCKCHAIN FOR CYBERSECURITY

Blockchain has the capabilities as a cybersecurity solution but it also draws parallel measures of risk associated with cybersecurity.

Strengths of Blockchain for cybersecurity are discussed in Fig. (**2**) as major pros of blockchain for cybersecurity. Blockchain records data that provide secure data storage and processing. It also enables secure and safe data transfers. Decentralized systems make them more resilient so there is no single point of failure. The history of transactions can be easily traced in blockchain due to data transparency and traceability feature. Blockchain network also provides user confidentiality that authenticates users by verifying users through their signature. Data privacy and transparency increase customer trust in different businesses.

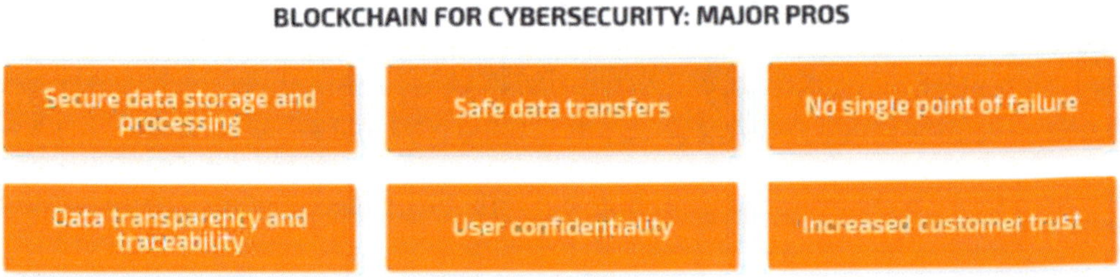

Fig. (2). Major Pros of Blockchain for cybersecurity. Source: https://www.apriorit.com/dev-blog/462-blockchain-cybersecurity-pros-cons.

Drawbacks of blockchain in cybersecurity are discussed in Fig. (**3**) as major cons of blockchain for cybersecurity. Scalability issues can occur during the number of transactions processed in a second as blockchain has different limits. Blockchain networks provide high security with private keys but reliance on private keys can be a drawback if the user loses the key the data recovery will be impossible. Blockchain technology can be a challenging technology while adapting to any business because it may require the complete replacement of existing systems, so adaptability challenges may occur. Although blockchain technology removes the possibilities of any malicious activity still it is not completely curable for cyber threats. High operation and customization costs are associated with blockchain. The development of blockchain technology requires a large skill set as well as different technical knowledge, so it is not easy to qualify as a blockchain developer.

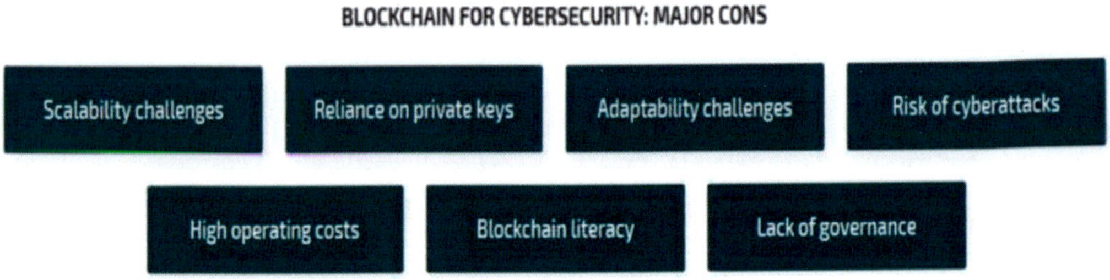

Fig. (3). Major Cons of Blockchain for cybersecurity. Source: https://www.apriorit.com/dev-blog/462-blockchain-cybersecurity-pros-cons.

ADVANTAGES AND DISADVANTAGES OF BLOCKCHAIN

The potential of blockchain technology for keeping the record is almost without limit. Providing high user privacy and security, blockchain technology has advantages as well as some disadvantages as discussed in Fig. (**4**). Blockchain and cybersecurity combination have captivating executives and technology experts even with their potential barriers. In a research report of Infosys published in 2020, respondents pointed out the use of blockchain as a top cybersecurity trend for the development of security solutions.

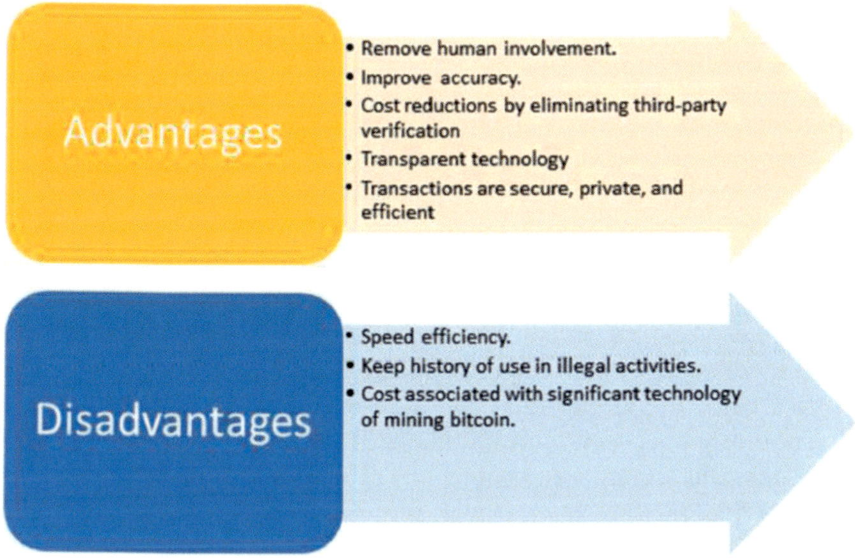

Fig. (4). Advantages and Dis-advantages of Blockchain in Cybersecurity. Source: Own development.

Advantages of Blockchain

- Remove Human Involvement: Transactions on the blockchain network remove almost all the human involvement because the transactions are approved by a network of thousands of computers.
- Improve Accuracy: Less human involvement results in an accurate record of information because it eliminates human errors.
- Cost Reduction: Blockchain removes the third-party verifications as well as the costs associated with that. In the case of bitcoin, there is a limited transaction fee associated.
- Transparent Technology: Blockchain technology works on open-source software that gives transparency to the users and anyone can view the code. Auditors can also review the cryptocurrencies like bitcoin for security.
- Secured Transactions: The authenticity of each transaction has been verified by the blockchain network. Details of purchasing went through the thousands of computers to check the accuracy; after the validation, the details were added to the blockchain block.
- Data protection: The technology of blockchain provides data protection and privacy by allowing selective access to information and transactions. It does not allow hackers to cut privacy at any level. It is hard to modify the information in the blockchain system.

- Public key Infrastructure management: Digital signatures are one of the core aspects of blockchain technology that provides security. The public key defines the digital identity and the private key authorizes the actions. The private key includes verification of transactions, secured encryption, and sign-in.

Disadvantages of Blockchain

- Speed efficiency: It has been estimated that blockchain networks can only manage seven transactions per second. Other cryptocurrencies are also available to give better performance and a Legacy brand visa can process 24,000 transactions per second.
- History of illegal activity: While protecting users from hacking and preserving privacy, blockchain network allows for such activities as trading that can be illegal in some way. Some websites allow browsing without being tracked which can be used by the user in the illegal purchasing of cryptocurrencies.
- Technology Cost: Consuming the computational power on higher-level results in high technology costs although blockchain saves the user money by saving transaction fees. But technology is not free and expenses that are associated with the technology make it costly.

CHALLENGES WITH BLOCKCHAIN

Blockchain-based cybersecurity is the new tool to adapt for multinational as well as government organizations but it doesn't seem easy for them to replace their existing toolkit smoothly. Blockchain and cybersecurity are still in their evolving stages and the characteristics of blockchain technology are not categorized by all types of businesses. Implementation of blockchain is not easy and its decentralized storage, securing edge devices, *etc.* are not aligned with all types of business needs and obstructions may occur while considering blockchain in cybersecurity strategy; some of them are mentioned below.

Regulations

It is a big challenge for organizations to understand how blockchain structure will fit into their data privacy, compliance, and regulations. Blockchain is a technology that prevents users from editing or deleting the data once it is stored. In some cases, there is a law to forget the data, in such cases, this technology will create risks of violating government laws and rules.

Privacy of Data

Public blockchain data is a concern for businesses as anyone can see and save the data in transactions. Those businesses that want to control the data and information sharing with the public will face these types of privacy issues. But this issue can be reduced by creating a permission blockchain where enterprises can control and give permission to trusted parties to view the transactions.

Interoperability

Low ability to exchange information between the systems or software lowers the scalability. Some of the platforms use a variety of ecosystems for their transaction schemes and smart contract logic. As per the developer's viewpoint, platform misconfiguration may create unwanted obstructions. But on the other side, the open protocols, algorithms, and multi-chain frameworks are reducing the issues by taking root in the blockchain.

Scalability

To give surety of privacy and security, all nodes store, process, and maintain the transactions in blocks. While implementing blockchain technology, scalability can restrict due to the size of the block or due to the time taken for responding. With the increase in transaction numbers, small size businesses starts struggling to store the number of transactions that growing speedily. This growing number of transactions may slow down the validation process.

Risks Associated with Technology

As blockchain has many benefits, on the other side it will come up with risks to the system if it will not be managed carefully. Efficiency, reduced cost, and improved security are the benefits of blockchain and the risks include the improper management of access control, inadequate encryption scheme selection and insecure operations, unintended chain split attacks and Application programming interface (API) integration.

I. The management of digital assets is dependent upon the end-users completely. Unauthorized access or theft of cryptographic keys may result in a loss that cannot be recovered. Improper key management and improper access control result in these kinds of losses.

II. By using cryptographic algorithms, saving sensitive data is not enough to protect it from attacks. Several factors make blockchain vulnerable, including inadequate encryption or inappropriate verification of digital signatures. Inadequate encryption scheme selection and insecure operations may result in the blockchain being unprotected.

III. There are chances tha nodes may not support the small changes made during the agreement phase while upgrading the smart contracts. In such cases when a new chain is split from the old and introduces risks, unauthorized parties can block and repeat the transactions. Unintended forks and chain split attacks may result in unauthorized parties' involvement.

IV. In private and public blockchain, third parties are required for Application programming interface (API) integration. API integration leads to unintentional leakage of information or sensitive data.

CONCLUSION

Blockchain technology has the ability of decentralization which makes it efficient to deal with cyber threats. Even in the coming days, it will be a trending technology that can be applied to every enterprise. There are challenges associated with the technology but they will lead to growth. Moving towards digitalization, companies need cybersecurity and privacy of their data and it can be managed by blockchain technology. It also gives the opportunities of maintaining data safety, network resilience, and scalability. To implement the blockchain technology model, a risk model should be developed so that risks associated with security threats can be evaluated. While enabling the private blockchain in any infrastructure, it should be secured and resilient. Automation of data storage eliminates human errors and can protect the data by dealing with unauthorized ways and cybercrimes. All layers' security is important so that it can be implemented more strategically and vulnerabilities can be considered at all the layers while bringing them into the operations. Cybercrime is a threat to any industry in the world and traditional security technologies are not able to deal with these vast cybercrimes. Blockchain has created trust in many industries to secure the data and gives potentially strong cybersecurity. Many industries are using blockchain technology to prevent their information and data from cybersecurity theft. To improve cybersecurity and make it more secure, Blockchain technology is the most reliable technology and also beneficial to almost all industries.

CONSENT FOR PUBLICATION

Not applicable.

CONFLICT OF INTEREST

The author declares no conflict of interest, financial or otherwise.

ACKNOWLEDGEMENTS

I would like to express my gratitude to my supervisor for guidance. I would also like to thank my family for their support and my sister Ritu Saini who helped me to follow the format guidelines of the chapter.

REFERENCES

[1] Martin. Arnold, "Five ways banks are using blockchain." Financial Times 16 (2017).

[2] S. Daily, *Wallets, hospitals and the Chinese military: 19 examples of blockchain cybersecurity at work.*, 2020.https://builtin.comhttps://builtin.com/blockchain/blockchain-cybersecurity-uses

[3] N. Kshetri, "Blockchain's roles in strengthening cybersecurity and protecting privacy", *Telecomm. Policy*, vol. 41, no. 10, pp. 1027-1038, 2017. [http://dx.doi.org/10.1016/j.telpol.2017.09.003]

[4] J. Kehrli, *Blockchain explained.*, 2016.https://www. netguardians. ch/news/2016/11/17/blockchain-explained-part-1

[5] J. Coward, "Meet the visionary who brought blockchain to the industrial IoT." IOT World News 14 (2016).

[6] S. Das, *Bitcoin Could Be Accepted at 300,000 Japanese Stores in 2017.*, 2017.https://www. cryptocoinsnews. com/bitcoin-accepted-300000-japanese-stores-2017/

[7] A. Farion, O. Dluhopolskyi, S. Banakh, N. Moskaliuk, M. Farion, and Y. Ivashuk, "Using blockchain technology for boost cyber security", [http://dx.doi.org/10.1109/ACITT.2019.8780019]

[8] R. Hackett, "How blockchains could save us from another Flint-like contamination crisis." (2017).

[9] M.V. Rijmenam, *What is the Blockchain and Why is it So Important?*, 2016. https://datafloq.com; https://datafloq.com/read/what-is-the-blockchain-and-why-is-it-so-important/2270

[10] G. Albeanu, "Blockchain technology and education", *The 12th International Conference on Virtual Learning ICVL*, 2017pp. 271-275

[11] Hsieh, Michael, and Samantha Ravich. "Leveraging Blockchain Technology to Protect the National Security Industrial Base from Supply Chain Attacks." Research memo, Foundation for Defense of Democracies (2017).

[12] R. Marley, *How Age Verification Protects the E-commerce Industry From Potential Risks.*, 2021.https://shuftipro.comhttps://shuftipro.com/blog/how-age-verification-protects--he-e-commerce-industry-from-potential-risks/

[13] N. Dey, *Role of Blockchain in Cybersecurity.*, 2021. https://www.geeksforgeeks.org/; https//www.geeksforgeeks.org/role-of-blockchain-in-cybersecurity/

[14] T. Salman, M. Zolanvari, A. Erbad, R. Jain, and M. Samaka, "Security services using blockchains: A state of the art survey", *IEEE Commun. Surv. Tutor.*, vol. 21, no. 1, pp. 858-880, 2019. [http://dx.doi.org/10.1109/COMST.2018.2863956]

[15] J. Legrand, *The Future Use Cases of Blockchain for Cybersecurity.*, 2020.https://www.cm-alliance.comhttps://www.cm-alliance.com/cybersecurity blog/the-future-use-ca-es-of-blockchain-for-cybersecurity

[16] P.J. Taylor, T. Dargahi, A. Dehghantanha, R.M. Parizi, and K.K.R. Choo, "A systematic literature review of blockchain cyber security", *Digital Communications and Networks*, vol. 6, no. 2, pp. 147-156, 2020. [http://dx.doi.org/10.1016/j.dcan.2019.01.005]

[17] M.E. Peck, "Blockchains: How they work and why they'll change the world", *IEEE Spectr.*, vol. 54, no. 10, pp. 26-35, 2017. [http://dx.doi.org/10.1109/MSPEC.2017.8048836]

[18] D. Schutzer, "CTO Corner: What is a Blockchain and why is it important? FSRoundtable." FS Roundtable, Washington, DC, USA, Tech. Rep 16 (2016).

[19] Chia, Vincent, Pieter Hartel, Qingze Hum, Sebastian Ma, Georgios Piliouras, Daniël Reijsbergen, Mark Van Staalduinen, and Pawel Szalachowski. "Rethinking blockchain security: Position paper." In

2018 IEEE International Conference on Internet of Things (iThings) and IEEE Green Computing and Communications (GreenCom) and IEEE Cyber, Physical and Social Computing (CPSCom) and IEEE Smart Data (SmartData), pp. 1273-1280. IEEE, 2018. [http://dx.doi.org/10.1109/Cybermatics_2018.2018.00222]

[20] S. Demirkan, I. Demirkan, and A. McKee, "Blockchain technology in the future of business cyber security and accounting", *Journal of Management Analytics,* vol. 7, no. 2, pp. 189-208, 2020. [http://dx.doi.org/10.1080/23270012.2020.1731721]

[21] https://www.ccn.comhttps://www.ccn.com/south-korean-exchange-youbit-declares-bankruptcy-after-second-hack-this-year

[22] P. Zhuang, T. Zamir, and H. Liang, "Blockchain for cybersecurity in smart grid: A comprehensive survey", *IEEE Trans. Industr. Inform.,* vol. 17, no. 1, pp. 3-19, 2021. [http://dx.doi.org/10.1109/TII.2020.2998479]

[23] H. Hasanova, U. Baek, M. Shin, K. Cho, and M.S. Kim, "A survey on blockchain cybersecurity vulnerabilities and possible countermeasures", *Int. J. Netw. Manage.,* vol. 29, no. 2, 2019.e2060 [http://dx.doi.org/10.1002/nem.2060]

[24] H. Wang, Y. Wang, Z. Cao, Z. Li, and G. Xiong, "An overview of blockchain security analysis", *China Cyber Security Annual Conference,* 2018pp. 55-72

[25] A. Razaque, A. Al Ajlan, N. Melaoune, M. Alotaibi, B. Alotaibi, I. Dias, A. Oad, S. Hariri, and C. Zhao, "Avoidance of cybersecurity threats with the deployment of a web-based blockchain-enabled cybersecurity awareness system", *Appl. Sci. (Basel),* vol. 11, no. 17, p. 7880, 2021. [http://dx.doi.org/10.3390/app11177880]

CHAPTER 3

Applications of Blockchain in Cyber Security Industry

N. Gupta[1,*] and **R. Agrawal**[1]

[1] *Manav Rachna International Institute of Research and Studies, Faridabad, Haryana, India*

Abstract: A blockchain is a decentralized record that is used to securely transfer digital currencies, make agreements, and trade. Everyone in the system goes to the most recent duplicate of the encoded record in order to authorize another transaction. A blockchain record is a collection of all prior bitcoin exchanges. Fundamentally, it is a suitable database that keeps up with a continually developing, highly organized information structure of blocks that hold a large number of individual transactions. Blockchain innovation has seen adoption in a variety of organizations, most notably in the use of digital currency. Regardless, innovation is useful in cyberspace. This chapter examined a few application cases of Blockchain in the cybersecurity industry. A majority of specialists are working on the acceptance of blockchain to safeguard IoT (Internet of Things) devices, systems, and information. The chapter has examined the methods proposed by previous analysts through which blockchain can carry the expense of security. Finally, the chapter has proposed the future of a single blockchain for building cyber security applications for coordination and consistency among security arrangements.

Keywords: Bitcoin, Blockchain technology, Cyber security.

INTRODUCTION

Blockchain is a cutting-edge innovation that has the potential to revolutionize the future of processing and challenge a few businesses with more imaginative arrangements. It is open, unchanging, and adequately adapted for all intents and purposes relevant to a variety of scenarios [1]. The rise of digital currency has increased interest in the idea, although it sees uses in a variety of fields other than finance. A blockchain is roughly equivalent to a few cryptographically attached blocks. A square alludes to a three-part information structure: information, the hash of the previous square, and the hash of the information and past hash. As a result, there is a demand for trust between blocks that can be used to ensure the integrity of the entire Blockchain. If the information in any of the blocks changes,

* **Corresponding author N. Gupta:** Manav Rachna International Institute of Research & Studies, Faridabad, Haryana, India; E-mail: neha.fca@mriu.edu.in

the hash value will change as well [2]. This will result in a spiraling impact in which the hashes of the resulting blocks will become invalid. This is why blockchain transactions are immutable. This foundation can be extremely useful in providing cyber security solutions in high-risk areas such as IoT gadgets, systems, and data storage and transmission.

Objectives of the Study

- To study the role of Blockchain in Cyber security.
- To study the future of Cyber security through Blockchain Technology.

Research Methodology

The chapter will illustrate the subjective investigation of supporting information to assess the relevance of blockchain innovation in the present cyber-security industry. It will concentrate on a recent report provided by Taylor *et al.* [18] that investigated 30 ongoing examinations contemplating on blockchain cyber security use cases.

ROLE OF BLOCKCHAIN IN CYBER SECURITY

The increased reliance on the web and innovation today has resulted in new revenue streams and plans of action for organizations; yet, this has also resulted in new gaps and open doors for programmers to exploit [3]. Cybercriminals have become increasingly perplexed and are attempting to take critical information like money, health records, individually identifiable data (PII), and licensed innovation, and are relying on exceptionally advantageous systems like disrupting a business's general operations through DDoS assaults, or adapting information access through the use of cutting edge ransom ware methods [4].

Given the current state of affairs, would blockchain innovation be an aid or a hindrance to cyber security? A blockchain, which employs Distributed Ledger Technology, is fundamentally a decentralized, digital, open record of all cryptographic money dealings [5]. This may aid to improve digital security because the platform may prevent deceptive exercises through agreement components and recognize information altering based on its fundamental attributes of operational flexibility, information encryption, auditability, straightforwardness, and permanence [6].

Blockchain resolves the 'lack of confidence' issue between counterparties at a critical level. Blockchain is a distributed database that is used in both private and open applications, as opposed to a centralized system in which all data is stored in a few extremely large databases [7]. The information pertaining to each cluster of valid trades is saved within its own block; each block is related to the block which is arranged in the situation before it and develops continuously as new data blocks are affixed.

ELIMINATING HUMAN FACTOR FROM AUTHENTICATION

Organizations can verify gadgets and clients without the requirement for a secret phrase with the assistance of blockchain innovation [8]. This disposes of human mediation from the procedure of confirmation, in this way maintaining a strategic distance from turning into a potential assault vector.

The use of a combined design and simple logins is a major drawback of standard frameworks. Regardless of how much money an organization invests in security, all of these efforts are pointless if employees and clients use passwords that are simple to steal or split. Blockchain provides reliable verification while also resolving a single point of attack. A security framework used in an organization can use a dispersed open key foundation for validating gadgets and customers with the assistance of blockchain [9]. Instead of a secret word, this security framework assigns a unique SSL endorsement to each device. Because the executives of endorsement information are finished on the blockchain, it is practically impossible for aggressors to utilize counterfeit authentications.

Decentralized Storage

Blockchain users can keep their data on their PC in their system. In this way, they can assure that the chain does not break. For example, if someone who isn't the owner of a piece of information (for example, an assailant) tries to meddle with a block, the entire framework examines every single information block to discover the one that differs from the rest [10]. If this type of block is found by the framework, it simply removes the block from the chain, marking it as fraudulent.

Blockchain is designed in such a way that there is no capacity area or focal authority. On the system, each client has a task to complete in terms of storing some or all of the blockchains [11]. Everyone in the blockchain network is responsible for verifying the information that is transmitted as well as keeping it up to ensure that existing information is not expelled and fake information is not incorporated.

Traceability

Each exchange that is uploaded to a private or open blockchain is meticulously time stamped and tagged. This means that companies can trace each trade back to a certain timeframe and locate the comparable party on the blockchain using their open location [12]. This aspect is associated with non-renunciation: the assurance that someone can't check the veracity of their mark on a document, or the starting of an exchange that they started. As each trade is cryptographically linked to a client, the current blockchain's utility improves the framework's steadfast quality. Any new transaction that is added to a blockchain changes the global state of the record. This means that with each new cycle of the framework, the previous state will be saved, resulting in a fully observable history log.

Blockchain's review capability provides companies with a level of security and transparency over each emphasis. From the standpoint of cyber security, this provides elements with an additional level of assurance that the information hasn't been tampered with and is correct [13].

Due to their communicated nature, blockchains provide no 'hackable' entrance or an essential issue of disappointment and, as a result, provide more security when contrasted with other current database-driven value-based structures [14].

In any case, it will look at the most recent applications of the developing blockchain innovation in cyber security. Second, it will investigate the methods available for transmitting blockchain cyber security arrangements. The main takeaways from the research discoveries and ideas from the broken-down papers will be used to build a discussion on how blockchain may bear the expense of security in current IT client settings [15].

The distributed form of recordkeeping is another important component of blockchain. Hubs in a blockchain system can store all of the system's information if necessary. Many hubs do this because it is necessary for either agreement or reference purposes [16]. This ensures that there is no combined data capacity. Any adversary attempting to trade the blockchain must bargain a significant number of the hubs that store decentralized bits of information. This is because the system examines the information blocks stored in decentralized areas to identify those that differ from the others. The advanced features of blockchain make it ideal for today's cyber security requirements. One way blockchain can be integrated into cyber security is through the development of devices that can prevent misrepresentation and data fraud [17]. Clients are constantly exposed to the risk of unauthorized access and alteration of information. This is due to the fact that various clients have gathered information stockpiling. It is thus straightforward for a coder to breach the information storage area and modify the information with malicious intent. With its dispersed storage of knowledge, blockchain prevents such instances. Oversensitive information, such as political decision results, may be stored in this manner on a large number of PCs, with each having a duplicate of the information.

Unless the programmer can bargain a large number of PCs with duplicates of information, the break and change of merely a couple of PCs will have no effect on the rest of the information in the system. Furthermore, Blockchain can be used to avoid data fraud [11]. According to NASDAQ, the current information robbery instances are the result of insufficient information on the board.

Clients are typically requested to show more than necessary information in order to obtain administrations from different enterprises. These organizations promise to protect the information, but programmers frequently end up identifying exploitable security gaps and infiltrating information storage facilities. Through decentralized identity architecture, blockchain can prevent fraud by ensuring that a client is whom they claim to be [12]. This can be completed by utilizing an all-inclusive framework in which all associations can check the personalities of clients without fundamentally requiring them to move their sensitive peculiarities. This reduces the possibility of a bargain and makes it more expensive for programmers.

HOW DOES BLOCKCHAIN PROVIDE CYBER SECURITY?

Because of the complicated structure of blockchain innovation, it is the most secure. As a result, trendsetters have begun implementing blockchain technology in a variety of fields to combat theft and improve information security. Bitcoin is expanding, but the blockchain is evolving. Bitcoin is a continual source of inspiration for blockchain innovation. Blockchain, on the other hand, is far more than just Bitcoin [14]. In terms of security, blockchain and its open record can provide solutions for Big Data management, endpoint assurance programming, monetary devices, and flexibly chain the executives' programming. Blockchain innovation has had an impact on the digital security business in several ways. The HYPR Corp is a New York-based firm that provides businesses with decentralized validation arrangements that enable consumers and representatives to use portable, Web, and Internet of Things (IoT) apps safely and consistently. It makes use of blockchain technology to decentralize accreditations and biometric data in order to incentivize risk-based verification. Every year, it spends US$ 10 million on this stage. NuCypher is another blockchain security firm that employs relayed blockchain frameworks intermediate re-encryption [15]. It also features an available control stage and employs open key encryption to safely move data and authorize access requirements.

Blockchain is one of the most prominent tech expressions in recent years, and the innovation is being touted as a solution for everything, including digital security. In March 2018, the US Ministry of Internal Affairs and Communications implemented a blockchain-based framework for drafting federal tenders. Each blockchain client has a private and public key. Any client who wishes to execute creates an advanced mark with the private key and the information to be transmitted. This newly created digital mark is given to the collector along with the transaction. The beneficiary has the sender's open key, which may be used to check the client [16].

For all of our digital security concerns, blockchain resembles the Swiss blade. Money exchanges are frequently guaranteed by a trusted outsider (for example, PayPal), and the blockchain can be used to computerise that procedure, decreasing overall expenses by removing the middle man with self-governing brilliant agreements and acting as a trusted middle person between parties on the system.

In the middle of the growing adoption of blockchain, the US-based Defense Advanced Research Projects Agency (DARPA) is also funding and supporting the use of Blockchains to help secure extremely sensitive information linked to everything from atomic bombs to nuclear power plants. Stocks, mutual funds, bonds, and annuities may one day be stored in a blockchain, and a number of financial institutions are researching this new technology.

Blockchain innovation is having a significant impact on the digital security business today. By removing a large portion of the human component from information storage, blockchain fundamentally reduces the risk of human errors, which is the leading cause of information leakage [17]. It is a decentralized distributed record architecture that is used to record information exchanges across various PCs. Blockchain technology can be used to prevent any type of data breach, data fraud, digital assaults, or unfavorable outcomes.

This ensures that the information remains private and secure. A few examples of how blockchain might aid with digital security are mentioned below:

- Guaranteed edge calculating with verification: Blockchain can help to reinforce confirmation, increase information attribution, and reorganize executive records.
- Propelled secrecy and information uprightness.
- Secure private information.
- Improved open key framework.

Unblemished Domain Name System (DNS): The DNS is an obvious target for noxious exercises because programmers can cut down the DNS specialized organizations for huge sites like Twitter, PayPal, and other administrations. A blockchain approach to dealing with solid DNS passes can increase overall security by removing that one point of failure.

Reduced DDoS assaults: A Distributed Denial of Service (DDoS) assault is one in which multiple compromised PC frameworks attack a target, for example, a server, website, or another system asset, and create a loss of administration for clients' targeted assets. This allows the framework to back off or possibly crash, denying assistance to genuine clients or frameworks. This issue can be resolved by integrating the blockchain into decentralized arrangements, which can provide protection against such attacks.

Blockchain does not require passwords because it relies on biometric information or private keys, as well as numerous steps for verification, to ensure that clients are who they claim to be. These frameworks provide more powerful data security than client names, passwords, and so forth. The rise of smart gadgets and other largely self-governing innovations has also given rise to increased levels of hacking. The Internet of Things has opened up a new avenue for hacking that is less prone to early detection and, as a result, may provide an alternative to phishing methods. Experts are now relying on blockchain innovation to detect erroneous or potentially degenerate instructions and inputs, and to keep a framework's usefulness from being completely terminated.

Information is all-inclusive cash. According to one source, a single buyer's information is worth at least US$ 240 every day and probably much more. Keeping information in a centralized database is popular these days, as it may easily be hacked by programmers. Because the blockchain is naturally decentralized, there is no one point of ingress for programmers to target.

We are living in a period of digital battle that is more dangerous than a ransomware disruption against a firm. In 2017, the national administration of the United States was the target of 61,000 digital assaults, each with varying degrees of danger. Elevated-level blockchains are well-known for their exceptional security features and their ability to limit the damage caused by digital disruption to the foundation. Blockchain DNA digital resistance security frameworks will provide another type of digital barrier framework.

USES OF BLOCKCHAIN TECHNOLOGY IN CYBER SECURITY

- **Protected Edge Computing with Authentication**

Edge processing is advantageous for IT performance, profitability, and force utilisation; nevertheless, it poses a security concern for CISOs, CIOs, and the larger corporation; thus, Blockchain is providing an option for secure IoT and Industrial IoT. It will aid in the reinforcement of verification, improved information attribution and stream, as well as the updating of executive records.

- **Ensures Confidentiality and Data Integrity**

Blockchain was created with no precise access limitations at first, as evidenced by its inclination for open conveyance. However, when the invention began to provide answers for various organizations, blockchain usage now has scope for information secrecy as well as access control. The blockchain's entire encryption ensures that information is not accessible to any unjust individual or organization while in transit.

- **Security in Private Messaging**

A large number of firms are investigating blockchain to ensure the security of their personal and private data traded across chats, informative applications, and internet networking. They desire to turn it into a secure stage that is impervious to faraway attacks by utilizing blockchain.

- **Improved Public Key Infrastructure (PKI)**

PKI, or Public Key Infrastructure, maintains apps, messages, websites, and all sorts of correspondence secure. They all, however, rely on outside testament specialists to issue, disavow, or store key sets. These authentication specialists can become a clear target for programmers using spoof characters attempting to breach encoded correspondences. However, when keys are distributed on a blockchain, there is no room for a false key age or widespread fraud because the applications validate the identity of the person you're dealing with.

- **Intact Domain Name System(DNS)**

The DNS is an obvious target for malicious activities because programmers can reduce DNS specialised co-ops for substantial sites like Twitter, Paypal, and other administrations. A blockchain approach to storing these DNS portions can increase security broadly since it eliminates the one particular purpose that can be subverted.

- **Decline in Denial of Service Attacks**

A distributed denial of administration (DDoS) assault is one in which numerous traded-off PC frameworks attack an objective, for example, a server, site, or another system asset, and cause a refusal of administration for clients of the targeted asset. This causes the framework to back off or perhaps crash and shut down, denying assistance to genuine clients or frameworks. This problem can be solved by integrating blockchain into decentralized arrangements that provide security against such attacks.

We can design and adopt numerous security measures, but threats also adapt and adjust in the same way. Nonetheless, with blockchain, we have a massive amount of assurance that information is secure.

As more people connect to the internet and technology advances, more data is created, and more programmers attempt to extract or degrade that data. Blockchain innovation is adaptable and astoundingly helpful for the final fate of the Internet, allowing clients to more easily ensure the accuracy of their data.

Innovative blockchain applications are gradually becoming a part of fields other than digital money and can be particularly useful in assisting cyber security. By implementing comprehensive encryption and information conveyance rules on a system, any organization may ensure that its data will remain secure, undamaged, and out of the reach of programmers.

FUTURE OF BLOCKCHAIN TECHNOLOGY: PREDICTIONS FOR 2030

For more than a decade, digital currencies and blockchain innovation have engulfed the world. Some argue that this is only the beginning. With several businesses across various industry verticals embracing blockchain at a rapid speed, it is apparent that blockchain is transforming into a development and is steadily progressing toward the next period of blockchain upheaval. Blockchain is quickly becoming an unavoidable marvel because of the fundamentally powerful improvements and enormous open doors it gives to computerized firms.

Blockchain will be Leveraged for a Majority of the World Trade

The global flexibility chain is one such encouraging area where blockchain might provide significant commercial value. There are a lot of wasteful features, misrepresentations, and errors in world exchange right now because it is directed through a disorderly arrangement of untrustworthy commercial connections. A rundown of this present reality flexibly affix issues which should be understood are:

- Fake automobile parts.
- Fake drugs.
- Corruption in the food flexibility chain.
- Counterfeit style attire and extravagant things.
- Fake electronic gear, including clinical gadgets.

These Markov chain problems are dangerous. This is mostly due to the fact that business biological systems are fragmented, only partially robotized, and lack a dependable focal point to ensure credibility and monitor provenance. Blockchain is one such breakthrough that will be resistant to disruption, bringing demand and acting as a force for unification. Blockchain will play a critical role in improving execution, adaptability, productivity, and growth.

Frictionless Flows And Digital Assets

In 2030, trillion-dollar tokens will outnumber trillion-dollar companies. At the present time, a race is taking place amongst Google, Apple, Microsoft, and Amazon, four highly regarded global corporations. These are valued at trillions of dollars. Blockchain will have a favorable impact on computerized businesses and will increase the incentive for financial transactions. The cost of trades and data streams is dramatically reduced thanks to blockchain. The blockchain facilitates the flow of tokens and other resources in a frictionless manner. Trillion-dollar tokens will play a crucial role in the future of blockchain technology. These are tokens that support a biological system of elements that is decentralized.

Blockchain Identity for All

Every individual and their virtual or actual resources will have blockchain personalities by 2030, if not sooner. By reaching a variety of character arrangements, blockchain will aid in the improvement of frameworks. Because current personality frameworks are ineffective and untrustworthy, blockchain innovation will serve as a single source of verification for both individuals and resources. This will help:

- Increment protection and productivity.
- Decentralize and confirm the information gathered.
- Store data in a solitary record.
- Diminish the danger of security penetration.

Make another character stage that is dispersed and not constrained by a focal power. This builds straightforwardness. Some utilization instances of blockchain in the character area are business records, charge distinguishing proof records, government records, authentications and human services records, and notoriety scores.

Considerable Improvements in the Global Standard of Living

Today, destitution and wage fraud are the most difficult concerns that humanity must deal with. Over 10% of the population, or over 750 million people, live on less than $2 each day. Over 2 billion people are considered unbanked since they do not use financial services. Blockchain has the potential to significantly reduce the gap in impoverishment. This is accomplished in three different ways, which are:

Reducing Corruption – The blockchain ensures the integrity of legitimate records. All subtleties, including land, will be recorded on permanent (sealed), plain, and secure digital records that will be completely open to the public. Susceptibility to any advantage reduces its recognizability potential and resource cost. Creating an allocated, resource-following framework will aid in the expansion of global wealth. Sifting through this maze will have enormous positive monetary consequences for the global economy.

Financial comprehensiveness – This is an evident benefit of digital currencies such as Bitcoin. Unbanked people can use cryptographic forms of money and blockchain to get banked and, as a result, receive payment. There is no compelling reason to rely on a consolidated institution, such as a bank or government, to offer approval to opening a financial account when blockchain innovation is used. It will provide easy access to a crypto exchange where users can buy and sell digital currencies using their smartphones. With a large number of shippers around the world tolerating cryptographic forms of money, digital currencies will become a true standard by 2030, similar to the United States Dollar, which is widely accepted now.

Tokenization of Value-Generating Assets – Tokenization refers to the use of sophisticated tokens to demonstrate resource accountability. The blockchain facilitates the tokenization of large-scale resources. This means that even a rancher from a rural area can become a part-owner of an income-generating resource, such as an inn or a gold mine. When compared to traditional protections, this will help open up a prospective financial specialized base to a larger market, reduce exchange time, and increase liquidity.

FINDINGS AND SUGGESTIONS

The results of the 30 research revealed that blockchain was becoming increasingly practical in IoT, system, and data storage security.

Because there are currently 9 billion such devices, the focus on blockchain IoT security is justified. These devices have weak security designs, and many of them are hacked and added to botnet networks. The Mirai Botnet, which has been used with great degrees of success against large targets such as Dyn DNS, one of the Internet's leading area name objectives firms, is one such botnet organization that has integrated IoT devices. As a result, a number of security researchers are looking at ways to ensure that these devices are secure using blockchain. The second major focus of blockchain cyber security research is information stockpiling. This is due to the increased number of data breaches in which programmers have had the ability to infiltrate information from corporations with billions of clients. For instance, the Yahoo data breach in 2014 resulted in the theft of information from three billion users. As a result, security researchers are investigating blockchain security solutions for information extra rooms, such as cloud stages. It can also be noticed that scientists are looking at the use of blockchain for ensuring the security of systems. Since current system safety attempts, such as security through WPA encryption, can be subverted, the significant majority of the examination in these territories is focused on verification. Finally, there is a lot of interest in blockchain security solutions for information security. The great bulk of the experiments are evaluating strategies for ensuring recognized data by using a widely used blockchain confirmation graphic. Clients will no longer be required to communicate their data to associations; instead, associations will confirm clients using the blockchain.

CONCLUSION

In the cutting-edge world, blockchain innovation continues to evolve and explore new application cases. Cybersecurity is one of the appropriate areas where it has been studied and used. The blockchain foundation allows it to be extremely practical in dealing with contemporary security concerns in areas such as IoT devices, systems, data transfer and capacity. Most blockchain security scientists appear to be concentrating their efforts on the adoption of blockchain security for IoT devices. Nearby this, other significant regions of blockchain security are systems and information. Blockchain technology can be utilized to ensure the security of IoT devices by utilizing increasingly solid confirmation and information transfer components. These can prevent programmers from breaking into these devices, which often have insecure security designs. The innovation can also be used to ensure the security of systems by utilizing the severe framework to prevent unauthorized connections and communication15. Finally, blockchain ensures information transmission and capacity through scrambled squares that can only be opened by the transmitting parties and are not subject to control. Despite the fact that other use cases are being concentrated, these three have become the primary focus. Future researchers should look into the feasibility of using a single blockchain to establish security arrangements, because the vast majority of current arrangements use several blockchains, which makes reconciliation difficult.

CONSENT FOR PUBLICATION

Not applicable.

CONFLICT OF INTEREST

The author declares no conflict of interest, financial or otherwise.

ACKNOWLEDGEMENT

Declared none.

REFERENCES

[1] W. Li, S. Andreina, J-M. Bohli, and G. Karame, Securing proof-of-stake blockchain protocols.*Data privacy management, cryptocurrencies and blockchain technology* Springer: Cham, 2017, pp. 297-315.
[http://dx.doi.org/10.1007/978-3-319-67816-0_17]

[2] D. Li, W. Liu, L. Deng, and B. Qin, "Design of multimedia blockchain privacy protection system based on distributed trusted communication", *Trans. Emerg. Telecommun. Technol.,* vol. 32, no. 2, p. e3938, 2021.
[http://dx.doi.org/10.1002/ett.3938]

[3] H.T.M. Gamage, H.D. Weerasinghe, and N.G.J. Dias, "A survey on blockchain technology concepts, applications, and issues", *SN Computer Science,* vol. 1, no. 2, p. 114, 2020.
[http://dx.doi.org/10.1007/s42979-020-00123-0]

[4] K. Karantias, A. Kiayias, and D. Zindros, "Proof-of-burn", *International conference on financial cryptography and data security,* 2020pp. 523-540 Cham
[http://dx.doi.org/10.1007/978-3-030-51280-4_28]

[5] L. Chen, L. Xu, N. Shah, Z. Gao, Y. Lu, and W. Shi, "On security analysis of proof-of-elapsed-time (poet)", *International Symposium on Stabilization, Safety, and Security of Distributed Systems,* 2017pp. 282-297 Cham

[6] N. Gupta, A Deep Dive Into Security and Privacy Issues of Blockchain Technologies.*Handbook of Research on Blockchain Technology* Academic Press, 2020, pp. 95-112.
[http://dx.doi.org/10.1016/B978-0-12-819816-2.00004-6]

[7] N. Gupta, Security and privacy issues of blockchain technology.*Advanced Applications of Blockchain Technology* Springer: Singapore, 2020, pp. 207-226.
[http://dx.doi.org/10.1007/978-981-13-8775-3_10]

[8] L. Kristian, J. Mattila, and T. Seppala, "Smart contracts–How will blockchain technology affect contractual practices?", *Etla Reports 68,* 2017.
[http://dx.doi.org/10.2139/ssrn.3154043]

[9] D. Macrinici, C. Cartofeanu, and S. Gao, "Smart contract applications within blockchain technology: A systematic mapping study", *Telemat. Inform.,* vol. 35, no. 8, pp. 2337-2354, 2018.
[http://dx.doi.org/10.1016/j.tele.2018.10.004]

[10] D. Efanov, and P. Roschin, "The all-pervasiveness of the blockchain technology", *Procedia Comput. Sci.,* vol. 123, pp. 116-121, 2018.
[http://dx.doi.org/10.1016/j.procs.2018.01.019]

[11] Y. Lu, "The blockchain: State-of-the-art and research challenges", *J. Ind. Inf. Integr.,* vol. 15, pp. 80-90, 2019.

[12] J. Truby, "Decarbonizing Bitcoin: Law and policy choices for reducing the energy consumption of blockchain technologies and digital currencies", *Energy Res. Soc. Sci.,* vol. 44, pp. 399-410, 2018. [http://dx.doi.org/10.1016/j.erss.2018.06.009]

[13] M. Niranjanamurthy, B.N. Nithya, and S. Jagannatha, "Analysis of blockchain technology: Pros, cons and SWOT", *Cluster Comput.,* vol. 22, no. S6, pp. 14743-14757, 2019. [http://dx.doi.org/10.1007/s10586-018-2387-5]

[14] X. Ling, Y. Le, J. Wang, Z. Ding, and X. Gao, "Practical modeling and analysis of blockchain radio access network", *IEEE Trans. Commun.,* vol. 69, no. 2, p. 1, 2020. [http://dx.doi.org/10.1109/TCOMM.2020.3029779]

[15] J. Bae, and H. Lim, "Random mining group selection to prevent 51% attacks on bitcoin", *2018 48th Annual IEEE/IFIP International Conference on Dependable Systems and Networks Workshops (DSN-W),* 2018pp. 81-82 [http://dx.doi.org/10.1109/DSN-W.2018.00040]

[16] M.R. Islam, M.M. Rahman, M. Mahmud, M.A. Rahman, and H.S.M. Muslim, "A review on blockchain security issues and challenges", *2021 IEEE 12th Control and System Graduate Research Colloquium (ICSGRC),* 2021pp. 227-232 [http://dx.doi.org/10.1109/ICSGRC53186.2021.9515276]

[17] C. Decker, and R. Wattenhofer, "Bitcoin transaction malleability and MtGox", *European Symposium on Research in Computer Security,* 2014pp. 313-326 Cham

[18] P.J. Taylor, T. Dargahi, A. Dehghantanha, R.M. Parizi, and K.K.R. Choo, "A systematic literature review of blockchain cyber security", *Digital Communications and Networks,* vol. 6, no. 2, pp. 147-156, 2020. [http://dx.doi.org/10.1016/j.dcan.2019.01.005]

CHAPTER 4

Overview of Attack Surfaces in Blockchain

S. Zalte[1,*], **H. Bhatia**[2], **R. Deshmukh**[3], **N. Gupta**[4] and **R. Kamat**[5]

[1] *Department of Computer Science, Shivaji University, Kolhapur, India*

[2] *School of Computer Science, Engineering and Applications, D Y Patil International University, Pune, India*

[3] *Department of Computer Science, Shivaji University, Kolhapur, India*

[4] *Manav Rachna International Institute of Research and Studies, Faridabad, Haryana, India*

[5] *Department of Computer Science, Shivaji University, Kolhapur, India*

Abstract: In blockchain technology, cybercriminals exploit new attack surfaces for non-legitimate persons who wish a dissemination of fake information, encourage cyber attacks, unethical behavior, *etc.* Attacks are believed to be attributed to the blockchain cryptographic architecture, the bottom-line architecture, and the substance in which they are applied. The main threat is focused on the progressive defense research activity. It is currently believed that other attacks on the blockchain can be launched without being able to withstand traditional defenses, a few of which may be used to deliver any other attack. By delineating these attacks and examining their countermeasures, it highlights the direction of new research that should be persisted for safer and more competent use of blockchain. In spite of vulnerabilities and attacks, this technology offers key features like hashing, immutability and digital signature, which enrich the blockchain. Researchers also contributed to developing a security shield for blockchain by using an intelligent combination of these features. Basically, these features are required to achieve CIA (Confidentiality, Integrity and Authentication). The contribution of this chapter would be systematically investigating the attack surface of Blockchain technology. The attack surface is the sum of all conceivable security risk exposures. It is also the total of all known and undiscovered threats, possible vulnerabilities, and controls, including all resources. To do this, we set attack vitality on the attack surface to a variety of attacks.

Keywords: Attack surface, Block chain, CIA, Defense research activity, Vulnerabilities.

* **Corresponding author S. Zalte:** Department of Computer Science, Shivaji University, Kolhapur, India; E-mail: sheetal.zaltegaikwad@gmail.com

Rashmi Agrawal and Neha Gupta (Eds.)

INTRODUCTION

Blockchain technology is an open-source, decentralized ledger, based on a peer-to-peer distributed network that records immutable and encrypted transactions which are verified between two entities without the involvement of a third party. Blockchain technology is secured as it is based on the concept of cryptography and peer-to-peer networks or distributed networks. The use of cryptography in blockchain technology enables to establish trust between entities of a network *via* digital signatures, enables integrity and immutability *via* hash functions and helps in transactions that are publicly verified and un-altered. On the other hand, the peer-to-peer network in blockchain eliminates the issue of single-point-of-failure and single point-of-trust, and allows for transaction ledger verification without the need for a centralized authority [1].

Apart from this, blockchain also supports other significant features like distributed ledger, consensus, availability and smart contracts *etc.,* as shown in Table **1**. Now, Blockchain technology is accustomed by the world and is being investigated in new and forthcoming novel applications [2]. Due to its vast application possibilities, blockchain has sparked a lot of curiosity among academics and industry. Blockchain technology is being employed in different domains like cryptocurrencies [5], Ethereum-based smart contract platforms and 'Decentralized Autonomous Organizations (DAOs)' like Dash and Bitshares [3, 4, 6], health care [7], Internet of Things [8, 9], financial systems [10], Vehicular Ad-hoc Networks (VANET), and edge computing [11, 12] and many more, *etc.*.

Table 1. Features of Blockchain.

Key Features	Description
Immutability	Allows to store transactions permanently and nobody can modify transactions once entered into the system.
Transparency	All Blockchain users have access to each public address's transactions, which are safe and secure.
Peer-to-peer network	Allows the execution and verification of transactions without the use of central authority or third party
Consensus	A fault-tolerant methodology and method of establishing consensus across all Blockchain participants
Smart contract	Self – executing contract allow the transaction without third parties
Distributed ledger	A decentralized database that is accessible to multiple users to create and update single, trusted transactions across multiple locations
Anonymity	The ability of node in the network to perform transaction or exchange data without revealing its identity.

The security of the blockchain is important as its use is not only limited to cryptocurrencies and smart contracts but used in large-scale systems which are used to hold delicate or user-specific sensitive data and information. In spite of the invulnerable security functionality of Blockchain technology that brings to applications, several attacks have been launched against this technology. For example, due to the popularity and capital tied to its system, blockchain-based cryptocurrencies are exposed to multiple activities that are fraudulent. Mt. Gox, a Tokyo-based Bitcoin exchange in Japan, was hacked by two malicious attackers who stole $ 460 million in bitcoins [13]. The hackers collected data from the Bitcoin blockchain and manipulated counterfeiting transactions that led to a surge in the market price. As a result of such activities, Mt. Gox suffered severe losses and, in the end, went ruined. Furthermore, the Bitcoin blockchain is overloaded with fraudulent or spam transactions, which causes legitimate transactions to be delayed. In 2017, Bitcoin storage pools were swamped by unethical transactions, which leads locks and delays in transaction verification, increasing the Bitcoin mining fee [14]. Furthermore, in June 2016, an unknown attacker managed to withdraw US $ 50 million from "The DAO", a decentralized autonomous organization that works on smart contracts based on blockchain or pre-programmed rules that govern the organization [15]. Bitfinex was temporarily blocked in June 2017 due to a distributed denial of service (DDoS) attack. Several Bitcoin and Ethereum (a Blockchain-based distributed computing platform) exchanges have been subjected to DDoS and DNS attacks on a regular basis, causing service outages for consumers.

A potential vulnerability in the Blockchain system could be launched in unanticipated attacks, jeopardising the system's overall security and privacy. As a result, the first step is to investigate the weaknesses in the technology that led to unethical activities. Furthermore, this research examines counterfeit solutions from a systemic perspective.

BLOCKCHAIN SECURITY ISSUES

The following are five of the most serious security concerns surrounding blockchain technology, as shown in Fig. (**1**).

Transaction Malleability

Due to the popularity and wealth invested in its system, blockchain-based cryptocurrencies are vulnerable to a variety of fraudulent operations. Mt. Gox, a Tokyo-based Bitcoin exchange, has been hacked by two people [16]. Transaction malleability is a form of attack that allows a user to alter the identification of a Bitcoin transaction prior to it being confirmed on the cryptocurrency network. This modification allows the individual to pretend that no transaction occurred. It may be used to make a double deposit or a double withdrawal on Bitcoin exchanges [17].

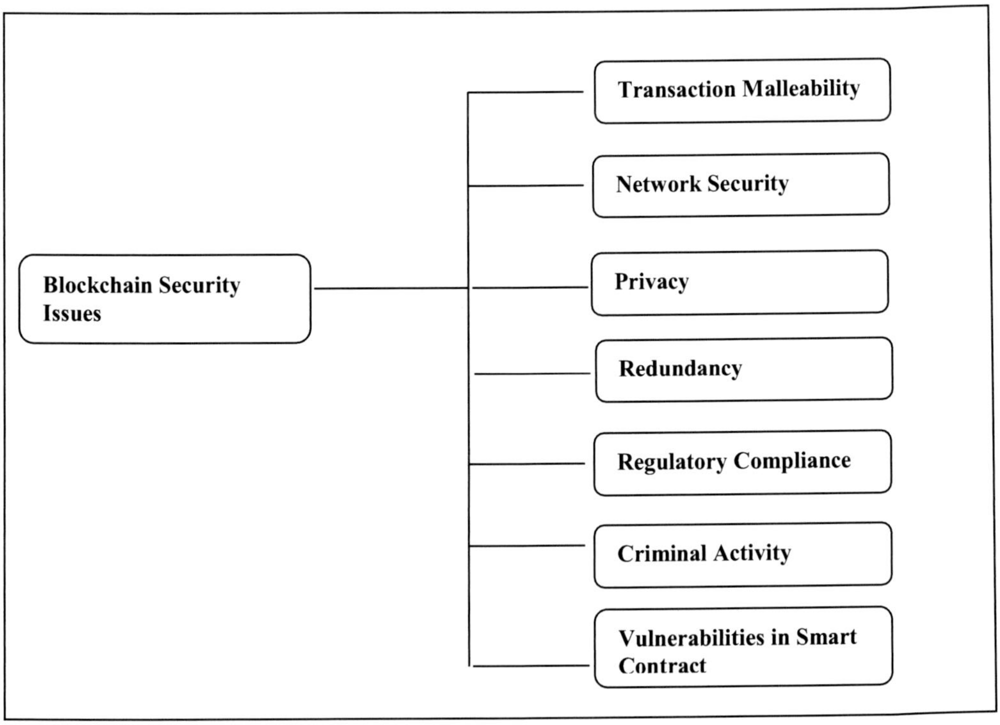

Fig. (1). Blockchain Security Issues.

Network Security

An Eclipse attack, which occurs when an adversary controls parts of the network and logically splits the network to raise the sync delay, is a basic denial of service attack intended to promote selfish mining and double-spending. In an Eclipse attack, the attacker selects information and hides it from one or more participants, possibly delaying the delivery of the block to the node [18].

Privacy

Data protection and secrecy are crucial components of blockchain transactions because each node can access the data of another node, and anyone looking at the blockchain can see all transactions. Various studies have offered solutions to this challenge; however, these solutions are only useful for a limited number of applications and do not solve all problems. Owing to the huge amount of data transmitted, attackers can target network communications, including sensitive data, with attacks, such as Maninthemiddle (MitM) and DoS / DDoS. Among the various unique privacy concerns that the Internet of Things brings with it are privacy and surveillance issues for mobiles and vehicles. Additionally, voice recognition is built so that devices can actively transfer data to cloud storage for processing while listening to calls [19].

Redundancy

Costly duplication to eliminate arbitrage so that every transaction is duplicated on every node in the network. However, duplicating brokerage services is impractical from both a financial and legal point of view; banks are reluctant to carry out any transaction with another bank or terminate the transactions of other banks. This duplication only adds costs but has little benefit.

Regulatory Compliance

Blockchains survive independently of the law, and their presence does not necessarily change the behavior of government officials. Apart from bitcoin, other currencies face regulatory hurdles when using blockchain technology in the legal and financial sectors, even though infrastructure regulation is very akin to blockchain regulation.

Criminal Activity

Users can buy and sell various things using external bitcoin markets. Due to the anonymity of these processes, it is impossible to track user behavior and present reasonable consequences. Bitcoin is often used for criminal activities, including ransomware, illegal markets, and money laundering. Due to illicit activity, certain underground marketplaces that trade online as T or hidden services utilize bitcoin as their medium of exchange, calling the blockchain's availability into doubt [20].

TAXONOMY OF ATTACK SURFACES

The entirety of all possible security vulnerabilities is referred to as the attack surface. It also comprises all hardware, software, and network components, as well as all known, unknown, and possibly exploitable flaws. An attacker can launch an attack by taking advantage of one or more vulnerabilities to gain access to the target system's numerous locations, components, and layers (including hardware and software). By getting access to many locations, components, and levels, for example, attackers can take secret information from a system (including hardware and software).

The kind and capability of the blockchain utility, the traits of its community structure, and the behaviour of peers and nodes all affect how various attacks manifest. It's essential to reflect on consideration on the way to guard a peer-t-

-peer or peer-by-peer structure from attacks. Reducing the vulnerability of systems and software program is one manner to enhance statistics safety. Many safety projects are targeted at the want to reduce attack surfaces. When it involves software program safety, maintaining the attack zones of software program environments as minimum as feasible is critical.

Your programmes' attack interface now represents their vulnerability to assault, not their vulnerability to assault. In a records system, an assault interface refers to the virtual footprint, which comprises hundreds of assets, components, and controllers. In a software programme environment, the assault interface is the sum of all the many assault factors through which unauthorised users or attackers can try to input or extract data from the environment.

Cryptocurrencies have a bigger assault floor than non-blockchain packages, which is concerning. Blockchain packages with assault surfaces are essential for cryptocurrencies, tokens, and clever contracts. To permit peer-to-peer transactions with virtual foreign money and make sure safety to users, blockchains rely upon secure software program code. As in their application-precise rules and peer-t--peer (P2P) networks, blockchains are steady in their realistic use as a cryptographic assemble, however liable to several attacks.

A blockchain community consists of nodes that create and run transactions and offer different services. For the occasion, the network is fashioned with the aid of using nodes that ship and get hold of transactions and miners that upload accredited transactions to blocks. Cybercriminals search for network communication threats and make the most of them with the subsequent kinds of attacks.

The blockchain has five attack vectors, as shown in Fig. (**2**).

a. Blockchain Network Attacks

Transaction Malleability Attack

An attack on the malleability of the transaction aims to make the victim pay double. In blockchain network, a hash digest every is a transaction identifier for each transaction. Before committing an original transaction, if attackers manage to change the ID of a transaction, you can try to send the transaction to the network with a modified hash and verify it before the original transaction [21]. If successful, the sender assumes the original transaction was unsuccessful, but the funds are still withdrawn from the sender's account. If the sender repeats the transaction, the same amount will be charged both times. Once both transactions have been validated by the miners, the hack is complete [22].

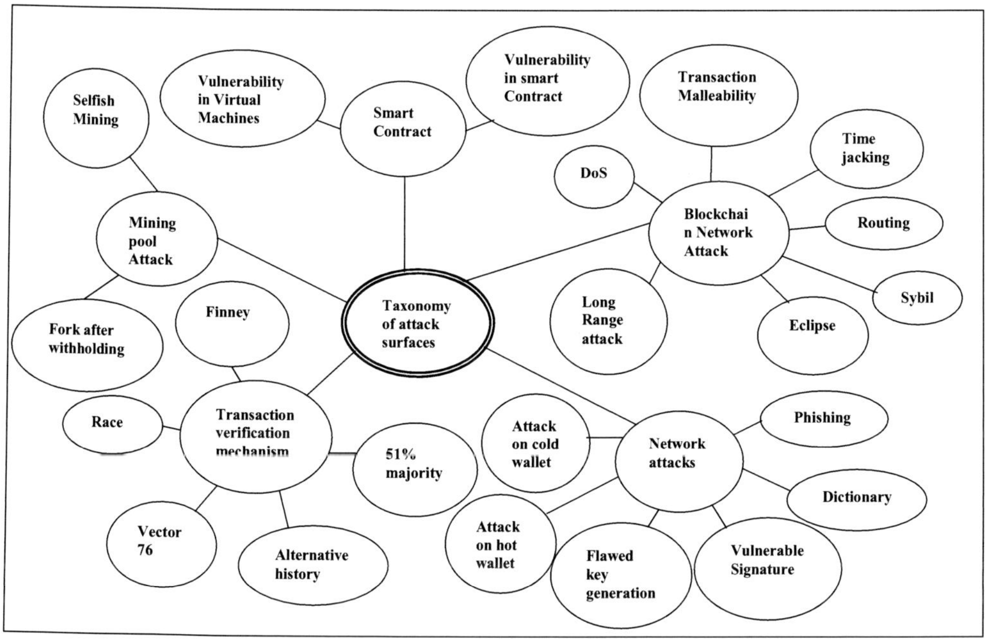

Fig. (2). Taxonomy of Attack Surface.

Timejacking

When dealing with Bitcoin timestamps, time jacking uses a theoretical flaw. A hacker adjusts the node's network clock and forces it to accept an alternate blockchain during a time jacking attack. If a malicious person adds a large number of bogus peers to the network with inaccurate timestamps, this is possible. A timejacking attack, on the other hand, can be avoided by limiting the time ranges that are permissible or by using timestamps [23].

DDOS Attack

Eventhough this type of attack is difficult to accomplish on blockchain technology, it is workable. DDoS attackers aim to convey down a server *via* way of means of ingesting all its processing sources with several requests. Their goal is to detach technology's mining pool, e-wallets and digital currency exchange different monetary services. DDoS at the utility layer of a blockchain can also be attacked *via* DDoS botnets.

Routing Attacks

Aattacker alters the node's network timer and forces it to respond in timejacking attack. Individual nodes and the entire network can be the target of a routing attack. The goal of this technique is to modify transactions before sending them to colleagues. Since the hacker is dividing the network into areas that cannot connect to each other, it is almost difficult for other nodes to notice this manipulation. Routing attacks are actually two different attacks. i. A partition attack that splits network nodes into different groups. ii. A delay attack interrupts the propagation of the message and transmits it to the network.

Sybil Attack

When numerous identifiers are assigned to the same node, a Sybill attack is launched. There are no trusted nodes in blockchain networks, and each request is sent to many nodes. During Sybil attack, Multiple identifiers are assigned to the same node in the Sybil attack. Each request is forwarded to several nodes in blockchain networks since there are no trusted nodes. A hacker takes control of many network nodes during a Sybil assault. The victim is then surrounded by phoney nodes that finish all the victim's transactions. After a while, the victim becomes exposed to double-contribution assaults. Sybil assaults are difficult to detect and avoid, however, increasing the cost of creating a new identity, maintaining a certain level of trust to join the network, and determining user reputation can all help [24].

Eclipse Attacks

An Eclipse attack necessitates a huge number of IP addresses or a sparse botnet for the hacker. The attacker then overwrites the addresses in the victim node's "attempted" database and waits for the victim node to resume. After restarting the target node, all outbound connections will be redirected to the attacker's IP addresses. This prevents the victim from obtaining transactions that they are interested in. Boston University researchers launched an eclipse assault on the Ethereum network, which they were able to achieve with only one or two workstations [25].

Long-range Attacks

These are directed at networks that use the proof of stake (PoS) consensus method, which allows users to mine or validate block transactions based on their asset in terms of the coin.

Three types of attacks can be distinguished:

1. Simple — when nodes don't check block timestamps, this is a simple version of the proof of stake protocol.

2. Posterior corruption — attempting to mint more blocks in a particular time frame than the main chain.

3. Stake leakage — duplicating a transaction from a properly kept ledger.

When initiating a remote attack, a hacker utilises a purchased or stolen private key from a big token balance that has previously been utilised for verification. The hacker can modify the blockchain's history and receive rewards based on PoS validation [26].

b. User Wallet Attacks

In fact, until individuals interact with blockchains and cybersecurity, they're like salt and pepper. It may come as a surprise, but blockchain users are the most dangerous to security. People tend to overvalue the blockchain's security and overlook its flaws. Cybercriminals are mostly interested in user wallet credentials.

Hackers attempt to get wallet credentials using both old tactics, such as phishing and dictionary attacks, as well as more complex ones, such as identifying flaws in cryptographic techniques. Here's a rundown of popular ways to get into people's wallets [27].

Phishing

In 2018, iotaseed.io (now offline), a phoney online seed generator, was used to launch an attack on IOTA wallets. Hackers used this service to execute a phishing campaign and obtain logs, including secret seeds. As a result, hackers were able to steal more than $4 million worth of IOTA from victims' wallets in January 2018 [28].

Dictionary Attacks

During these attacks, a hacker tries to hash values of common passwords like password1 to decrypt a victim's cryptographic digest and salt. Attackers can find wallet credentials by converting clear text passwords to cryptographic hashes [29].

Vulnerable Signatures

Blockchain networks establish user signatures using a variety of cryptographic algorithms, but they may be vulnerable. Bitcoin, for example, employs the ECDSA cryptographic technique to produce unique private keys automatically. However, ECDSA does not appear to have enough entropy, resulting in the same random value appearing in multiple signatures. IOTA's former Curl hash algorithm also had cryptographic issues [30].

Flawed Key Generation

In December 2014, a hacker known as Johoe got access to secret keys by using flaws in the key creation. During a code upgrade, a coding mistake resulted in inadequate randomization of inputs for creating public user keys, resulting in the attack. Despite the fact that the weakness was promptly patched, the ECDSA algorithm still has a vulnerability.

Attacks on Cold Wallets

These wallets can be hacked as well. For example, researchers used flaws in the Nano S Ledger wallet to launch an Evil Maid attack. Researchers received the victims' secrete keys, PINs, recovery seeds, and passwords, as a result of this incident.

Cryptocurrency exchange UPbit began moving funds to a cold wallet in 2019, which was one of the most recent cold wallet hacks. When you are expecting a cyberattack, this is a standard approach to freeze crypto. The hackers were able to take 342,000 ETH because they were aware of the transaction's timing [31].

Attacks on Hot Wallets

Hot wallets are web-based applications that store private cryptographic keys. Though cryptocurrency exchange owners maintain that their users' data is kept in wallets that aren't connected to the internet, a $500 million attack on Coincheck in 2018 demonstrated that this is not always the case, though [32].

An attack against GateHub in June 2019 resulted in the theft of crypto assets and unauthorized access to dozens of native XRP wallets. Due to a system weakness, Bitcoin, a Singapore-based cryptocurrency exchange, was also exposed to a hot wallet attack around the same time. As a result, hackers were able to take XRP, valued at over $4.5 million and ADAIt, worth $237,500.

c. Smart Contract Attacks

Smart contract development and penetration testing are two areas where Apriorit has teams working. We have extensive experience detecting and preventing problems in smart contracts built on the Ethereum, EOS, and NEO platforms. Errors in the source code, the virtual machine on a network, the smart contract execution environment, and the blockchain are the most common vulnerabilities associated with smart contracts. Let's take a look at each of these attack vectors one by one.

Vulnerabilities in Contract Source Code

The parties signing the smart contract are at risk if the contract's source code is defective. For example, errors found in the Ethereum deal cost its owners $ 80 million in 2016. The re-entry attack, which is one of the most common vulnerabilities in Solidity, allows untrusted functions from other smart contracts to delegate control to them. Contract A calls a function from contract B, whose behavior during this attack is undefined. Contract B, on the other hand, may use the function of contract A for harmful purposes [33].

Vulnerabilities in Virtual Machines

Ethereum Virtual Machine (EVM) is a distributed stack computer on which all smart contracts based on the Ethereum blockchain are executed. Below are some of the most common EVM errors [34].

Immutable Defects

Since blockchain blocks are inherently immutable, once a smart contract has been formed, it can no longer be changed. However, if there are errors in the code of a smart contract, they cannot be fixed either. As with the DAO attack, there is a risk that hackers could detect and steal ether or create a new fork, and take advantage of programming faults.

Cryptocurrency Lost in Transfer

When ether is moved to an orphan address with no owner or contract, you can do this.

Bugs in Access Control

In Ethereum smart contracts, a missing modifier hole allows a hacker to gain access to critical contract functionality.

Short Address Attack

This is feasible due to the EVM's ability to accept improperly padded parameters. Hackers can take advantage of this flaw by sending specially designed emails to prospective victims. A modification to the Coindash Ethereum address, for example, caused victims to send their Ether to the hacker's address during a successful attack on the Coindash ICO in 2017.

d. Transaction Verification Mechanism Attacks

Double Spending Attack

Blockchains, unlike financial institutions, only confirm transactions after approval by all nodes in the network. The transaction is considered unverified until the block containing the transaction is verified. On the other hand, verification takes time, making it an ideal vector for cyber attacks. A typical blockchain attack using a transaction validation mechanism is twice as high. To be valid, all blockchain transactions need to be validated by users, which takes time. System latency can be used by attackers to mislead the system into utilising similar crypto-coins or tokens in repeated transactions [35].

Finney Attacks

When the transaction is converted to a block, and another identical transaction is performed prior to that block being published prior to network exploration, the other same transaction becomes invalid.

Race Attacks

When an attacker makes two mismatched transactions, it is called a racing attack. The money is sent to the victim in the first transaction. (and ships the merchandise, for example) before the transaction is verified. At the same time, the conflicting transaction is sent to the network, causing the attacker to return the same amount of bitcoins, effectively canceling the original transaction.

Vector76

Vector76 is the result of combining two prior attacks. A malevolent miner constructs two nodes in this situation; one is just connected to the exchange node, while the other is connected to the blockchain network's well-connected peers. After that, the miner creates two transactions, one with a high value and one with a low value. The attacker makes preemption and then holds the lock from an exchange service that contains a high-value transaction. After an accident announcement, the attacker quickly delivers the precast block to the operator's service. He and some miners will confirm this transaction by treating the pre-mined block as the main chain. Therefore, this attack takes advantage of the fact that one part of the network sees the transaction that the attacker has inserted into a block, while the other does not see the transaction [36].

The attacker transmits a low-value transaction to the main network after the exchange service approves the high-value transaction, which is eventually rejected. As a result, the amount of the high-value transaction is credited to the attacker's account. Though this form of attack has a high possibility of succeeding, it's not widespread because it requires a hosted e-wallet that takes payments after one confirmation and a node that receives incoming transactions.

Alternative history attacks

An alternate history attack, also known as a blockchain reorganisation assault, can occur even when there are numerous confirmations, although it needs a significant amount of computer power on the part of the hacker. A malevolent user in this example, sends a transaction to a recipient while simultaneously mining an alternative fork with another transaction that yields the same currency. Even if the recipient accepts the transaction after n confirmation and delivers a product, if the attacker releases a longer chain and collects the coins, the recipient may lose money.

In August 2020, one of the most recent blockchain rearrangement assaults occurred when a miner employed obsolete software and lost internet access for a period of time while mining Ethereum Classic. When two versions of the blockchain contended for legitimacy from network nodes, a restructuring occurred, resulting in around a 3000-block insertion. It was first published on [37].

51% or Majority Attacks

A majority assault happens when a hacker gets control of 51% of the network's hash rate and launches a new fork that eventually replaces the existing forks. This attack was the only known blockchain vulnerability at the time, and it appeared to be unachievable in the near future. Verge, ZenCash, Monacoin, Bitcoin Gold, and Litecoin Cash are among the cryptocurrencies that have previously been targeted at a 51 percent rate. Cybercriminals amassed enough hashing power in each of these situations to hack the network and take millions of dollars [38].

In August 2020, a 51 percent assault on Ethereum Classic (ETC) resulted in the double-spending of around $5.6 million worth of ETC coins. The hacker apparently had an extensive understanding of the ETC protocol and mined 4,280 blocks over the course of four days before the platform detected an attack. ETC was hit by a second 51 percent attack just five days after the first, in which a miner reorganised the network by 4,000 blocks.

e. Mining Pool Attacks

Individual miners can no longer profit from large cryptocurrencies, such as bitcoin, so miners pool their processing resources to form mining pools. This allows them to mine more blocks and distribute the prize evenly. BTC.com, AntPool and ViaBTC are currently the top three Bitcoin mining pools. According to Blockchain.com, they account for over 52% of the total hash rate of the Bitcoin network. Mining pools are a tempting target. By exploiting vulnerabilities in the blockchain consensus system, Malicious miners attempt to gain internal and external control of mining pools. The following are the most frequent mining pool assaults.

Selfish Mining

Malicious miners attempt to raise their part of the reward by not delivering the blocks to the network for a set length of time and then releasing several blocks at once, resulting in other miners losing their blocks. Randomly assigning miners to different branches of the pool, preferring a block with the latest timestamp, and creating blocks within the maximum time allowed are all possible countermeasures. Block holding is another name for this type of attack.

Miners lost 300 BTC in 2014 due to a selfish mining assault on the Eligius pool. Selfish mining has a high success rate and may occur with any coin. Only trustworthy miners will be registered, and the existing Bitcoin protocol will be modified to hide the distinction between partial and complete proof of work are two possible preventative methods against selfish mining [39].

Fork After Withholding

FAW (Fork After Hold) is a form of selfish kicking that seems more profitable for attackers. During a FAW attack, a hostile miner conceals the winning block and steals it, depending on the situation, either rejects it or publishes it later, creating a fork. A team of researchers led by Ugin Kwon has elucidated the concept of this attack in detail [39].

MEANS OF PROTECTION AGAINST CYBER ATTACK INTERFACE

When it comes to defending your business against cybercrime and cyberattacks, it can be tough to know where to start. There is so much information available that it can be overwhelming, especially when the information is contradictory. There is a need to take some preventive security measures against cyber attacks, as shown in Fig. (**3**).

- Make Cybersecurity a top priority by implementing a security strategy to examine and classify the information you manage and, as a result, the type of security you want to protect it with. Every day, conduct a security audit.
- Raise your employees' understanding of cyber-security and the need for data protection.
- Create a one-of-a-kind password to obtain access to the system, secure password combination and pair it with two-factor authentication.
- Invest in cybersecurity solutions, such as antivirus software, firewalls, and other privacy tools, to scan threats automatically. Set up and keep your antivirus software up to date.
- Establish a solid backup policy. It will protect you against ransomware.
- End-to-end encryption can be used to protect sensitive information.
- Try to hack yourself! This might aid you in determining the system's vulnerabilities.

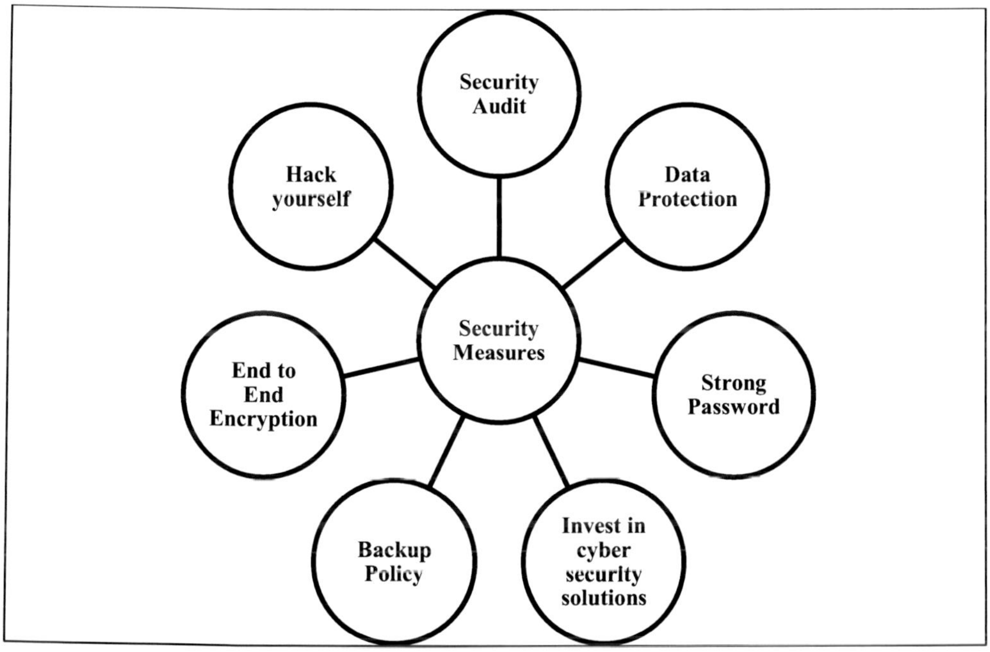

Fig. (3). Security Measures.

CONCLUSION

Blockchains have emerged as a new paradigm in distributed systems and allow the secure exchange of assets between companies with competing interests. Blockchain technology is rapidly gaining ground, particularly in the form of cryptocurrencies like Bitcoin and Ethereum, which together have a market capitalization of more than $ 850 billion. Due to its huge market capitalization, opponents often target blockchain-based cryptocurrencies to make money. The attack surface of the blockchain was thoroughly examined in this chapter. We found that the attack surface of the blockchain can be divided into three types of attacks.

Authentication and encryption technologies can help prevent assaults, but they aren't the sole way to keep the system safe. Outdated security and defence methods can't handle complex new threats like zero-day malware campaigns, which have changed the scope of cybercrime.

Finally, this chapter contributes to the security of distributed systems by exposing a series of novel vulnerabilities related to application-specific regulations and the complexity of the network layer of blockchain systems. Our theoretical modeling, measurements, attacks, and countermeasures pave the way for new approaches to assessing blockchain security.

The attack surfaces for blockchain technology have been explored. Attacks on cryptographic designs, peer-to-peer network architecture, and blockchain technology applications are taken into account. The report reviewed the latest security research on decentralized systems based on blockchain technology and identified the main weaknesses of decentralized systems based on blockchain. Although despite current countermeasures, some attacks can be carried out with a high degree of probability, the work also sheds light on the connection between different attack sequences.

CONSENT FOR PUBLICATION

Not applicable.

CONFLICT OF INTEREST

The author declares no conflict of interest, financial or otherwise.

ACKNOWLEDGEMENT

Declared none.

REFERENCES

[1] A. Back, M. Corallo, L. Dashjr, M. Friedenbach, G. Maxwell, A. Miller, A. Poelstra, J. Timón, and P. Wuille, *Enabling blockchain innovations with pegged sidechains.*, 2014. http://www. Opensciencereview. com/papers/123/enablingblockchain-innovations-with-pegged-sidechains

[2] S. Zalte, and R. Kamat, "Blockchain Technology: Developers Cultivate Novel Applications for Societal Benefits", *Transforming Cybersecurity Solutions Using Blockchain,* 215. [http://dx.doi.org/10.1007/978-981-33-6858-3_11]

[3] S. Nakamoto, *Bitcoin: A peer-to-peer electronic cash system.* Decentralized Business Review, 2008, p. 21260.

[4] Tim Ruffing, Pedro Moreno-Sanchez, and Aniket Kate, "P2P mixing and unlinkable bitcoin transactions", *Cryptology ePrint Archive,* 2016.

[5] L. Mauri, S. Cimato, and E. Damiani, *A Comparative Analysis of Current Cryptocurrencies.*, 2018. [http://dx.doi.org/10.5220/0006648801270138]

[6] A. Kosba, A. Miller, E. Shi, Z. Wen, and C. Papamanthou, *Hawk: The blockchain model of cryptography and privacy-preserving smart contracts.*, 2016.

[7] M. Saad, J. Spaulding, L. Njilla, C. Kamhoua, and S Shetty, DaeHun Nyang, and Aziz Mohaisen, "Exploring the attack surface of blockchain: A systematic overview", *arXiv preprint arXiv:1904.03487,* 2019.

[8] E.F. Jesus, and R.L. Vanessa, "Chicarino, Célio VN De Albuquerque, and Antônio A. de A. Rocha. "A survey of how to use blockchain to secure internet of things and the stalker attack", *Secur. Commun. Netw.,* p. 2018, 2018.

[9] M.S. Ali, M. Vecchio, M. Pincheira, K. Dolui, F. Antonelli, and M.H. Rehmani, "Applications of blockchains in the Internet of Things: A comprehensive survey", *IEEE Commun. Surv. Tutor.,* vol. 21, no. 2, pp. 1676-1717, 2019. [http://dx.doi.org/10.1109/COMST.2018.2886932]

[10] H. Hyvärinen, M. Risius, and G. Friis, "A blockchain-based approach towards overcoming financial fraud in public sector services", *Bus. Inf. Syst. Eng.,* vol. 59, no. 6, pp. 441-456, 2017. [http://dx.doi.org/10.1007/s12599-017-0502-4]

[11] Rakesh Shrestha, Rojeena Bajracharya, Anish P. Shrestha, and Seung Yeob Nam, "A new type of blockchain for secure message exchange in VANET", *Digital communications and networks,* vol. 6, no. 2, pp. 177-186, 2020. [http://dx.doi.org/10.1016/j.dcan.2019.04.003]

[12] R. Casado-Vara, F. de la Prieta, J. Prieto, and J.M. Corchado, "Blockchain framework for IoT data quality *via* edge computing"., *Proceedings of the 1st Workshop on Blockchain-enabled Networked Sensor Systems,* 2018pp. 19-24 [http://dx.doi.org/10.1145/3282278.3282282]

[13] T.P. Keenan, "Alice in blockchains: Surprising security pitfalls in PoW and PoS blockchain systems", [http://dx.doi.org/10.1109/PST.2017.00057]

[14] M. Saad, M.T. Thai, and A. Mohaisen, "POSTER: Deterring ddos attacks on blockchain-based cryptocurrencies through mempool optimization", *Proceedings of the 2018 on Asia Conference on Computer and Communications Security,* 2018pp. 809-811 [http://dx.doi.org/10.1145/3196494.3201584]

[15] S.S. Shetty, L. Njilla, and C.A. Kamhoua, *Journal: Blockchain for Distributed Systems Security, 2019, p. 1-24.*, 2019. [http://dx.doi.org/10.1002/9781119519621]

[16] Islam, Md Rafiqul, Muhammad Mahbubur Rahman, Md Mahmud, Mohammed Ataur Rahman, and Muslim Har Sani Mohamad. "A Review on Blockchain Security Issues and Challenges." In 2021 IEEE 12th Control and System Graduate Research Colloquium (ICSGRC), pp. 227-232. IEEE, 2021. [http://dx.doi.org/10.1109/ICSGRC53186.2021.9515276]

[17] C. Decker, and R. Wattenhofer, "Bitcoin transaction malleability and MtGox", *European Symposium on Research in Computer Security,* 2014pp. 313-326

[18] Pradip Kumar Sharma, Seo Yeon Moon, and Jong Hyuk Park, "Block-VN: A distributed blockchain based vehicular network architecture in smart city", *Journal of information processing systems,* vol. 13, no. 1, pp. 184-195, 2017.

[19] C. Mann, and D. Loebenberger, "Two-factor authentication for the Bitcoin protocol", *Int. J. Inf. Secur.*, vol. 16, no. 2, pp. 213-226, 2017. [http://dx.doi.org/10.1007/s10207-016-0325-1]

[21] K.M. Khan, J. Arshad, and M.M. Khan, "Simulation of transaction malleability attack for blockchain-based e-Voting", *Comput. Electr. Eng.*, vol. 83, p. 106583, 2020. [http://dx.doi.org/10.1016/j.compeleceng.2020.106583]

[22] G. Ma, C. Ge, and L. Zhou, "Achieving reliable timestamp in the bitcoin platform", *Peer-to-Peer Netw. Appl.*, vol. 13, no. 6, pp. 2251-2259, 2020. [http://dx.doi.org/10.1007/s12083-020-00905-6]

[23] P. Swathi, "Preventing sybil attack in blockchain using distributed behavior monitoring of miners", In: *10th International Conference on Computing, Communication and Networking Technologies (ICCCNT)* IEEE, 2019, p. 1p. 6.

[24] S. Zhang, and J-H. Lee, "Eclipse-based stake-bleeding attacks in pos blockchain systems", *Proceedings of the 2019 ACM International Symposium on Blockchain and Secure Critical Infrastructure,* 2019pp. 67-72 [http://dx.doi.org/10.1145/3327960.3332391]

[25] P. Gaži, A. Kiayias, and A. Russell, "Stake-bleeding attacks on proof-of-stake blockchains", *2018 Crypto Valley Conference on Blockchain Technology (CVCBT),* 2018pp. 85-92 [http://dx.doi.org/10.1109/CVCBT.2018.00015]

[26] S. Jarecki, A. Kiayias, H. Krawczyk, and J. Xu, "Highly-efficient and composable password-protected secret sharing (or: How to protect your bitcoin wallet online)", In: *IEEE European Symposium on Security and Privacy (EuroS&P).* IEEE, 2016, pp. 276-291. [http://dx.doi.org/10.1109/EuroSP.2016.30]

[27] N. Bodziony, P. Jemioło, K. Kluza, and M.R. Ogiela, "Blockchain-Based Address Alias System", *J. Theor. Appl. Electron. Commer. Res.*, vol. 16, no. 5, pp. 1280-1296, 2021. [http://dx.doi.org/10.3390/jtaer16050072]

[28] "An Approach to Defense Dictionary Attack with Message Digest Using Image Salt", In: *International Conference on Ubiquitous Information Management and Communication* Springer: Cham, 2019, pp. 769-777.

[29] O. Ajayi, M. Cherian, and T. Saadawi, "Secured cyber-attack signatures distribution using blockchain technology", In: *IEEE International Conference on Computational Science and Engineering (CSE) and IEEE International Conference on Embedded and Ubiquitous Computing (EUC)* IEEE, 2019, pp. 482-488. [http://dx.doi.org/10.1109/CSE/EUC.2019.00095]

[30] https://www.welivesecurity.com/2019/11/27/upbit-cryptocurrency-exchange- hack/

[31] https://www.qredo.com/blog/proofofkeys-7-ways-private-keys-have-been-

[32] P. Tantikul, and S. Ngamsuriyaroj, *Exploring Vulnerabilities in Solidity Smart Contract.*, 2020. [http://dx.doi.org/10.5220/0008909803170324]

[33] F. Ma, M. Ren, Y. Fu, M. Wang, H. Li, H. Song, and Y. Jiang, "Security reinforcement for Ethereum virtual machine", *Inf. Process. Manage.*, vol. 58, no. 4, p. 102565, 2021. [http://dx.doi.org/10.1016/j.ipm.2021.102565]

[34] H. Lee, M. Shin, K.S. Kim, Y. Kang, and J. Kim, "Recipient-oriented transaction for preventing double spending attacks in private blockchain", In: *15th Annual IEEE International Conference on Sensing, Communication, and Networking (SECON)* IEEE, 2018, pp. 1-2. [http://dx.doi.org/10.1109/SAHCN.2018.8397151]

[35] A. Panwar, and V. Bhatnagar, A Research on Different Type of Possible Attacks on Blockchain: Susceptibilities of the Utmost Secure Technology.*Machine Intelligence and Smart Systems.* Springer:

Singapore, 2021, pp. 537-551.
[http://dx.doi.org/10.1007/978-981-33-4893-6_46]

[36] X. Ling, Y. Le, J. Wang, Z. Ding, and X. Gao, "Practical modeling and analysis of blockchain radio access network", *IEEE Trans. Commun.,* vol. 69, no. 2, p. 1, 2020.
[http://dx.doi.org/10.1109/TCOMM.2020.3029779]

[37] J. Bae, and H. Lim, "Random mining group selection to prevent 51% attacks on bitcoin", In: *48th Annual IEEE/IFIP International Conference on Dependable Systems and Networks Workshops (DSN-W)* IEEE, 2018, pp. 81-82.
[http://dx.doi.org/10.1109/DSN-W.2018.00040]

[38] I. Eyal, and E.G. Sirer, "Majority is not enough: Bitcoin mining is vulnerable", *International conference on financial cryptography and data security,* 2014pp. 436-454
[http://dx.doi.org/10.1007/978-3-662-45472-5_28]

[39] S-Y. Chang, Y. Park, S. Wuthier, and C-W. Chen, "Uncle-block attack: Blockchain mining threat beyond block withholding for rational and uncooperative miners", *International Conference on Applied Cryptography and Network Security,* 2019pp. 241-258
[http://dx.doi.org/10.1007/978-3-030-21568-2_12]

CHAPTER 5

Review of Anti-Counterfeit Solutions in Blockchain

H. Bhatia[1,*], **S. Zalte**[2], **I. Chatterjee**[3] and **D. Mantri**[4]

[1] *School of Computer Science, Engineering and Applications, D Y Patil International University, Pune, India*

[2] *Department of Computer Science, Shivaji University, Kolhapur, India*

[3] *Department of Computer Engineering, Tongmyong University, Busan, South Korea*

[4] *Sinhgad Institute of Engineering, Lonavala, Pune, India*

Abstract: Blockchain technology offers a data format that has built-in security. It is built on cryptography, decentralization, and consensus concepts to ensure transaction confidence. Decentralization is enabled by blockchain technology, which allows members to participate in a dispersed network. No single user can alter the transaction, as all transactions are transparent and visible to all other users on the network. However, there are some significant security differences between blockchain and other systems. Nowadays, there are so many potential attacks found on the blockchain. The contribution of this chapter would be to match the effective defence taken by blockchain technology or a patch for related vulnerabilities offered by researchers to reduce the impact of these attacks. To keep the network secure and resilient, an overview of these security solutions for various vulnerabilities and attacks helps to reduce the attack surface in the blockchain.

Keywords: Cryptographic, Decentralization, Consensus, Security, Defense, Attacks.

INTRODUCTION

Blockchain is the first type of decentralization technology with no central controlling authority and is based on secure and distributed decentralized protocols. All nodes that are part of the network are responsible to generate, add and confirm the transactions within the data blocks. Blockchain technology inherits several security qualities like decentralization, hash functions, consensus mechanism, digital signatures and smart cards, which enhance and secure blockchain technology.

* **Corresponding author H. Bhatia:** School of Computer Science, Engineering and Applications, D Y Patil International University, Pune, India; E-mail: heenakbhatia@gmail.com

Blockchain technology has enormous potential for a wide range of applications and offers numerous options for diverse infrastructure. A blockchain transaction uses hash functions to secure the records, and each transaction is linked to previous transactions or records. The data integrity of transaction data is protected using hash functions. Consensus algorithms on the blockchain nodes validate transactions. Since blockchain networks operate in a decentralized manner, a single entity cannot start the transaction. Each participant has the ability to view transactions at any time. Thus, blockchains enable transparency. Digital signatures are a crucial building element of blockchains that is used to authenticate the validity of transactions. A smart contract is a self-executing set of instructions, which automates the execution of transactions without third-party involvement. Ethereum is a decentralized system for executing smart contracts.

Even with such adequate and strong significant security capabilities, blockchain is still establishing itself in the market. Blockchain technology is susceptible to a variety of attacks. Attackers exploit the vulnerability present in the blockchain. As a result, Blockchain adoption has been slower than anticipated. Hence, identifying the solutions for the main reasons for such delayed adoption becomes a critical issue. In this paper, we investigate and provide counterfeit solutions for the various blockchain security-related issues and risks associated with blockchain implementation for attacks like User wallet attacks, blockchain nctwork attacks, transaction verification mechanism attacks, Smart contract attacks and Mining pool attacks.

COUNTERFEIT SOLUTIONS FOR ATTACK SURFACES

This section will present a summary of countermeasures against the existing attack surfaces in Blockchain.

Countermeasure against Blockchain Network Attacks

Countermeasures against Distributed Denial of Service Attack

In a recent study, countermeasures focussed on multi-field coordination to alleviate DDoS attacks. In order to detect an anomalous network flow, high detection and low false alarm rate were proposed by Cheng *et al.* [1]. The Credit Bonus Penalty Strategy (CBPS) was introduced by Yang *et al.* [2] to offer an IoT confidante environment that can successfully protect against DDoS attacks. SDNs are a significant aspect of network administration because they separate control planes and data and offer novel ways to resist DDoS attacks. Saad *et al.* [3] proposed cost-effective and age-effective remedy designs, which maximize the memory pool size for a new sort of DDoS attack that affects bitcoin systems in their memory pools underlined, which lead to a significant backlog of transaction backlogs and higher mining charges.

Fig. (1). Types of Blockchain attacks and its countermeasures. [Rounded rectangle represents type of blockchain attack and oval represent its countermeasures].

Countermeasures against Transaction Malleability Attack-

The malleability of transactions caused substantial loss and reputation damage to the community of Bitcoin. The value of Bitcoin has been decreasing since this issue, and millions of dollars in Bitcoins have been stolen. Rajput *et al.* [4] proposed a robust solution that includes a transaction Id consisting of a combination of the signature-free transaction script's hash and the ultimate transaction. This final joint hash is used for both checking and identifying the transactions. This approach is feasible and identifies any attempt at the transaction.

Countermeasures against Timejacking

To validate new blocks to the Blockchain, network time is used. A Timejacking attack occurs when an attacker writes incorrect timestamps, modifies the time clock of the node, and fools it into accepting a block from another Blockchain instead of one from its own. This is a fictitious attack. Boverman [5] provides the following solutions as

- Instead of using network time for timestamps, the node's system time is used.
- 70 to 140 minutes is the maximum initial attack timeframe.
- 70 to 140 minutes is the maximum initial attack timeframe. This time is cut in half, to 30 to 60 minutes, bringing the network node time down to around 30 minutes. This strategy will not be able to entirely eliminate attacks, but it will help to reduce them.
- Blocking untrusted peers and establishing a safe node can help to minimise the scope of an attack, however, it will not solve the problem of global problem related to time agreement.
- In order to accept a transaction, the number of confirmations required is being increased.

Time-jacking attacks are rare, so no new strategies to combat them have been devised. As it is always related to double-spending, the majority of double-spending security measures also hold products for time-jacking attacks.

Countermeasures against Routing Attacks

There are numerous strategies for defending against routing attacks [6]. Multi-homed bitcoin is recommended since it makes it more difficult to conduct attacks when there are more connections. Attackers must either know both IP addresses or abort all cryptographic communication, which is easily discovered, in order to interrupt links between nodes. In the second approach, during the attack, the round-trip time (RTT) to hijacked destinations increases. A node could notice abrupt changes in the RTT towards its peers. As a protective strategy, the node will make random connections as a result of the outlier identification. Using another approach, UDP packets between nodes can also be updated regularly to identify if traffic has been withdrawn in part and in case it is connected to the network.

Countermeasures against Sybil Attacks

The development of anti-Sybil methods placed a greater emphasis on the environment for the application. Blockchain-based cyber threat intelligence (CTI) platform, suggested by Gong and Lee [7], successfully mitigates the strength of the Sybil attack. When the attacker launches the attack, he or she will suffer a severe loss of property, limiting their ability to introduce false or fake data into the system. Otte *et al.* [8] suggested Trustchain, a scalable blockchain featuring a unique mechanism to defend against Sybil attacks.

Countermeasures against Eclipse Attacks

The following are countermeasures against eclipse attacks offered by Heilman *et al.* [9] to increase the difficulty of successfully launching eclipse attack.

Random Node Selection:

By constructing a peer-to-peer network, a blockchain architect can dramatically limit the probability of a node connecting to a malicious node, even if it had recently joined as if each node is connected to a random range of IP addresses synchronizes with the network rather than sticking to set of repeatable, exploitable nodes.

Deterministic Node Selection:

When a node connects to the network, this strategy involves placing specific IP addresses into their respective fixed slots. If the network's connections are fixed, an adversary will have a harder time managing hostile nodes around the network and converging around a target. An eclipse attack attempt will not be successful if addresses under the attacker's control are inserted repeatedly. Similarly, a blockchain might include node identities to reconnect with genuine nodes with a greater level of trust in its network connection requirement. The blockchain network will be safer and less vulnerable to outside interference if node connections are made using identifying information rather than contextual data such as timestamps and availability; they deviate from authorised network activity. However, the network may suffer scalability if connections may only be made to specified nodes that other peers have authorised.

Increased Node Connections:

A network can raise the possibility by increasing the required number of node-t--node connections; a node can connect to a genuine user. However, bandwidth restrictions limit how many node connections a network can add without sacrificing speed, making this strategy ineffective as a self-contained solution against eclipse attacks.

Restrictions on New Nodes:

By increasing the cost or difficulty of construction of new nodes inside a network, the blockchain architect can raise the standard for malicious actors to saturate the network with malicious nodes. This strategy frequently entails restricting the number of nodes that can connect to a single IP address or device. This precautionary measure can be evaded by an attacker building a botnet comprised of devices with unique IP addresses.

Countermeasures against Long-Range Attacks on Proof of Stake Networks

A Long-Range attack is one in which the adversary returns to the genesis block and splits the network. The new branch is filled with people with a distinct history from the main chain. The attack is successful when the adversary's branch grows longer than the main chain and overtakes it. Longest chain rule, Moving Checkpoints, Key-evolving cryptography, context-aware transactions and plenitude rule are countermeasures against long-range attacks [10].

Defence Mechanism against User Wallet Attacks

Countermeasures against Phishing

To resist phishing attacks, Imperva offers a combination of login management and online application security solutions: Imperva Login Safeguard provides two-factor authentication to protect URL addresses on your website or online application. This includes URL parameterized addresses and AJAX pages, which are typically a greater challenge to safeguard with 2FA. The solution can be implemented in a matter of seconds with just a few mouse clicks. It requires no additional hardware or software and allows you to modify user roles and rights directly from the Imperva dashboard [11]. The Imperva Web Application Firewall (WAF), which runs in the cloud, prevents malicious requests at the network edge. This involves preventing attempts by insiders to inject malware which have been infiltrated, as well as duplicating XSS attacks caused by phishing campaigns.

Countermeasures against Dictionary Attacks

A dictionary attack is a brute-force assault in which attackers try to guess passwords by running them through a dictionary of popular words and phrases. To prevent offline Dictionary attacks, Canetti *et al.* [12] proposed using many human-only solvable puzzles (HOSPs) generated and saved on disk without their answers. The password provided by the user is then used to choose a small number of puzzles from the database. The key is extracted from the password and the puzzle solutions once a legitimate user completes these puzzles to acquire access to the information that has been encrypted. The goal is to challenge the attacker to solve a large number of puzzles for each password guess, restricting its ability to look for the password in a comprehensive manner

Countermeasures against Vulnerable Signatures

To resist attacks against signatures, Zhu *et al.* [13] presented an Interactive Incontestable Signature that might prevent the falsification of the holder's information while also preventing the information of the merchant from being refused. This signature protocol was primarily utilised to create a blockchain system that was more precise and performed better than current blockchain systems. As the system's core, IIS could verify that the transaction was both confirmed and unambiguous. With this signature, the merchant may guarantee the owner that the transaction will be permanently recorded on the blockchain system. The signature method has proven to be a reliable security mechanism for the merchant's non-repudiation and the owner's unforgeability. This solution overcomes the problem of delivering speedy non-repudiation confirmation during blockchain deployment.

Countermeasures against Flawed key generation

In the blockchain world, key leakage is a crucial problem. Zheng *et al.* [14] explore mixing and anonymity as two ways proposed to improve blockchain anonymity. It is still possible to discover the genuine user's identity even if the user's addresses are pseudonymous using mixing. Mixing adds the ability to route a transaction through several input and output locations. For example, when a sender X wants to send funds to a recipient X, the sender X transfers funds to trusted x1, x2, x3, and so on users, who then transfer the funds to the intended recipient Y, rather than making a direct transaction from X to Y, which could allow the attackers to discover the relationship between users. To improve anonymity in the bitcoin network, the origin of the payment is separated from its transactions to prevent the examination of transaction graphs, which can lead to the identification of the true user identity.

Countermeasures against Cold Wallets and Hot Wallets Attacks

To resist hot attacks, the trust Zone-based wallet encrypts data with a key that is only available at the hardware level. There are two partitions: one called Global Partition, which stores general hardware wallet information, and another called Account Partition, which stores all wallets. Each wallet is then divided into two parts, one containing sensitive data encrypted with AES XEX128, the password plus a cryptographic salt are used to generate keys and the other containing unencrypted information about the wallet. Even though the most sensitive data is encrypted, this part is vulnerable to dictionary-based attacks, in which an attacker attempts to decrypt a huge number of popular passwords until he discovers one that works [15]. Cold wallets are offline wallets for storing bitcoins. Two issues are related to cold wallets.

1. The presence of private keys in at least one cold device;

2. The exposure of all private keys to a single trusted cold wallet administrator.

To address these challenges, Ebrahimi *et al.* [16] create a novel system for handling cold wallet assets that makes use of native multi-signature schemes. For both wallet creation and signature generation, the proposed cold wallet system includes at least two different devices and their respective administrators. The strategy makes certain that no final private key is stored on any device. To that objective, no single authority may spend from exchange assets.

Mechanism against Smart Contract Attacks

In the proposed solution, Alkhalifah *et al.* [17] calculate the difference between the contract balance and the sum of the balance of all participants in the smart contract balance (noted as a1 before the transaction and a1 ′ after the transaction). The result is computed by calculating the difference between a1 and b1 before and a1 ′ and b1 ′ after each procedure in a smart contract transaction. The transaction is recorded as T1 and the pre-trade difference as x1, while the post-trade difference is recorded as x1 ′. If the difference is equal to (x1 = x1 ′), then the operation is genuine; otherwise, the operation is malignant. This operation is blocked, and the transaction is considered a malignant operation.

Defense Mechanism against Transaction Verification Mechanism Attacks

Countermeasures against Finney Attacks

Finney's attack targets the merchant who does not wait for transaction confirmation.To counteract this assault, the Vendor must obtain several confirmations before transferring items or offering a service to the client. While waiting for several confirmations does not eliminate the possibility of a double-spending attack, it does reduce the risk and makes it more difficult for the attacker to spend the same coins twice.

Countermeasures against Race Attacks

Race Attack occurs when a vendor or recipient accepts unconfirmed transactions as payment. In a Race attack, the target is the Vendor (V) that accepts transactions without completely confirming the authenticity of blocks. The three detecting methods are as follows:

- **Listening period:** In this method, each received transaction is associated with a listening period, during which the Vendor monitors all receiving transactions. Only if the Vendor observes no attempt at double-spending throughout the listening period, will he deliver the product or provide the service.
- **Inserting observer nodes:** In this case, the Vendor inserts observer nodes into the network. The main task of the observer node is to transmit all transactions received to Vendor. This enables the Vendor or its observers to notice a double-spending attempt within seconds. To detect this attack, the Vendor must deploy a large number of observer nodes capable of connecting numerous nodes. The Vendor will incur costs as a result of implementing this countermeasure.
- **Sending out Warning or Alert Messages:** To counteract double-spending on rapid Bitcoin transfers, an efficient defense strategy has been developed. Peers on the Bitcoin network send out alarm messages when they receive two additional transactions with similar inputs but distinct outputs.

Countermeasures against Vector76

Vector76 attack is an attack in which attackers aim to fraudulently withdraw or steal the coins from the target using an invalid transaction. Using the mechanism that does not accept transactions with a single confirmation, the user node in the network should avoid having inbound connections, which prevents the attacker from injecting false information into the network; outgoing node connections should be monitored as well, and only well-known nodes should be permitted to join, and notifying the merchant about the ongoing double-spend could be preventive actions.

Countermeasures against Alternative History Attacks

In the case of repeated confirmations, an alternate-history attack is still conceivable, but it necessitates a high hash rate and the danger of largely lost electricity to the attacking miner. Incoming connections are not permitted; implementation of explicit outbound connections to well-known nodes, placing observer nodes in the network, and notifying the merchant about the ongoing double-spend are all feasible safeguards [11].

Countermeasures for 51% Or Majority Attacks

Several countermeasures are recommended to mitigate 51 percent of attacks or the Majority of attacks. Miller *et al.* [18] recommended adjustments to Bitcoin's PoW puzzle in order to minimise coalitions of mining pools for majority attacks. In

PoW, they proposed that mining pools that outsource their mining processes risk losing mining profits if the design involves non-outsourceable difficulties. To detect selfish mining activity in PoW-based Blockchains, Saad *et al.* [19] calculated transaction confirmation height and the block publication height and constructed a "truth state" for each published block using the relationship between the two attributes to discern between a valid block and a selfishly mined block.

Bastiaan [20] proposed the concept of "two-phase proof-of-work" in response to the 51 percent attack (2P-PoW). 2P-PoW is a continuous-time Markov chain (CTMC) model with two problems to solve instead of one. The CTMC states keep the pool from becoming uncontrollably large by lowering the incentive for miners to participate in the pool. 2P-PoW prevents huge pools from gaining hegemony by either outsourcing a large portion of their hash rate or disclosing the pool operator's private keys.

Sayeed and Marco [21] proposed five security protection techniques against the 51 percent attack. The penalty system for delayed block submission is a PoW-based security technique that makes the attack far more expensive to carry out. The delayed block method requires the attacker to mine a significant number of blocks in a row before joining the legitimate chain. The penalty imposed on the attacker may not be adequate to completely mitigate the attack. The addition of transactions to the delay blocks will not be confirmed until the penalty is lifted. As a result, certain transactions may take a few hours and days, to finalise. As a result, this strategy is not suitable for use in a real network, it is ineffective against 51 percent of attacks, and it has a medium level of risk.

Komodo proposed Delayed Proof of Work (dPoW) as a security solution. Notary nodes are appointed by the Komodo blockchain for notarization. Nodes collect data from Komodo and store it on the bitcoin blockchain. An attacker must alter the Komodo chain and bitcoin checkpoints in order to perform double-spending. The attacker must also get control of the bulk of the notary network [22]. As a result, the entire process makes the technique highly resilient. However, because there are a limited number of nodes, this security mechanism becomes centralised, introducing the well-known issue of a "single point of failure," where attackers know exactly what to attack. The dPoW is not cost-effective because it requires a fee to be implemented in the blockchain. It can only be applied to coins that use UTXO-based blockchains.

The notarization process is done every 10 min. This 10-minute checkpoint period provides attackers with plenty of time to carry out the 51 percent attack on crypto-coins, when the block confirmation time is only a few seconds [22]. This security approach has a minimal attack risk.

PirlGuard was created to protect against 51 percent exploitation. It works in a similar fashion as compared to the Penalty System and dPoW. As a result, attackers face a penalty. Master nodes are involved in notarization. As a centralised technique, the master nodes amplify it. This security method is solely dependent on only the Ethash algorithm. PirlGuard mitigates the 51% attack to approximately 0.03%. As a result, the penalty mechanism and the master node feature are both low risks.

ChainLocks is a Dash-specific security solution that tries to protect users from a 51 percent assault. Dash, with only 4100 master nodes, is an ideal target for a 51 percent assault because of its limited hashing power [23]. The 51 percent attack against low hashing currencies is highly likely to be carried out by simply renting the necessary hashing power [24]. As a result, ChainLocks' security mechanisms are insufficient to prevent the double-spending attack. The double-spending attack can be carried out by attackers with less than 51 percent hashing power because just one confirmation is required to publish a block which makes the Dash blockchain more susceptible. As a result, the level of risk is considered to be high.

Merged mining is a technology that allows several coins to be mined concurrently [25]. Merged mining is not a safe method of mining, but it can help to mitigate the 51 percent attack when used. This strategy combines the hashing power of two crypto-coins, increasing the cost of the attack. This method has the potential to greatly boost low-quality coins. The main constraint of this method is that the combined crypto-coins must be on the same consensus. Another problem is that if two crypto-coins with low hashing power collide, they can still be attacked if the attacker has enough hashing power. As a result, merged mining is simply a method of increasing the attacking cost by combining hashing power. As a result, it does not give a practical solution, and the risk level is judged to be significant.

Defense Mechanism Mining Pool Attacks

Countermeasures against Selfish Mining

Researchers have carried out research beforehand and proposed numerous viable solutions to tackle the problem of selfish mining [26 - 29]. Solat and Potop-Butucaru [30] support block 'lifes,' which prohibits greedy minors from retaining blocks. The network will refuse the estimated lifespan of a block (measured by honest miners). Heilman [27] is hindering the profitability of greedy miners by adopting a “Freshness Preferred” defense strategy. Heilman [27] adds unforgivable timelines to block, and in comparison to older blocks, it prefers more recent timestamps in blocks, in addition to the prior works by Eyal and Sirer [29]. The author shows through his research that miners who store their blocks for a long time have lower motivation than opportunistic miners.

Countermeasures against fork after withholding (FAW) Attack-

To solve the FAW attack problem, Kwon *et al.* [31] time-controlled beacons are introduced by the pool operators assigned to miners. In response to each assignment, the miners find and determine how much POW they have and send the answer, together with the beacon value, to the pool operator. After a few seconds, the beacon value is updated to find a rogue miner if the valid solution is retained and later propagated across the web. However, the authors also observed that this technique might not be practicable in some scenarios, concluding that research and academic communities are still grappling with the issue of FAW attacks.

Chang and Park [32] proposed Silent Timestamping as a defense mechanism against the FAW attack that ensures share ordering and essentially negates the FAW's incentive effects. The behaviour of the ideal attacker against silent timestamping was studied, and it was discovered that the best FAW attacker approach is forced to decrease to ethical mining. Silent Timestamping removes the requirement for networking and does not require any modifications to the miner's code. As a result, silent timestamping provides a feasible, backward-compatible, and effective protection option. Table **1** summarizes various blockchain attack surfaces and their countermeasures.

Table 1. Summarizes Blockchain attack surfaces and their countermeasures.

S. No	Categories of Attacks	Types of Attacks Under Each Category	Counterfeit Solutions for Each Attack
1	Blockchain network Attacks	Distributed denial of service	A high rate of detection and a low percentage of false alarms [1] Credit Bonus Penalty Strategy (CBPS) [2] Increase block size [3]
		Transaction malleability attacks	Soft fork [5]
		Timejacking	Synchronized clocking
		Routing attacks	Mining Pool-Multihoming [6]
		Sybil attacks	Cyber Threat Intelligence platform [7] Trustchain [8]
		Eclipse attacks	Peer monitoring [9]
		Long-range attacks on proof of stake networks	Longest chain rule, Moving Checkpoints, Key-evolving cryptography, context-aware transactions, and plenitude rule [10]

(Table 1) cont.....

S. No	Categories of Attacks	Types of Attacks Under Each Category	Counterfeit Solutions for Each Attack
2	User wallet Attacks	Phishing	Imperva Web Application Firewall (WAF) [11]
		Dictionary attacks	Use of human-only solvable puzzles (HOSPs) [12]
		Vulnerable signatures	Interactive Incontestable Signature [13]
		Flawed key generation	Mixing and anonymous operation [14]
		Attacks on hot wallets	TrustZone wallets [15]
			native multi-signature schemes [16]
3	Smart Contract Attacks	Vulnerabilities in contract source code and virtual machines	Before and after any operation that modifies the state of a contract, result of difference between the contract balance and the total balance of all participants must be the same [8]
4	Transaction verification mechanism attacks	Finney attacks	Wait for multi-confirmations of transactions.
		Race attacks	1. Listening period. 2. Placing observer nodes in the network 3. Peer-to-peer communication of double-spending alerts [25].
		Vector76	wait for multi-confirmations for transactions
		Alternative history attacks	1. There are no inbound connections 2. Outgoing connections to a well-connected node must be explicit. 3. The merchant is notified of the ongoing double-spend by placing observers in the network [11].
		51% or the majority attacks	Two-phased proof-of-work [20]
			Penalty System [21]
			DPoW [22]
			PirlGuard [21]
			ChainLocks [23, 24]
			Merged Mining [25]
5	Mining pool attacks	Selfish mining	Time-stamping blocks [26 - 29]
		Fork after withholding	Time controlled beacons [31]
			Silent-Timestamping [32]

CONCLUSION

There is no doubt that blockchain has grown in popularity throughout the world. It has had a lasting influence on the globe, rather than merely being famous. The unique features of blockchain technology make its implementation appealing in a variety of commercial domains, including monetary transactions, healthcare, and smart contracts. The blockchain has the potential to allow a new breed of decentralized apps that do not require intermediaries, as well as serve as the foundation for critical components of Internet security infrastructures. As a result, identifying existing research especially connected to the application of blockchain to the problem of cyber security, is critical in order to address how developing technologies might offer solutions to reduce emerging risks.

Understanding and managing blockchain network risks are important to blockchain security. A blockchain security model is a blueprint for making these controls secure. The security model for blockchain should be created in a way that all essential security safeguards are protected with all necessary security measures. To execute a security model for a blockchain solution, administrators must establish a risk model capable of managing all industry, governance, technical, and process risks. Thus, examine the risks associated with blockchain. Then, based on the three types below, administrators must develop security measures to limit risks and threats: Implement blockchain-specific security mechanisms, use standard security measures, and make sure there are business controls in place on the blockchain.

CONSENT FOR PUBLICATION

Not applicable.

CONFLICT OF INTEREST

The author declares no conflict of interest, financial or otherwise.

ACKNOWLEDGEMENT

Declared none.

REFERENCES

[1] J. Cheng, R. Xu, X. Tang, V.S. Sheng, and C. Cai, "An abnormal network flow feature sequence prediction approach for DDoS attacks detection in big data environment", *Comput. Mater. Continua,* vol. 55, no. 1, pp. 95-119, 2018.

[2] H. Yang, J. Yuan, H. Yao, Q. Yao, A. Yu, and J. Zhang, "Blockchain-based hierarchical trust networking for JointCloud", *IEEE Internet Things J.,* vol. 7, no. 3, pp. 1667-1677, 2020. [http://dx.doi.org/10.1109/JIOT.2019.2961187]

[3] M. Saad, M.T. Thai, and A. Mohaisen, "POSTER: deterring ddos attacks on blockchain-based cryptocurrencies through mempool optimization", *Proceedings of the 2018 on Asia Conference on Computer and Communications Security,* 2018pp. 809-811 [http://dx.doi.org/10.1145/3196494.3201584]

[4] U. Rajput, F. Abbas, and H. Oh, "A solution towards eliminating transaction malleability in bitcoin", *Journal of Information Processing Systems,* vol. 14, no. 4, pp. 837-850, 2018.

[5] Alex Boverman, "Timejacking & bitcoin", *Culubas blog,* 2011.

[6] M. Apostolaki, A. Zohar, and L. Vanbever, "Hijacking bitcoin: Routing attacks on cryptocurrencies", *2017 IEEE Symposium on Security and Privacy (SP),* IEEE, pp. 375-392, 2017. [http://dx.doi.org/10.1109/SP.2017.29]

[7] S. Gong, and C. Lee, "Blocis: blockchain-based cyber threat intelligence sharing framework for sybil-resistance", *Electronics (Basel),* vol. 9, no. 3, p. 521, 2020. [http://dx.doi.org/10.3390/electronics9030521]

[8] M. Samaniego, U. Jamsrandorj, and R. Deters, *"Blockchain as a Service for IoT." In 2016 IEEE international conference on internet of things (iThings) and IEEE green computing and communications (GreenCom) and IEEE cyber, physical and social computing (CPSCom) and IEEE smart data (SmartData).* IEEE, 2016, pp. 433-436.

[9] E. Heilman, A. Kendler, A. Zohar, and S. Goldberg, "Eclipse attacks on bitcoin's peer-to-peer network", In 24th {USENIX} Security Symposium ({USENIX} Security 15), pp. 129-144. 2015.

[10] E. Deirmentzoglou, G. Papakyriakopoulos, and C. Patsakis, "A survey on long-range attacks for proof of stake protocols", *IEEE Access,* pp. 28712-28725, 2019.

[11] P. Gaži, A. Kiayias, and A. Russell, "Stake-bleeding attacks on proof-of-stake blockchains", *2018 Crypto Valley Conference on Blockchain Technology (CVCBT),* 2018pp. 85-92 [http://dx.doi.org/10.1109/CVCBT.2018.00015]

[12] R. Canetti, S. Halevi, and M. Steiner, "Mitigating dictionary attacks on password-protected local storage", *Annual International Cryptology Conference,* 2006pp. 160-179 [http://dx.doi.org/10.1007/11818175_10]

[13] Y. Zhu, R. Guo, G. Gan, and W-T. Tsai, "Interactive incontestable signature for transactions confirmation in bitcoin blockchain", In: *40th Annual Computer Software and Applications Conference (COMPSAC)* vol. 1. IEEE, 2016, pp. 443-448. [http://dx.doi.org/10.1109/COMPSAC.2016.142]

[14] Z. Zheng, S. Xie, H. Dai, X. Chen, and H. Wang, An overview of blockchain technology: Architecture, consensus, and future trends.*In 2017 IEEE international congress on big data (BigData congress).* IEEE, 2017, pp. 557-564. [http://dx.doi.org/10.1109/BigDataCongress.2017.85]

[15] M. Gentilal, P. Martins, and L. Sousa, "TrustZone-backed bitcoin wallet", *Proceedings of the Fourth Workshop on Cryptography and Security in Computing Systems,* 2017pp. 25-28 [http://dx.doi.org/10.1145/3031836.3031841]

[16] Shahriar Ebrahimi, Parisa Hasanizadeh, Seyed Mohammad Aghamirmohammadali, and Amirali Akbari, "Enhancing Cold Wallet Security with Native Multi-Signature schemes in Centralized Exchanges", 2021.

[17] Alkhalifah, Ayman, Alex Ng, Paul A. Watters, and A. S. M. Kayes. "A Mechanism to Detect and Prevent Ethereum Blockchain Smart Contract Reentrancy Attacks." Frontiers in Computer Science 3 2021. [http://dx.doi.org/10.3389/fcomp.2021.598780]

[18] A. Miller, A. Kosba, J. Katz, and E. Shi, "Nonoutsourceable scratch-off puzzles to discourage bitcoin mining coalitions", *Proceedings of the 22nd ACM SIGSAC Conference on Computer and Communications Security,* 2015pp. 680-691 [http://dx.doi.org/10.1145/2810103.2813621]

[19] M. Saad, L. Njilla, C. Kamhoua, and A. Mohaisen, "Countering selfish mining in blockchains", *2019 International Conference on Computing, Networking and Communications (ICNC),* 2019pp. 360-364 [http://dx.doi.org/10.1109/ICCNC.2019.8685577]

[20] M. Bastiaan, *Preventing the 51%-attack: a stochastic analysis of two phase proof of work in bitcoin.,* 2015. http://referaat.cs.utwente.nl/conference/22/paper/7473/preventingthe-51-attack-a-stochasticanalysis-oft

wo- phase-proof-of-work-in-bitcoin.pdf

[21] S. Sayeed, and H. Marco-Gisbert, "Assessing blockchain consensus and security mechanisms against the 51% attack", *Appl. Sci. (Basel),* vol. 9, no. 9, p. 1788, 2019. [http://dx.doi.org/10.3390/app9091788]

[22] N.A. Akbar, A. Muneer, N. ElHakim, and S.M. Fati, "Distributed Hybrid Double-Spending Attack Prevention Mechanism for Proof-of-Work and Proof-of-Stake Blockchain Consensuses", *Future Internet,* vol. 13, no. 11, p. 285, 2021. [http://dx.doi.org/10.3390/fi13110285]

[23] N. G. Edmund, *A Dash to Mitigate 51% Attacks with ChainLocks. 2018..*

[24] https://www.nicehash.com/

[25] https://www.cryptocompare.com/mining/guides/what-is-merged-mining-bitcoin-namecoinlitecoin-dogecoin/

[26] A. Sapirshtein, Y. Sompolinsky, and A. Zohar, "Optimal selfish mining strategies in bitcoin", *International Conference on Financial Cryptography and Data Security,* 2016pp. 515-532

[27] E. Heilman, "One weird trick to stop selfish miners: Fresh bitcoins, a solution for the honest miner", *International Conference on Financial Cryptography and Data Security,* 2014pp. 161-162 [http://dx.doi.org/10.1007/978-3-662-44774-1_12]

[28] N.T. Courtois, and L Bahack, "On subversive miner strategies and block withholding attack in bitcoin digital currency", *arXiv preprint arXiv:1402.1718,* 2014.

[29] I. Eyal, and E.G. Sirer, "Majority is not enough: Bitcoin mining is vulnerable", *International conference on financial cryptography and data security,* 2014pp. 436-454 [http://dx.doi.org/10.1007/978-3-662-45472-5_28]

[30] S. Solat, and M. Potop-Butucaru, "Zeroblock: Timestamp-free prevention of block-withholding attack in bitcoin", *arXiv preprint arXiv:1605.02435,* 2016.

[31] Y. Kwon, D. Kim, Y. Son, E. Vasserman, and Y. Kim, "Be selfish and avoid dilemmas: Fork after withholding (faw) attacks on bitcoin", *Proceedings of the 2017 ACM SIGSAC Conference on Computer and Communications Security,* 2017pp. 195-209 [http://dx.doi.org/10.1145/3133956.3134019]

[32] S-Y. Chang, and Y. Park, "Silent timestamping for blockchain mining pool security", *2019 International Conference on Computing, Networking and Communications (ICNC),* 2019pp. 1-5 [http://dx.doi.org/10.1109/ICCNC.2019.8685563]

CHAPTER 6

Preserving the Privacy of Wearable IoT Device Data Using Blockchain

K.K. Sowjanya[1,*], **K.P.B. Madavi**[2] and **G. Thahniyath**[3]

[1] *CMR Institute of Technology, Bangalore, India*

[2] *GITAM University, Bangalore, India*

[3] *Dayananda Sagar University, Bangalore, India*

Abstract: Personal healthcare has become the most important part of present human life due to the COVID-19 pandemic. The awareness of one's health is made easily available by adopting IoT wearable devices like Fitbit, smart watches, oximeters, *etc.* All these devices store sensitive information like a heartbeat, BP, distance traveled, calories burnt, stress levels, location details, *etc.*, and are stored in third-party data servers. These servers are vulnerable to illegitimate users and also have a single point of failure. The personal data of the individuals should be protected along with its integrity. At the same time, the data stored in the servers should be decentralized to overcome the problem of a single point of attack. The objective of this article is to provide a framework that uses SHA-56 for generating the hash code and Blockchain technology to store the data. Thus, providing privacy, security, and integrity for the data.

Keywords: Blockchain, Fitbit, Fitbit data, Encryption, Hashing, IoT, Mining, Privacy, Security, Wearable devices.

INTRODUCTION

Smart homes, smart cities, and smart devices are driving the future generation with the help of IoT. IoT has gained so much popularity because of its heterogeneous forms and heterogeneous applications. It is changing our normal world into a digital world where interconnected devices communicate with each other through a network without human interaction [1]. Adopting this Internet of Things has introduced many technological advancements such as smart security home systems, which provide security alerts for the houses; smart agriculture systems, which provide information about the land, soil, *etc.*; and smart health care systems, which provide the health status of individuals [2]. Since it can be

* **Corresponding author K.K. Sowjanya:** Dayananda Sagar University, Bangalore; E-mail: ksowjanya-cse@dsu.edu.in

Rashmi Agrawal and Neha Gupta (Eds.)

used in day-to-day activities, the usage of these IoT devices is enormous in various fields like health care, industries, agriculture, cities, *etc.* The usage statistics of IoT devices in various fields in 2020 are represented in Fig. (**1**) as follows:

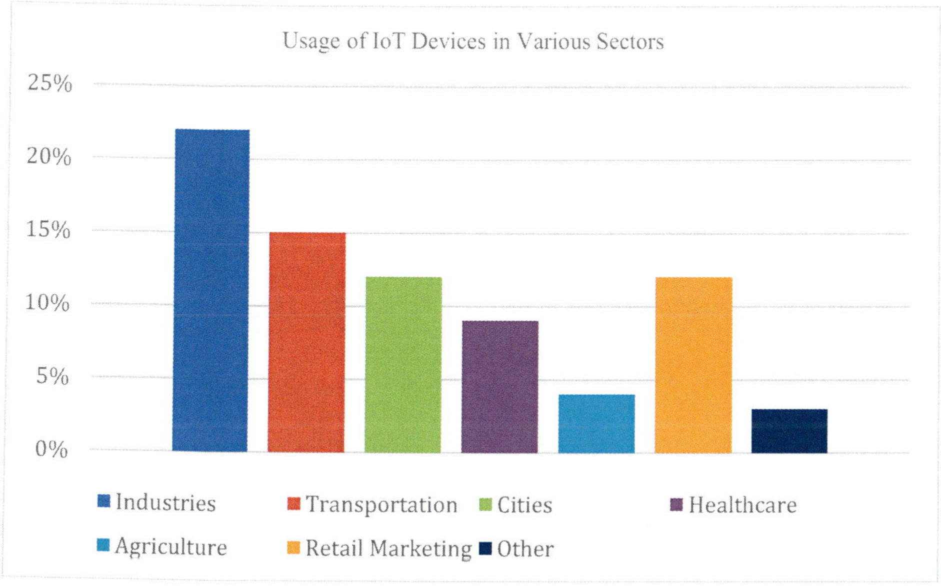

Fig. (1). Usage of IoT Devices in Various Sectors [3].

IOT ARCHITECTURE

Fig. (**2**) depicts the IoT's core three-layer architectural structure in terms of the devices and technology that each layer encompasses. Each layer in the IoT is characterized by the functions it performs and the devices it employs. Many experts believe that the IoT is primarily based on three layers: perception, network, and application [4].

Perception Layer: It is the architecture's physical layer. This is where the sensors and connected devices come together when they collect different amounts of information according to the project requirements. The edge devices, sensors, and actuators which interact with their environments can be used.

Network Layer: All of the data gathered by these devices must be transferred and processed. This is the role of the network layer. These devices are linked to other smart things, servers, and network devices. The transmission of all the data is also handled. Cloud computing platforms, Internet gateways, switching and routing devices, and other devices at this layer use cutting-edge technologies, including Wi-Fi, LTE, Bluetooth, 3G, and Zigbee.

Application Layer: The user interacts with the application layer. It's responsible for providing the user with application-specific services. This might be a smart home application where users tap a button in the app to switch on a coffee machine, for example. The data's validity, integrity, and confidentiality are all guaranteed by the application layer. The goal of IoT, or the establishment of a smart environment, is accomplished at this layer.

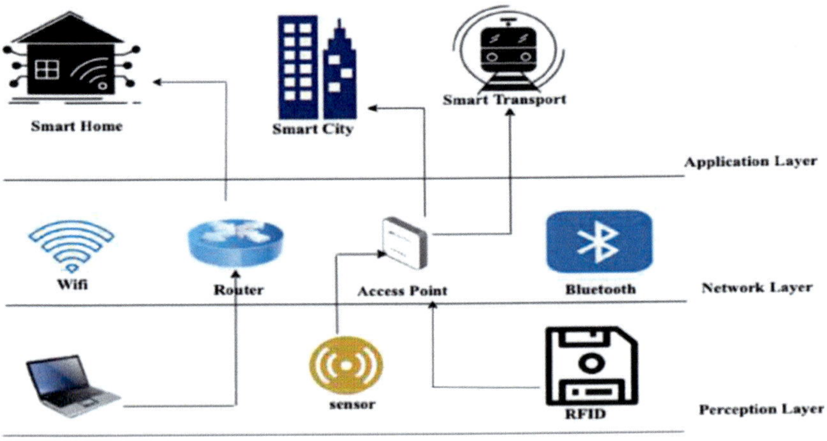

Fig. (2). Three-Layer IoT Architecture [5].

IOT FITBIT INTRODUCTION

James Park and Eric Friedman launched Fitbit Incorporated in 2007 as Healthy Metrics Research Incorporated. The initial goal of the company was to incorporate accelerometers into wearable technology. Accelerometers are small sensors that measure the forces of acceleration. The Fitbit Tracker, the company's first product, was released to the public in 2009. The first Fitbit was a wristband that was attached to the wearer's clothing. The little device could count and track the number of steps taken, and it was followed by a slew of other Fitbit gadgets with a variety of features. An accelerometer is used in Fitbit devices to track your movements. Fitbit counts your steps and monitors the distance you've gone, calories burnt, and sleep quality using the accelerometer, which converts movement data into digital measures. Fitness tapes include a touchscreen, smartphone notifications, activity, and medical monitoring, automatic exercise detection, and water resistance to swimming. It has a built-in heart rate monitor and sleep tracking. Calls, texts, and calendar reminders are also available for notifications on the band. During the day, the Fitbit Tracker could be fastened to the user's clothing. It also came with a wristband so you could wear it at night. The device was linked to a website where users could log their workouts, eat their meals, and keep track of their weight. It also included a charging station that allowed customers to wirelessly upload data from their Fitbits.

Fitbit has been around since 2007, and it is the most well-known fitness tracker brand. As a result, they're regarded as one of the top items available. There are numerous alternatives available to suit all budgets and feature requirements. We've compared the latest Fitbit models in a side-by-side comparison chart. As the version of Fitbits is advancing, so is the data it collects from the user. An overview of various metrics generated from IoT Wearable devices is displayed in (Table **1**).

Table 1. Overview of various Metrics generated from IoT Wearable Devices.

BASIC FEATURES	ZIP 2012	FLEX 2 2013	ALTA 2016	ALTA HR 2017	CHARGE 3 2018	VERSA 2019	Sense 2020
Steps & Activity	✓	✓	✓	✓	✓	✓	✓
Calories Burned	✓	✓	✓	✓	✓	✓	✓
Floors Climbing					✓	✓	✓
Clock/Time	✓		✓	✓	✓	✓	✓
Female Health Tracking						✓	✓
Sleep Tracking		✓	✓	✓	✓	✓	✓
Smart Track		✓	✓	✓	✓	✓	✓
Built-in GPS					✓	✓	✓
Heart Rate Tracking				✓	✓	✓	✓
Cardio Fitness Level				✓	✓	✓	✓
Oxygen					✓	✓	✓
Stress Tracking							✓
ECG							✓

Fitbit Architecture

Fig. (**3**) is an example of how fitness wearable technology can be utilized for lifestyle applications, as shown in an architecture that includes weight, calories burned, heart rate, speed, *etc.* The users' activities will be tracked *via* sensors, and they will be able to input part of the data themselves, which will subsequently be transmitted to a smartphone and the provider's cloud service. The data is subsequently processed, making it easier for the user to comprehend. Depending on the type of display, this is transmitted back into either the associated smartphone or the wearable itself.

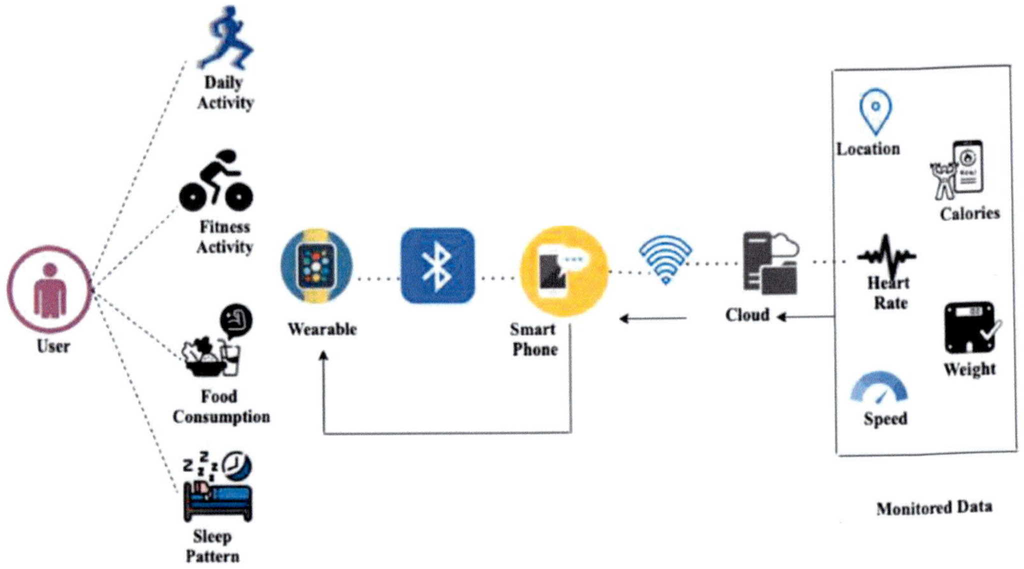

Fig. (3). Fitbit Architecture.

Challenges of IoT Devices

IoT devices come in a wide range of varieties. These devices communicate with other devices in different ways, such as wired or wireless communication, using different protocols depending on the end communication device. Due to the heterogeneity of the devices, there is no standardization of the communication protocols. This raises a concern in terms of the security, integrity, and confidentiality of the device and its associated data. And also, these devices are more easily prone to security attacks because of their limited resources and computational capacity. Due to the wide range of devices, IoT devices face many challenges, which are tabulated in Table **2**.

Table 2. Challenges of IoT Devices.

S.No.	Challenge	Description
1	Confidentiality	As the Devices maintain sensitive information about the user, there is a need to maintain the confidentiality of the data.
2	Integrity	As the devices communicate with other devices or servers, it is transmitted through a network. Hence the integrity of the data is necessary
3	Authentication	Data transmission or reception happens between various IoT devices to enhance functionality. Hence a proper authentication mechanism is needed before setting up the communication.
4	Power Efficient	Many small-range IoT devices lack the resources to maintain the power for computation and working.

(Table 2) cont.....

S.No.	Challenge	Description
5	Single point of attack	All the data generated from these devices will be stored in the respective device data centers that are of centralized architecture. It acts as a single point where an illegitimate user can access the data.
6	Vulnerability	Many IoT devices are vulnerable because of wireless communication from end to end.

INTRODUCTION TO BLOCKCHAIN

Blockchain is a P2P (peer-to-peer) secure distributed network that maintains the transaction records of the network and exchange of digital information without a third-party intervention or a central server, or a trusted agent. It is a database structure that holds the information in chunks. The block of data is chained to the previous block of data with a given time stamp. A block is a set of transactions that are put on the chain at the same time after it has been verified by the standard users in the network. A block mainly consists of the following:

- The reference to the previous block
- The Proof of Work: nonce value (a random value generated only once at a particular time)
- The time-stamp
- The Merkle tree root for the transactions: Each of the transactions is a leaf node in the tree. The transaction is each hashed, combined, and rehashed till all the transactions are combined in one root.

Each of the nodes has a duplicated copy of the block. Hence Blockchain is a duplicated ledger of transactions that have been agreed upon by the standard nodes and distributed across nodes.

There are two types of Blockchain [6] user's public key is permissionless e.g. (Bitcoin or Ethereum), which is public, and only one can join the network, and Permissioned Blockchain (Hyperledger Project by The Linux Foundation) [7]. Permissioned Blockchain, where the consensus of valid peers about the transaction is required and is gaining a lot of interest in applications other than financial use cases.

Characteristics of the Blockchain

Immutability of data: Once the Blockchain is formed, it is difficult to tamper with the block.

Transparency: All transactions in the Blockchain can be viewed by any participant.

Decentralization: The Blockchain is managed across multiple sites, making it more reliable.

Security: blockchain technology mainly uses public key infrastructure and hashing techniques for authentication and integrity of the data, respectively.

BLOCKCHAIN ARCHITECTURE

Blockchain technology was first introduced by the author Satoshi Nakamoto [8]. The main intention behind this is to make online payments without third-party server authentication. This led to the invention of the current trending bitcoin and cryptocurrencies. This technology enables the user to exchange any digital information online. It provides high security, reliability, and availability because the Blockchain is immutable and secure. Because of these features, blockchain technology is used in a wide range of applications where there is a need for security. The data in the Blockchain is maintained in the form of nodes. Each node represents a transaction or a digital data entry. Each entry is encrypted with the private key of the user and is sent to the chain; the consensus algorithm checks the validity of the transaction and adds it to the chain. Thus, all the nodes/transactions are added to the Blockchain, which forms a chain-like structure. This technology follows the architecture in which each node is connected to every other node in the network. It is represented in Fig. (**4**).

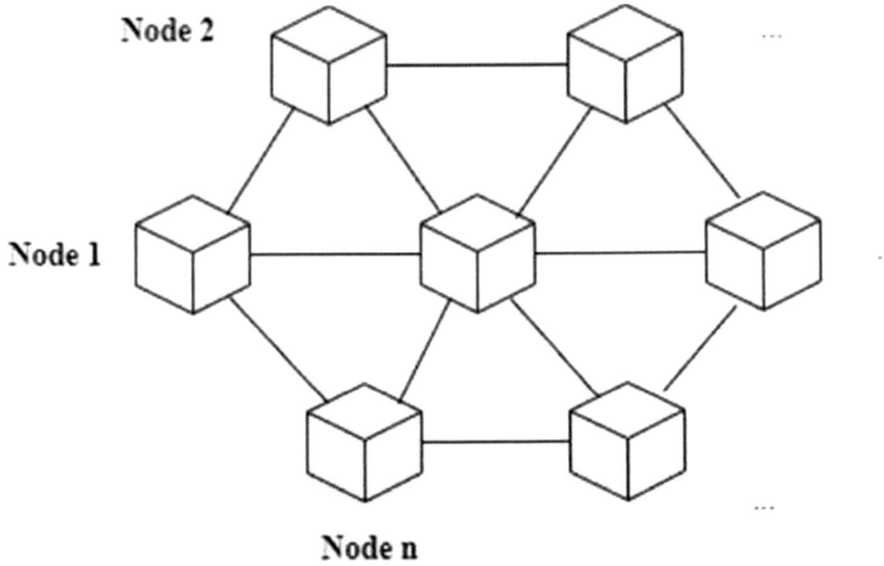

Fig. (4). Architecture of typical Blockchain [9].

Components of Blockchain

The blockchain functionality is based on basic core components such as node, transaction, block, mining, and consensus.

Transaction: Transaction is the basic data that is sent to the nodes for validity and is added to the chain. When new data is generated, that is considered a transaction and broadcasted to all the nodes.

Block: Group of transactions is called a block. The transactions are grouped based on validity and are distributed across the chain. This block contains information about the transactions/data. Every block that is added to the chain will contain the hash value of the previous block.

Node: Node is a component for the validity of a new transaction or digital entry. Every node in the Blockchain will have a copy of all the nodes of the chain. When a new transaction comes, the node checks its previous history and sends it to the remaining nodes to check its validity. If the transaction is valid, it is added to the chain; otherwise, it is denied.

Mining: Mining is the core functionality of the Blockchain. It is a process of creating a block, validating it, and adding a hash valuc to it. Aftcr adding thc hash value, it is distributed across the network.

Consensus: The whole process of validating, adding, and distributing a block in the network is called consensus. Various Consensus algorithms like proof-o--work and proof-of-stake are already available that define a set of rules to maintain the Blockchain.

Based on all the components and their properties, the Blockchain can be either private, public, or hybrid. The overall working of the Blockchain, along with the components, are represented in Fig. (**5**):

SECURITY USING BLOCKCHAIN

Blockchain decentralized [11] and distributed processes, when applied to IoT, reduce the cost and risk associated with IoT device data management and data transfer as there is no central repository of the data [12]. The IoT gateway for data exchange can be eliminated with blockchain technology, thus reducing the cost and delay associated with IoT networks.

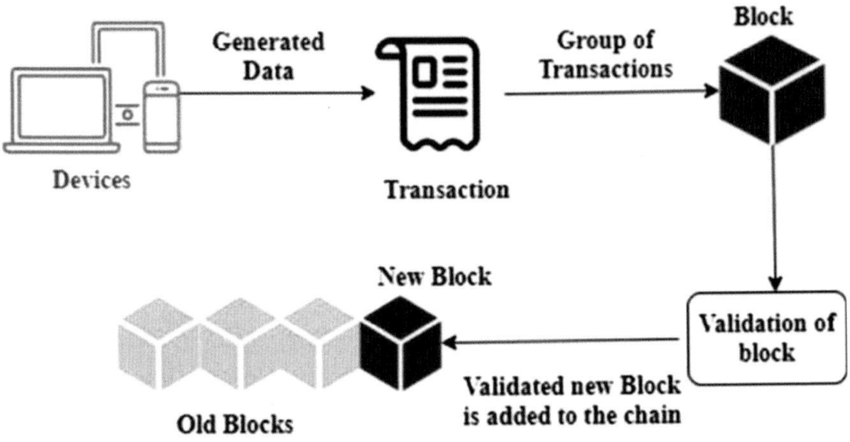

Fig. (5). Overall working of the Blockchain [10].

Authentication of IoT device

The IoT device that should take part in the transaction should be authenticated. The Authentication process can be done *via* Hardware Authenticator, which can be an offline device. The Hardware Authenticator (HA) has important functions like creating the initial block, assigning a digital signature to the IoT device, and creating new blocks with a private key.

Each of the authenticated devices can take part in the transaction with another authenticated device by looking into the block database given by HA. The database has the identification of all authenticated devices and valid previous transaction records. The other already standard devices in the network validate the newly joined device. Once validation is confirmed by 51% of the standard users in the network, the new authenticated device can take part in the transaction using its private key.

Integrity: The hash value of the block identifies the particular block of information, and this characteristic makes the block of data immutable. The hash value of each block references the previous block of information to form a chain, and the time is recorded. Each block thus has the hash value of the previous block of data, thus making it hard to alter a particular block of data. The Overall hash value of the block is formed by considering the previous block's hash value, the hash value of the transactional data, and Metadata. If any of the blocks of data is altered, it breaks the chain. The initial block has no valid previous hash as there is no previous block. This chunk of data is called Genesis Block, and the previous hash is set to a string of one or more zeros. There are two methods employed to make the data secure.

Method 1: In this method, the inventors of the Blockchain have framed a set of rules that makes the recalculation of hash value difficult and time-consuming in case of any modification and an attempt to recalculate the hash of the following blocks. The rule to be followed for a harder calculation of the hash in each block should have X number of leading zeroes.

Method 2: The second method is Consensus-based, wherein the peer-to-peer network is followed [13]. Any participant can join the network. Each of the participants gets a full copy of the Blockchain. The Blockchain is distributed across different sites. Each authenticated device sends the block of data to all the peers of the network. More than 51 percent of the peers should validate the transaction, and then the block is added to the chain. In case of any modification of the data, recalculation of the hash and getting validation by more than 50 percent of the standard devices is very difficult.

The Process of Transaction: (Fig. **6**) gives an overview of the Blockchain.

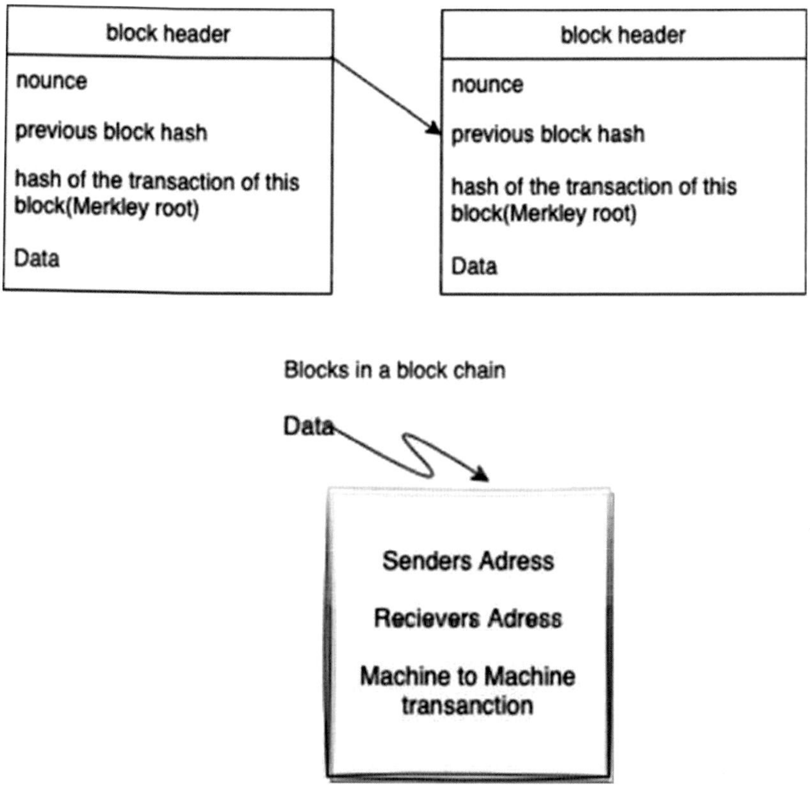

Fig. (6). Blockchain.

Encryption [14]: Blockchain Technology uses Hashing. Hashing of the transaction uses mainly the SHA-256 algorithm to secure the data. The public key of the sender, the transaction information, and the receiver's address are encrypted by the SHA-256 algorithm to generate the fixed-length encrypted information. This process of verification done in the Blockchain is called Encryption. Each of the users in the Blockchain has a private and a public key. A private key is used to authenticate the user and to confirm the origin of the transaction is legitimate. The public key of the user is the key that is shared across the peer network for verification of the transaction.

Verification of the sender

Once the Hash key or a message digest is generated, a digital signature is created, and along with the private key, a digitally signed document is created. The original message, digitally signed document and a public key are sent to the receiver. The receiver retrieves the hash value from the digitally signed document along with the shared public key of the sender compared with the hash value created at the receiver side by considering the original message.

Proof of Work

Validation of the data is done by using a method called Mining [15]. The miners determine the nonce value, i.e., the random value combines it with the hash of the previous block, rehash the value, and compare this to the target hash. If the miners correctly determine the hash value and if it is less than the target value, the transaction is said to be validated by the user and the block is added to the Blockchain, and the transaction is processed. If one of the miners can determine the nonce value and decrypt the information. The other users can just validate the transaction so that the block is added to the Blockchain. The mathematical puzzle required to find the right nonce value such that the generated hash value meets the requirement, say it has to be less than the target value, requires an enormous amount of computation power as it has to be done using the Brute force method. And such an enormous amount of computation can be attempted only by standard users. As the nonce value is "Number only used Once", Proof of Work is used to determine that the transaction done by the user is only once and is depicted in Fig. (7).

Smart Contract

To have a more secure and automatic machine-to-machine transaction in IoT, a Smart contract is built over the Blockchain [16]. Smart Contract is an executable script that allows the automatic execution of multiple steps: the agreement to be met and the transaction to be carried over by all the peers in the network. It enables automatic transactions that are initiated by an action. Smart contracts built on Blockchain inherit the properties of Blockchain, hence will validate, capture and see that the agreement is met by multiple parties involved in the transaction without the need for a third party. Every device in the IoT gets a copy of the smart contract. On the receipt of an action to its address, a smart contract is executed. Ethereum provides the concept of smart contracts and Solidity (the programming language used to write these contracts) that enables decentralized applications. A low-latency and low-computation consumption protection model based on a smart contract has been researched [17]. Each node that has to send the block as a transaction in the network has to get registered in the smart contract. The smart contract issues a token that validates the transaction, and it is stored in the block. This token acts as proof of validity, and the block can be considered to be added to the Blockchain.

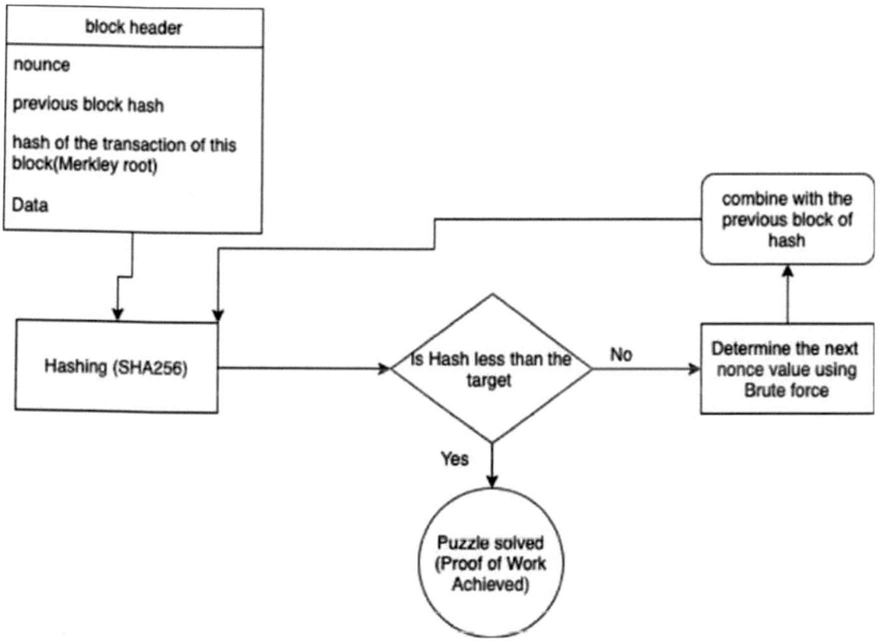

Fig. (7). Proof of Work.

RELATED WORKS

To preserve the privacy of the data generated by IoT devices, many authors have proposed many algorithms and techniques [18], proposing a hybrid approach that involves homomorphic encryption to encrypt the sensor data during the transmission and blockchain technology to maintain privacy. However, there is a storage overhead for this technique which can be resolved by maintaining only the hashes instead of the entire chain. Not only preserving the sensor data but

Blockchain can also be used to preserve the privacy of medical IoT data [19]. proposed a four-layer architecture to provide security for the medical data which is retrieved from the IoT devices. The data generated is stored in the databases using blockchain technology; if the third party wants to retrieve the data, they have to use a smart contract that provides the authenticity of the user. This model could provide security but lacks inefficient image retrieval systems and has storage overhead and computational complexity. To address the problems of extensive computational complexity, and storage overhead [20], proposed a modified blockchain framework that uses the cloud for storing the blocks generated, which in turn reduces the storage overhead. All the blocks that belong to one Blockchain are given a unique identifier which makes the retrieval process authenticated. The users or the doctors who want to access the data can send a request using the smart contract and the public key. In addition to the Blockchain, many cryptographic techniques were also implemented to provide security from different kinds of attacks. Similar to the above method [21], proposed a four-layered architecture that includes many technologies such as cloud for storage, Blockchain for privacy, and IoT for monitoring the health of a person. The data generated by these sensors are stored in the cloud using a NoSQL database and is hashed using blockchain technology which makes the retrieval process fast [22]. extended the usage of Blockchain to provide security to smart cities using mobile edge computing as every person has a mobile device with a cellular network area. This technique uses already existing mobile computing to generate the data and includes Blockchain to provide secure peer-to-peer communication [22]. Also proposed a similar framework for smart cities by storing the data in a blockchain to provide reliability, using somewhat homomorphic encryption for providing security, and machine learning algorithms to classify the data and use it for predictions. Most of the mentioned techniques provide security for the generated data, whereas, they have used blockchain technology to provide a reliable and secure platform to exchange the data between the device to device and the human to a device. In addition, many authors have used machine learning algorithms to classify the data into two categories: critical and non-critical, data before giving access to third-party servers. Extra security is provided by encrypting critical or non-critical data using different encryption algorithms.

PROPOSED METHOD

The proposed method involves implementing blockchain technology to provide security for the data generated from IoT devices, as mentioned in Tables **1** and **3**.

Day to Day, the data is generated from the device, and each day's data is considered as one transaction. Initial data, i.e., Day 1 data, is considered as one block, and it is hashed with the hash value of the genesis block using the SHA-

256 algorithm. The newly generated block is added to the chain, and then it is uploaded to the data center cloud. Similarly, in Day n, the block is hashed with the hash value of block n-1 and is added to the chain. Every block generated daily is considered a block, and the chain is maintained by adding the hashed block to the chain. The process of maintaining the chain is represented in (Fig. **8**), and the algorithm is represented in Table **4**.

Table 3. Typical data generated from IoT.

Date	Activity	Steps	Distance km	Time	Heart Rate	Stress Levels	Calories
06/01/2021	Walking	10,000	7.62	6:00 AM	85	HIGH	409
06/02/2021	Jogging	7,500	5.7	6:15 AM	84	MEDIUM	261
06/03/2021	Walking	3,000	2.2	6:05 AM	77	LOW	153
06/04/2021	Walking	9,000	6.8	6:00 AM	85	LOW	334
06/05/2021	Jogging	9,000	6.8	6:20 AM	88	LOW	334
06/06/2021	Running	7,800	5.9	6:12 AM	85	MEDIUM	272
06/07/2021	Walking	5,678	4.32	6:17 AM	77	LOW	204
06/08/2021	Walking	7,998	6.09	6:00 AM	80	LOW	284
06/09/2021	Walking	9,087	6.92	6:03 AM	85	LOW	344
06/10/2021	Jogging	5,009	3.8	6:04 AM	78	MEDIUM	190
06/11/2021	Walking	8,009	6.1	6:00 AM	82	LOW	284
06/12/2021	Walking	12,000	9.1	6:14 AM	88	HIGH	614

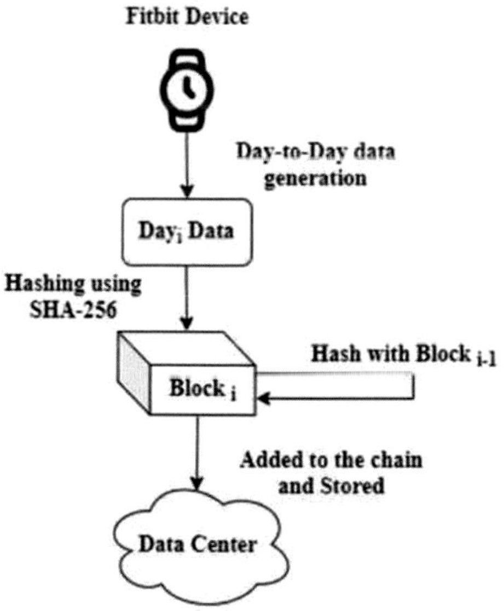

Fig. (8). Proposed Method to Preserving Privacy.

Table 4. Proposed Algorithm for Data Privacy Using Blockchain

Step1: Data for a day i is generated and considered as a transaction
Step2: Block i is combined with the hash value of Block i-1 using SHA-256
Step3: New generated block with hash value is added to the chain and uploaded to the server

Chain Validation

Blockchain is popular because of the high security provided. The integrity of the data in the Blockchain is maintained high using the process of mining. Mining the chain includes adding a new block to the chain by recalculating the hashes of the existing blocks and checking for the validity of the newly calculated hash value with the previous existing hash values. If there is any discrepancy in the hash values, that can be identified easily using the process of mining. The process of identifying the modified/tampered block can be done in two ways. One, using the present block hash, by comparing the present block hash with the recently computed present block hash. If these two values are equal, then the data is not modified/tampered with. Else the data is tampered with. Two, using the previous block hash, by comparing the previous hash of the present block with the computed hash of the previous block. Similarly, if these two hash values are the same, then there is no modification; else, the data is tampered with. The process of chain validation is represented in Figs. (**9** and **10**) as follows.

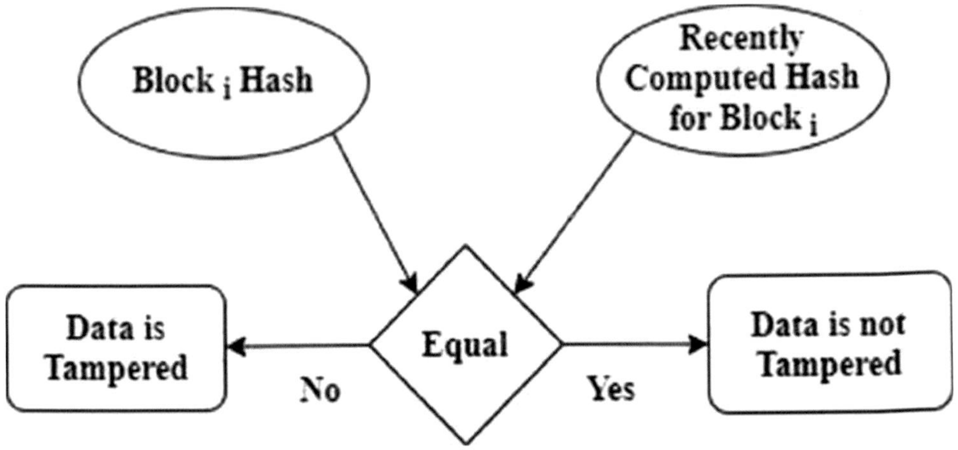

Fig. (9). Validation using Present Block Hash.

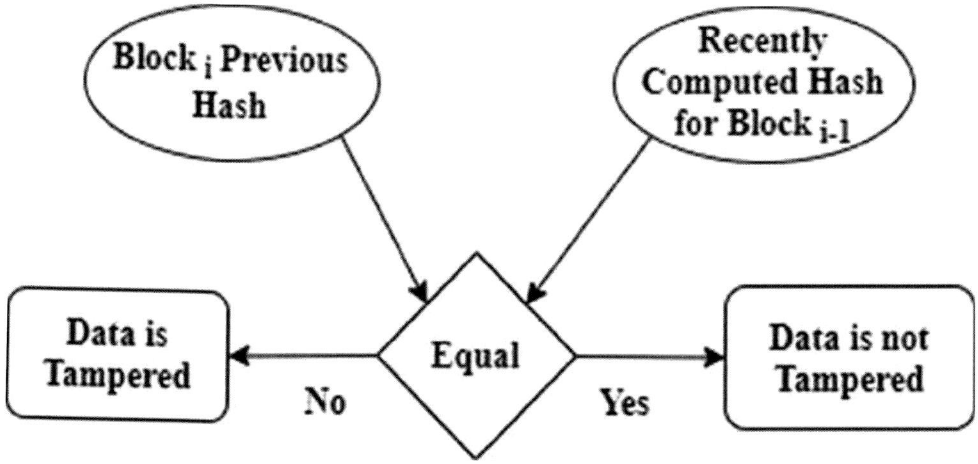

Fig. (10). Validation using Previous Block Hash.

RESULTS

Static sample data such as Serial number, Heart rate, Step count, BP, Stress levels, and Date are considered to create and maintain in a blockchain. The genesis block contains the initial information given by the user, and the later data is generated from the IoT device on a day-to-day basis and is added to the chain by hashing with SHA-256 with character set UTF-8 and the generated results are tabulated in Table **5**.

Table 5. Blockchain hash generation using SHA-256

	Data	Previous Hash	Hash Generated
Genesis Block	"0", "75", "10000", "120/75", "Medium", Date,	Null	C69/G6YCWFsrH7/dZsJjIJ2JdXB6 fgbr5ktcx1AYPbU=
Block 1	"1", "75", "10000", "125/85", "high", Date	C69/G6YCWFsrH7/dZsJjIJ2JdXB6 fgbr5ktcx1AYPbU=	M0cAs1SA51+ZVXqV3wdDIaGHi j9v5KoNoGCwaDKNs3U=
Block 2	"2", "80", "8000", "110/70", "low", Date	M0cAs1SA51+ZVXqV3wdDIaGHi j9v5KoNoGCwaDKNs3U=	pnkbcFsuEusZ1iR0uB8HRNznGenl rk+i6pBj7w+k0rE=
Block 3	"3", "85", "7500", "120/90", "Medium", Date	pnkbcFsuEusZ1iR0uB8HRNznGenl rk+i6pBj7w+k0rE=	j/BwMAnRRCq8hWfNoMdFXQV6 2sVP++ezHbQ2Odffcdk=
Chain is valid			

For the blockchain validation, the previous hash of the latest block has been tampered with, and in the mining process, it is identified as an invalid chain and represented in Table **6**.

Table 6. Blockchain Validation using the Previous Hash

	Data	Previous Hash	Hash Generated
Genesis Block	"0", "75", "10000", "120/75", "Medium", Date,	Null	C69/G6YCWFsrH7/dZsJjIJ2JdXB6 fgbr5ktcx1AYPbU=
Block 1	"1", "75", "10000", "125/85", "high", Date	C69/G6YCWFsrH7/dZsJjIJ2JdXB6 fgbr5ktcx1AYPbU=	M0cAs1SA51+ZVXqV3wdDIaGHi j9v5KoNoGCwaDKNs3U=
Block 2	"2", "80", "8000", "110/70", "low", Date	M0cAs1SA51+ZVXqV3wdDIaGHi j9v5KoNoGCwaDKNs3U=	pnkbcFsuEusZ1iR0uB8HRNznGenl rk+i6pBj7w+k0rE=
Block 3	"3", "85", "7500", "120/90", "Medium", Date	ABCDEFG (Tampered Hash)	j/BwMAnRRCq8hWfNoMdFXQV6 2sVP++ezHbQ2Odffcdk=
The chain is NOT valid			

In the case of data tampering, the hash value generated will be changed with the change in the data values. So, even if the data is modified/tampered with, that can peer-to-peer be easily identified using blockchain technology, as represented in Table **7**.

Table 7. Blockchain Validation using the Previous Hash (Data value Tampered)

	Data	Previous Hash	Hash Generated	
Genesis Block	"0", "75", "10000", "120/75", "Medium", Date,	Null	C69/G6YCWFsrH7/dZsJjIJ2JdXB6 fgbr5ktcx1AYPbU=	-
Block 1	"1", "75", "10000", "125/85", "high", Date	C69/G6YCWFsrH7/dZsJjIJ2JdXB6 fgbr5ktcx1AYPbU=	M0cAs1SA51+ZVXqV3wdDIaGHi j9v5KoNoGCwaDKNs3U=	-

(Table 7) cont.....

	Data	Previous Hash	Hash Generated	
Block 2	"2", "100", "8000", "150/120", "high", Date (Tampered Data)	M0cAs1SA51+ZVXqV3wdDIaGHi j9v5KoNoGCwaDKNs3U=	**98fLH2eG8qsnpo9F6s+Myaqo DsTfailGi4UJbcfDROg=**	**Mis match of Present and Previous Hashes**
Block 3	"3", "85", "7500", "120/90", "Medium", Date	**pnkbcFsuEusZ1iR0uB8HRNznGenl rk+i6pBj7w+k0rE=**	j/BwMAnRRCq8hWfNoMdFXQV6 2sVP++ezHbQ2Odffcdk=	-

Thus, by the implementation of the Blockchain, integrity and utmost privacy can be provided to the sensitive data generated by IoT devices. The results show that any attempt to hack or modify the data by third-party servers/third-party persons can be easily identified using this technology.

CONCLUSION & FUTURE WORKS

Many smart devices like smartwatches, and smart home devices are emerging in the present digital world. This paper presents an overview of the Fitbit devices along with the type of data generated from those devices. In addition to this, various challenges of IoT security have also been discussed. Privacy and security are the primary concerns regarding IoT devices as it stores sensitive data about the person using them. Due to the advancement of high computational units, the servers can be hacked if they are protected with traditional security algorithms and centralized architecture. The proposed model provides security and privacy of the data and a single point of attack using blockchain technology, and any anomaly can also be detected using the same. The proposed model consumes more energy which is not ideal. This can be solved by implementing lightweight blockchains that consume less energy. In future works, the proposed model can be implemented for real-time data.

CONSENT FOR PUBLICATION

Not applicable.

CONFLICT OF INTEREST

The author declares no conflict of interest, financial or otherwise.

ACKNOWLEDGEMENT

Declared none.

REFERENCES

[1] G. Aroganam, N. Manivannan, and D. Harrison, "Review on wearable technology sensors used in consumer sport applications", *Sensors,* vol. 19, no. 9, pp. 1-26, 20191983. [http://dx.doi.org/10.3390/s19091983]

[2] F. Loukil, C. Ghedira-Guegan, K. Boukadi, and A.N. Benharkat, "Privacy-preserving IoT data aggregation based on blockchain and homomorphic encryption", *Sensors,* vol. 21, no. 7, p. 2452, 20212021. [http://dx.doi.org/10.3390/s21072452]

[3] M. Shen, Y. Deng, L. Zhu, X. Du, and N. Guizani, "Privacy-preserving image retrieval for medical IoT systems: A blockchain-based approach", *IEEE Netw.,* vol. 33, no. 5, pp. 27-33, 2019. [http://dx.doi.org/10.1109/MNET.001.1800503]

[4] A. D. Dwivedi, G. Srivastava, S. Dhar, and R. Singh, "A decentralized privacy-preserving healthcare blockchain for IoT", *Sensors,* vol. 2019, vol. 19, no. 2, p. 326, 2019. [http://dx.doi.org/10.3390/s19020326]

[5] D.H. Wang, "IoT based clinical sensor data management and transfer using blockchain technology", *Journal of ISMAC,* vol. 2, no. 3, pp. 154-159, 2020. [http://dx.doi.org/10.36548/jismac.2020.3.003]

[6] I. Makhdoom, I. Zhou, M. Abolhasan, J. Lipman, and W. Ni, "PrivySharing: A blockchain-based framework for privacy-preserving and secure data sharing in smart cities", *Comput. Secur.,* vol. 88, no. 101653, p. 101653, 2020. [http://dx.doi.org/10.1016/j.cose.2019.101653]

[7] M. Shen, X. Tang, L. Zhu, X. Du, and M. Guizani, "Privacy-preserving support vector machine training over blockchain-based encrypted IoT data in smart cities", *IEEE Internet Things J.,* vol. 6, no. 5, pp. 7702-7712, 2019. [http://dx.doi.org/10.1109/JIOT.2019.2901840]

[8] B. Le Nguyen, E.L. Lydia, M. Elhoseny, I. Pustokhina, D.A. Pustokhin, and M.M. Selim, "Privacy preserving blockchain technique to achieve secure and reliable sharing of IoT data", *Comput. Mater. Continua,* vol. 65, no. 1, pp. 87-107, 2020. [http://dx.doi.org/10.32604/cmc.2020.011599]

[9] S. Nakamoto, "Bitcoin P2P e-cash paper", In: *The Cryptography Mailing List* Nakamoto Institute, 2008, pp. 1-7.

[10] R. Mahmoud, T. Yousuf, F. Aloul, and I. Zualkernan, "Internet of things (IoT) security: Current status, challenges and prospective measures", *2015 10th International Conference for Internet Technology and Secured Transactions (ICITST),* 2015pp. 1-6

[11] G.M. Gandhi, "Artificial intelligence integrated blockchain for training autonomous cars", *2019 Fifth International Conference on Science Technology Engineering and Mathematics (ICONSTEM),* 2019pp. 1-5 [http://dx.doi.org/10.1109/ICONSTEM.2019.8918795]

[12] D. Puthal, N. Malik, S.P. Mohanty, E. Kougianos, and G. Das, "Everything you wanted to know about the blockchain: Its promise, components, processes, and problems", *IEEE Consum. Electron. Mag.,* vol. 7, no. 4, pp. 6-14, 2018. [http://dx.doi.org/10.1109/MCE.2018.2816299]

[13] C.H. Lau, K.H.Y. Alan, and F. Yan, "Blockchain-based authentication in IoT networks", *IEEE Conference on Dependable and Secure Computing (DSC),* 2018pp. 1-8

[14] R. Zhang, R. Xue, and L. Liu, "Security and privacy on blockchain", *ACM Comput. Surv.*, vol. 52, no. 3, pp. 1-34, 2020. [CSUR]. [http://dx.doi.org/10.1145/3316481]

[15] S. Nakamoto, "Bitcoin: A peer-to-peer electronic cash system", *Decentralized Business Review,* vol. 21260, pp. 1-9, 2008.

[16] A. Pinna, and W. Ruttenberg, "Distributed ledger technologies in securities post-trading revolution or evolution?", *ECB Occasional Paper,* vol. 172, pp. 1-36, 2016.

[17] A. Reyna, C. Martín, J. Chen, E. Soler, and M. Díaz, "On blockchain and its integration with IoT. Challenges and opportunities", *Future Gener. Comput. Syst.,* vol. 88, pp. 173-190, 2018. [http://dx.doi.org/10.1016/j.future.2018.05.046]

[18] H. Malviya, "How blockchain will defend IoT", *SSRN,* p. 2883711, 2016.

[19] A. Maseleno, M. Othman, P. Deepalakshmi, K. Shankar, and M. Ilayaraja, Hash function based optimal block chain model for the Internet of Things (IoT).*Handbook of multimedia information security: Techniques and applications.* Springer: Cham, 2019, pp. 289-300. [http://dx.doi.org/10.1007/978-3-030-15887-3_12]

[20] S. Ali, G. Wang, B. White, and R.L. Cottrell, "A blockchain-based decentralized data storage and access framework for PingER", *2018 17th IEEE International Conference On Trust, Security And Privacy In Computing And Communications/ 12th IEEE International Conference On Big Data Science And Engineering (TrustCom/BigDataSE),* 2018pp. 1303-1308

[21] G. Schmitt, A. Mladenow, C. Strauss, and M. Schaffhauser-Linzatti, "Smart contracts and internet of things: A qualitative content analysis using the technology-organization-environment framework to identify key-determinants", *Procedia Comput. Sci.,* vol. 160, pp. 189-196, 2019. [http://dx.doi.org/10.1016/j.procs.2019.09.460]

[22] S. Zhang, and J.H. Lee, "Smart contract-based secure model for miner registration and block validation", *IEEE Access,* vol. 7, pp. 132087-132094, 2019. [http://dx.doi.org/10.1109/ACCESS.2019.2940551]

CHAPTER 7

Blockchain Based Access Control Systems

R. Agrawal[1,*] and **N. Gupta**[1]

[1] *Manav Rachna International Institute of Research and Studies, Faridabad, Haryana, India*

Abstract: While accessing data through the Internet of Things (IoT), privacy and safety are the most important features. IoT developers have a challenging job of securing and protecting the data of the users during the development process due to the complicated nature of decentralisation and heterogeneity of the environment present in IoT. There are several access control models for the IoT available in the literature which rely on centralized architecture and raises security concerns because IoT devices can spontaneously and dynamically interact with one another. The need for secure and distributed access control architecture to overcome the single point of failure problem of a centralized entity becomes a big challenge when coupled with scalability and lightweight features. It is possible to achieve this through the use of Blockchain technology, which has recently been used to provide access control services. IoT device management would be used to manage distribution, heterogeneity, scalability, the ability to tolerate failure, security and privacy aspects of IoT devices at scale in the near future as it is useful.

Keywords: Blockchain, Access control system, Policy creation transaction, Distributed access management, Internet of things.

INTRODUCTION

There seems to be a reliance on the presence of a trusted authority in the current digital economy. To conduct any online transaction, we need to trust that the information we receive is accurate. Whether that be an email service provider informing us of delivery or a certification authority telling us to trust a particular digital certificate; on the other hand, a social network, for instance Facebook, might tell us our posts about life are only shared with our friends, or a bank might tell us we can put our trust in our dear ones in another country. We live in a world that is precarious, where we have to rely on a third-party institution to keep us safe and to keep our individual information private. Third parties, as always, are susceptible to hacking, manipulation, or compromise. Blockchain technology offers a solution to these problems. With distributed consensus enabled by this

* **Corresponding author R. Agrawal:** Manav Rachna International Institute of Research & Studies, Faridabad, Haryana, India; E-mail: rashmi.fca@mriu.edu.in

technology, it is possible to verify any online transaction involving digital assets at any time, allowing the world of digital to undergo revolutionary change. Digital assets and party identities are protected without compromising privacy. Blockchain technology is distinguished by its distributed consensus as well as its anonymity. Regulation issues and technical challenges are outweighed by the benefits of Blockchain technology.

Blockchain technology has proven to be a highly transparent and incorruptible method of storing data. Decentralized technology ensures encryption and security end-to-end, making it ideal for networks with lots of users. Blockchain's decentralized nature eliminates the possibility of human error and offers protection against hacker attacks altogether due to its distributed nature. In the context of Access Control, especially Access Control as a Service, all of the above is of paramount importance.

Cryptocurrencies and financial transactions were the first blockchain applications. There is a wide range of applications for smart contracts, such as healthcare, internet of things, supply chains and more. Study [1], a review of many research studies on blockchain and smart contracts, shows that many of the applications presented were aimed at providing an efficient and secure way to control access.

An Access Control System is used to control access to data and services that are perceived as critical or valuable by the public. Furthermore, it is also used to manage computing systems, storage space, and other coprocessors. Access control policies are used in general to express the rights of subjects to access resources. These policies are evaluated based on the context of the request at the time. ABAC (Attribute-Based Access Control) [2] is a form of access control that consists of a set of conditions that describe the inherent characteristics of subject areas, resources, environments, *etc.,* involved in the access request. As examples of subject attributes, one can find his ID, the company's ID, his title within that organization, the names of the projects he is working on, the number of resources he is currently using, and so on.

It may be necessary to transfer the access right between subjects for a variety of reasons in some cases due to certain circumstances. An individual who owns an access right could, for instance, sell it to someone else. The same holds true for an example of an employee of a company who is supposed to perform a particular procedure on a Virtual Machine, yet chooses rather delegate the responsibility of the task to another employee who also needs to access the Virtual Machine.

BACKGROUND

A blockchain is a digital ledger of data that can be accessed by anyone at any time. Blockchains are decentralized databases that are secure, easy to use, and can be accessed by anyone. This system is based on trustless principles, which means that users accept the data and analyze the data, whether it is secure or not, without any third-party intervention. Initially, it was planned to provide secure cryptocurrencies, such as Bitcoins, but nowadays, researchers are exploring the possibility of applying the technology to a wide range of fields [3]. As part of the method, tokens are exchanged in the form of transactions on the blockchain in exchange for tokens. A blockchain is an example of a peer-to-peer network consisting of several nodes that uses a cryptographic protocol. By verifying the transactions and passing between these nodes, these nodes handle the communication between them. Blockchain has a lot of interesting features that make it easy to use [4]. Basically, it is a distributed ledger that is only appended to. The data, once inserted into a database, cannot be changed once they have been added, nor can they be deleted after they have been added. On the blockchain, anyone can be added to the network, so they will be able to see all the transactions that are by nature public, as blockchain transactions are public by nature.

With the help of the blockchain, bitcoin, like many other cryptocurrencies, stores value exchanges referred to as transactions on the public ledger [5]. Every single block in this ledger is a collection of non-conflicting transactions that were made in that block. In order to create the link between blocks, the hash of the header of the previous block is stored in the header of the next block of the chain. The root of a Merkle tree derived from the block transaction hashes is included in the block header of each block as a function of its block header (and hence it is hash). This is done to make the block headers dependent on all transactions contained in that block. The decision of which block to add to the ledger at each step is made by a distributed consensus algorithm known as the 'Nakamoto consensus', which is based on the HashCash Proof-of-Work [6] system.

A simple way to look at the Bitcoin blockchain from a data point of view is to see it as a list of transactions. Users exchange funds using their wallet addresses, which serve as the address of their wallet. A public key that derives from an ECDSA key pair [7] is derived as a two-way hash (first applying SHA-256 and then applying Ripemd-160 as the second step) to establish an address.

In the case of Bitcoin, the address (and therefore the public key) is used by the users to send and receive payments, while the private key is used to provide proof of ownership (through digital signatures). Since creating new ECDSA key pairs is as cheap as creating new addresses, each user can create and use multiple ECDSA key pairs. A user is also encouraged to use different addresses because even the failure to use different addresses makes Bitcoin an insecure, non-anonymous currency.

Having the blockchain as the sole means of keeping track of all transactions in the system, the only way to manage funds is to keep track of those transactions. The only way to divide or aggregate funds is to spend them. A transaction can originate from more than one input address and output more than one address, meaning that a transaction can withdraw funds from more than one address and send funds to more than one address. Furthermore, each input is signed by the owner of the private key that corresponds to the address where the funds will be spent.

As part of a transaction, a voluntary fee can also be specified to cover the costs associated with the validation process. The purpose of this fee is to act as an incentive for users to participate in the consensus protocol that was previously mentioned. It is possible to see each output as a couple (amount, recipient address) in the context of a transaction. Inputs instead specify where to withdraw the funds, *i.e.,* the previous transaction (through its hash) where the funds were created and where the funds will be withdrawn. In addition to the scripting language used in the Bitcoin protocol to specify conditions for the redemption of funds, Bitcoin's protocol uses a stack-based scripting language, which is not Turing complete.

Despite the fact that blockchain technology is mostly known for applications in cryptocurrencies [8], such as Bitcoin, it can be used outside of the monetary domain as well, for example, to trace the origins and transformations of products in a supply chain. Huckle *et al.* [9] discuss how blockchain can be used to create decentralized, shared economy applications that will enable people to monetize their things in a secure manner in order to become more wealthy. A study conducted by [10] notably notes that having a worldwide-available, verifiable, and untamperable source of data will enable anyone who wishes to offer trusted third-party services to do so in a cost-effective and robust way.

Most digital resources nowadays are exposed to the Internet, which necessitates a well-designed security framework that provides protection. Users with actual rights to access the information. There are systems that deal with access control specifically designed to deal with these types of situations, and they look after expressing the rights of subjects to access resources through the use of policies, which are then evaluated against the prevailing access context for each access request. Sometimes, authorization to perform access is continuously validated during the access, so that previously authorized accesses are interrupted as soon as these rights expire.

In the scientific literature, different types of control models have been proposed for defining different types of controls. One of the most popular ABAC schemes represents the access context through a set of attributes that describe their relevant characteristics in relation to the subjects, resources, and the environment, and the Access Control policies consist of a set of conditions over these attributes. It is possible for the Access Control systems to be deployed, managed and operated on the premises of the resource owners or by third parties trusted by the resource owners.

As a resource owner, the cost of maintaining an Access Control system can be a notable constraint. To avoid this cost, it is possible to outsource the evaluation of its security policies to external systems. For instance, over the last few years, a number of Access Control systems have been proposed and implemented as independent services on top of the Cloud following the Software as a Service (SaaS) paradigm. It is common for these services to use an open-platform API, so that users are not locked into using one specific implementation, and they can use them to have a uniform configuration for controlling all their resources with the same policy. As for the other Cloud services, each user pays for the usage of the Access Control Services on a per use basis.

BLOCKCHAIN-BASED ACCESS CONTROL FOR IOT

According to the authors [11], the Blockchain is the mechanism used to generate and manage access tokens representing a subject's rights to access a resource. The model introduces a new type of subscription transaction. PCT (Policy Creation Transaction) and RTT (Right Transfer Transaction). The resource owner must first perform a transaction when the resource attributes comply with the individual access policies, in order to generate and transfer an access token. Access requests may be evaluated for approval by two different systems (the resource owner and the external authorization system). Both systems must interact for the process to be successful. An access token can also be passed from one subject to another in the second type of transaction. This process is called access delegation. Based on the XACML standard, an external authorization system is implemented using the Bitcoin platform to manage user access tokens.

Novo [12] provides a design for offering a decentralized access control system that is composed of a network of sensors that are operational in multiple parts of the world. Smart contracts are designed to reduce the amount of communication overhead between nodes in order to provide real-time, decentralized access control for the benefit of users. Since IoT devices are not capable of connecting to the Blockchain due to their limited capabilities, the architecture instead specifies a new component called a management hub which can request access control information on the Blockchain from IoT devices. There are also two types of Blockchain nodes defined by the system architecture, namely managers and agents. A manager does not participate in mining, and is considered a lightweight Blockchain node. A single smart contract is deployed by the agent node to manage the access control permission of IoT devices. This specific smart contract comprises all of the capabilities of an access management system in one package. As soon as an IoT device receives an access request, it sends the request to the hub, which is connected directly to a Blockchain node, for example, to a miner that works together with the smart contract to determine whether the requestor is authorized to access the resource. In a proof-of-concept implementation, Blockchain technology has been used as a distributed access management technology for IoT.

Researchers identified two primary problems with IoT access control in [13]. The first is that of centralized architecture, and the second has to do with handling static policies. Using machine learning algorithms in conjunction with a blockchain architecture, the authors propose a framework for ensuring complete distributed access control while managing dynamic access policies based on machine learning algorithms. Utilizing a Smart Contract concept, this framework implements a resource owner's (RO) access control policy to manage access to a resource that he owns. It is important to remember that in order for the Policy Contract to properly execute, the requester must meet policies regarding accessing the data in question, thus allowing the Policy Contract to generate and issue an authorization token allowing him access to the resource. Every time the Policy Contract is interacting with something; a transaction is generated, which is recorded in the Blockchain register. The resource owner will also receive feedback information about the system's current state after the contract is executed by using Reinforcement Learning (RL) algorithms. The feedback information can be used to dynamically improve security parameters such as trust and integrity. A Proof of Concept is required to validate the proposed model.

IoT Chain is a Blockchain-based architecture called by the authors in [14] for securing End to End access management to IoT resources. Resources that are stored on the resources servers will be encrypted and signed and will be stored on a proxy server that the owners of the resources will own. It is, therefore, the client who requests access to the protected resources on behalf of a third party. Upon requesting the decryption key, it checks the Blockchain to verify if the client has been authorized before requesting the decryption key. Authorization takes place in the following manner: the resource owner creates a smart contract for clients and publishes it to the Blockchain. Upon meeting certain conditions, the client calls the corresponding smart contract to generate an access token. A contract will keep the token stored in persistent memory on the contract's server rather than transmitting it to the client. Tokens are stored in the internal contract storage, and then clients request the key to decrypt them from the key server, which is a blockchain node that maintains a copy of the Blockchain ledger. The key server verifies a client's access token on the blockchain and transmits the key using DTLS channels after checking the smart contract storage on the Blockchain. The client then downloads the encrypted resource from the proxy server and decrypts it.

Researchers in the study [15] used smart contracts to solve the scaling problem associated with IoT authentication. Typically, an individual owns one or more IoT devices, and each device requires its own set of credentials. Therefore, it is necessary for the user to authenticate to every device individually from this point onward. As a consequence, this method causes an authentication overhead and is difficult to scale. Smart contracts are used primarily for authenticating users and providing them with a token that allows them access to the IoT devices which they own. Users authenticate to the smart contract using their Ethereum wallet address, which allows the smart contract to verify the user's identity. A contract is subsequently negotiated if the user is allowed access to the resources, and the key is then communicated to the end user and to the IoT device. The user will then sign the received token using his private key, send it to the IoT device that will take the token and confirm its integrity by comparing it with the instance received earlier from the contract and then grant access. The Ethereum blockchain has been used to implement and test this approach. A general approach for blockchain-based access control for IoT has been shown in (Fig. **1**).

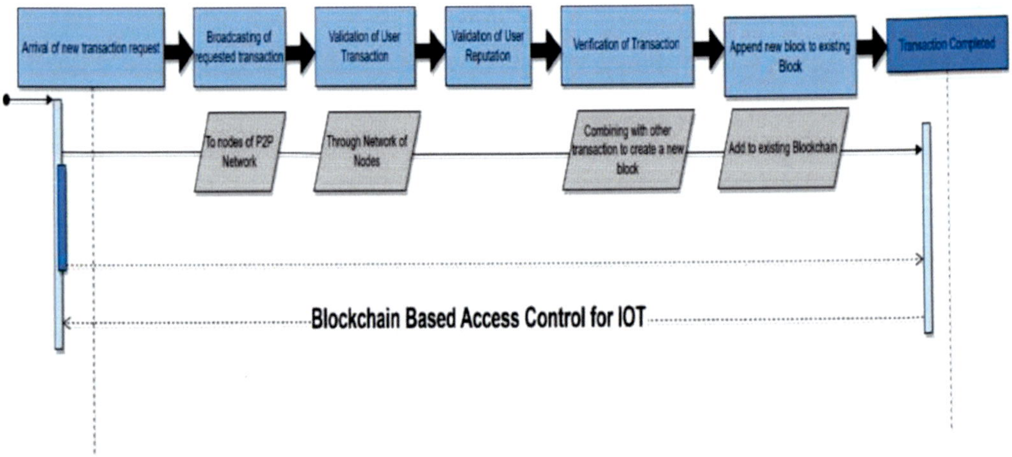

Fig. (1). Blockchain-Based Access Control for IoT.

CONCLUSION & FUTURE SCOPE

The blockchain is built on an existing network, cryptographic, and recordkeeping technologies but applies them completely differently. Organizations must take into account both the advantages and disadvantages of using the technologies while assessing whether they will be suitable for their requirements. The implementation and adoption of a blockchain may be so widespread that it may be difficult to change it once it is in place. When data is recorded in a blockchain, it usually remains there forever. Even if a mistake is made, the data is usually a part of the blockchain. There are a number of applications that make use of the blockchain for data storage, but understand that actual data on the blockchain cannot be altered. In such cases, the later blocks and transactions act as updates or updates to previous transactions and blocks. The software abstraction is able to allow for modifications to working data, while also providing the ability to track the history of those changes. Such capabilities can be useful for certain organizations. Some may find that these are deal breakers that prevent the adoption of this technology by others.

We can consider the use of Blockchain technology as a new trend in access control for IoT, based on the literature survey. A major motivation for the exploitation of the Blockchain is to gain access to its secure distributed architecture since it can handle the security requirements of the Internet of Things. Blockchain is clearly the driving force behind future access control in terms of privacy, security and production. The architecture has interesting mechanisms and properties that may help solve some of the major problems associated with distributed systems. However, the approach is at the beginning of the process, and a test should be done in order to evaluate the performance of the approach. An approach based on Blockchain needs to be developed for standardizing access control that represents the future of distributed systems. According to our study, the transactions mainly serve the purpose of managing secure access tokens, and the use of a smart contract provides the benefit of resolving the problem of centralized access control, which is to eliminate a single point of failure. To guarantee the success of the proposed approaches, they should nevertheless be evaluated and tested in real-life IoT domains to evaluate their performance and create a standard for managing IoT access *via* Blockchain.

We may need to rethink the current static access control methodology and adopt a dynamic approach, where each resource can define its own access control, to meet the needs of future systems. A future investigation could involve integrating blockchain technologies with dynamic access control approaches.

CONSENT FOR PUBLICATION

Not applicable.

CONFLICT OF INTEREST

The author declares no conflict of interest, financial or otherwise.

ACKNOWLEDGEMENT

Declared none.

REFERENCES

[1] S. Rouhani, and R. Deters, "Security, performance, and applications of smart contracts: A systematic survey", *IEEE Access,* vol. 7, pp. 50759-50779, 2019. [http://dx.doi.org/10.1109/ACCESS.2019.2911031]

[2] Vincent C. Hu, David Ferraiolo, Rick Kuhn, Arthur R. Friedman, Alan J. Lang, Margaret M. Cogdell, Adam Schnitzer, Kenneth Sandlin, Robert Miller, and Karen Scarfone, "Guide to attribute based access control (abac) definition and considerations (draft)", *NIST special publication,* vol. 800, no. 162, pp. 1-54, 2013.

[3] R.C. Merkle, "A digital signature based on a conventional encryption function", In: *Conference on the theory and application of cryptographic techniques* Springer: Berlin, Heidelberg, 1987, pp. 369-378.

[4] C. Dwork, and M. Naor, "Pricing *via* processing or combatting junk mail", In: Annual international cryptology conference Springer: Berlin, Heidelberg, 1992, pp. 139-147.

[5] NIST, US, Descriptions of SHA-256, SHA-384 and SHA-512,

[6] Preneel, Bart, Antoon Bosselaers, and Hans Dobbertin. "The cryptographic hash function RIPEMD-160." (1997): 9-14.

[7] D. Johnson, A. Menezes, and S. Vanstone, "The elliptic curve digital signature algorithm (ECDSA)", *Int. J. Inf. Secur.,* vol. 1, no. 1, pp. 36-63, 2001. [http://dx.doi.org/10.1007/s102070100002]

[8] M. Pilkington, Blockchain technology: Principles and applications.*Research handbook on digital transformations* Edward Elgar Publishing, 2016. [http://dx.doi.org/10.4337/9781784717766.00019]

[9] S. Huckle, R. Bhattacharya, M. White, and N. Beloff, "Internet of things, blockchain and shared economy applications", *Procedia Comput. Sci.,* vol. 98, pp. 461-466, 2016. [http://dx.doi.org/10.1016/j.procs.2016.09.074]

[10] M. Michael, and M. Smith, "Sharing ledgers for sharing economies: An exploration of mutual distributed ledgers (aka blockchain technology)", *Journal of financial perspectives,* vol. 3, no. 3, 2015.

[11] D.D.F. Maesa, P. Mori, and L. Ricci, Blockchain based access control.*IFIP international conference on distributed applications and interoperable systems* Springer: Cham, 2017, pp. 206-220.

[12] O. Novo, "Blockchain meets IoT: An architecture for scalable access management in IoT", *IEEE Internet Things J.,* vol. 5, no. 2, pp. 1184-1195, 2018. [http://dx.doi.org/10.1109/JIOT.2018.2812239]

[13] A. Outchakoucht, H. Es-Samaali, and J. Philippe, "Dynamic access control policy based on blockchain and machine learning for the internet of things", *Int. J. Adv. Comput. Sci. Appl.,* vol. 8, no. 7, pp. 417-424, 2017.

[http://dx.doi.org/10.14569/IJACSA.2017.080757]

[14] O. Alphand, M. Amoretti, T. Claeys, S. Dall'Asta, A. Duda, G. Ferrari, F. Rousseau, B. Tourancheau, L. Veltri, and F. Zanichelli, "IoTChain: A blockchain security architecture for the internet of things", *2018 IEEE wireless communications and networking conference (WCNC),* 2018pp. 1-6

[15] A.Z. Ourad, B. Belgacem, and K. Salah, "Using blockchain for IOT access control and authentication management", In: *International Conference on Internet of Things* Springer: Cham, 2018, pp. 150-164. [http://dx.doi.org/10.1007/978-3-319-94370-1_11]

CHAPTER 8

Multi-chain Deployment over Smart Contracts to Enhance Security

N. Gupta[1,*] and **R. Agrawal**[1]

[1] *Manav Rachna International Institute of Research and Studies, Faridabad, Haryana, India*

Abstract: A blockchain is a data structure in which each block is linked to the next in a time-stamped chronological manner. Each block is cryptographically linked to the others. This is a global distributed ledger that contains an immutable public record of financial transactions. Every new record will be reviewed across the distributed network before being saved in a block. All information is verifiable and auditable once it is deposited on the ledger, but it cannot be edited. It will be an underestimation to say that Blockchain Technology is one of the most inventions of this 21st century. More people are considering that the decentralization and translucence that comes along with blockchain technology have the prospective to jiggle multiple industries to its very staple. This article reconnoiters different blockchain applications and their deployment approaches. In other facets, Multichain is a platform for the creation and distribution of private blockchains, either within or between organizations. Likewise, there are many more blockchain applications than just cryptocurrency, and they can unsettle way more sectors than just the finance sector. We intentionally avoided showing the Blockchain's impact on the banking sector to keep the list as non-fintech as possible. Smart contracts are well customary as the greatest enabling technology for blockchains. With them, a blockchain ecosystem becomes self-governing, open, consent, and credible. It is through a compilation of smart contracts that blockchains can operate without human intervention.

The smart contracts are established to deploy at the predefined blockchain nodes. They can be entreated by the call-backs either from the blockchain system, the other smart contracts, or the participants' information systems.

Usually, blockchain operations and application-related rules can be predetermined as smart contracts. The use cases and their real-world functions differ, but the benefits derived from using the technology remain unchanged: immutability, transparency, redundancy, and security.

Keywords: Multi chain, Block chain, Real world applications, Decentralization, Smart contracts.

* **Corresponding author N. Gupta:** Manav Rachna International Institute of Research & Studies, Faridabad, Haryana, India; E-mail: neha.fca@mriu.edu.in

INTRODUCTION

The Blockchain is a series of blocks, each of which holds valuable data that is not supervised by a central authority. It is unchangeable and cryptographically secure. Linked Lists and Pointers are two significant data structures used in a blockchain. The Blockchain is redefining ways of handling trustworthy transactions. The internet is incredibly vulnerable, and Blockchain [1] has been released as a result of this. Blockchain defines the confidence liability lines as one challenge for AI and IoT. The majority of IoT devices communicate with one another on public networks, and it is superfluous to discuss how vulnerable public networks are. Blockchain [2] overcomes this challenge by allowing users to create linear and long-lasting indexed records. They can also make the business process go more smoothly by offering a payment mechanism and a communication channel. Any kind of hacking and tampering with the data, like captivating control of devices and records, is excruciating by the way blocks are stored and guarded in an unambiguous database in the Blockchain outline. Every IoT device is a point of vulnerability, and the hazards are still higher as even AI is intricate in making choices for users. Hence, Blockchain can provide a safe, scalable, and certifiable platform with superlative security implementations [3].

BLOCKCHAIN AND SMART CONTRACTS

Implementation Techniques for Blockchains

To develop a realistic and effective blockchain application environment, a number of fundamental concerns must be addressed [4]. The four levels of a unique blockchain ecosystem are smart contracts, Blockchain, services, and user interfaces. Enterprise network models, participants, ecosystem design, admission policies, nodes, polling systems, incentive mechanisms, smart contracts, and clients are all examples of blockchain implementation strategies. Furthermore, to solve the problematic issues of blockchain applications, data collecting and data processing methods are required.

The majority of current projects are struggling with the blockchain network concept [5]. Blockchain technologies are still changing, and no widely acknowledged technological pattern exists. Due to their inefficiency and high-performance costs, specific Bitcoin-based projects have not been recognised. Self-designed hybrid networks or alternative network architectures are being used in an increasing number of applications.

A typical blockchain ecosystem includes a blockchain infrastructure, participants' information systems with programming edges to the Blockchain, and a set of smart contracts for operation. All data and communications are stored in a decentralised and self-regulating data infrastructure provided by the blockchain system.

Participants should be identified based on their function and the blockchain network. The polling technique and operation objectives determine the number of nodes and evolution policies. The network model is used to establish the admission policies and required information in the consortium blockchain paradigm. To build the Blockchain and establish an effective consensus process, a realistic and efficient incentive mechanism should be developed.

Smart contracts are often regarded as the most advanced blockchain-supporting technology. A blockchain ecosystem that includes smart contracts improves autonomy, openness, consent, and credibility. Blockchains can work without the need for human intervention thanks to a collection of smart contracts. Smart contracts are created with the intention of being implemented at predetermined blockchain nodes. Call-backs from the blockchain system, other smart contracts, or the parties' information systems can all be used to activate them. Smart contracts may usually be used to programme both blockchain operations and application-related rules.

Blockchain Clients for Participants

There are three different types of blockchain clients, each of which interacts with the blockchain ecosystem *via* application programming interfaces. The first sort of client is created in the information systems of the participants; this includes both management information systems and embedded systems. Smart contracts, or those given by the Blockchain operating systems, such as blockchain browsers, are the second type of client. The Blockchain's third form of the client is public facilities, which provide a public user interface for both participants and potential participants.

To support blockchain-based enterprises, data collection approaches are precarious. The data in a blockchain is intended to be private and self-regulated by the members, which poses a number of common data collection difficulties, including data insufficiency, data scarcity, and data redundancy. For missing data attributes and irrelevant or redundant data, well-defined compensation methods must be developed. Simultaneously, weighing and cross-checking algorithms should be developed to take advantage of the assimilated participatory data from both inside and outside the Blockchain, on and off the Blockchain, which could be implemented as smart contracts to consolidate the data. When administering the data, there are a few additional concerns to consider. For example, to learn how to make use of data from previous blockchain ecosystems, the ecosystem is built to integrate both within and outside of the Blockchain, and the requester may benefit from the other blockchain ecosystem.

Application Development Environments for Blockchains

There are dozens of open-source general-purpose blockchain development environments. With the revolutionary principles of Bitcoin, miner, proof-of-work, transaction, and permissionless [6], the Bitcoin Blockchain was the first player in 2008. The Ethereum Blockchain is a fork of Bitcoin that has been in use since its inception, using terms like Ether, Ethereum miner, proof of stake, account, and permissionless [7]. Hyperledger Blockchain is a business-oriented blockchain. Asset, chain code (smart contracts), Practical Byzantine Fault Tolerance (PBFT), membership, and approval are among the topics introduced [8].

Hundreds of blockchain development environments have been developed for specific applications or situations, including supply chain financing, financial clearance, company regulation and supervision. They have been enhanced with better infrastructure, consent mechanisms, and design patterns in order to achieve higher performance and best-fit particular cases on general-purpose blockchain development platforms. For this reason, Beihangchain, an approved blockchain with distinctive consensus algorithms, interfaces, and design, has been established. For a number of applications, including copyright protection and digital payment, the Blockchain employed an account blockchain and a trade blockchain [9]. The Hyper chain is a self-contained, controllable blockchain platform that enables enterprise-level blockchain network development. It allows businesses to use, expand, and complete a blockchain network using existing cloud platforms, and it provides real-time visual monitoring of the network's operation condition [10].

Blockchains for Supply Chains with Smart Contracts

As there are various companies in a supply chain that require a creditworthy mechanism to connect for a business, it is one of the best-fit domains for blockchains. To avoid cheating or business oppression, the blockchain ecosystem can be enhanced to give creditworthy, secure, and complete information among supply chain members. Creditworthy data make it easier for small and medium-sized businesses to obtain financial services, which is a major problem in traditional industries. Similarly, the author learns from several interviews and collaborative projects with industry partners that several blockchain projects in China have been built to improve the efficiency of financial auditing and resolve the financial concerns of small businesses. Due to creditworthy buy remits, the financial agency can offer money to small suppliers and service providers, as shown in Fig. (**1**). Several supply chain finance blockchain developments can be found on information portals [10].

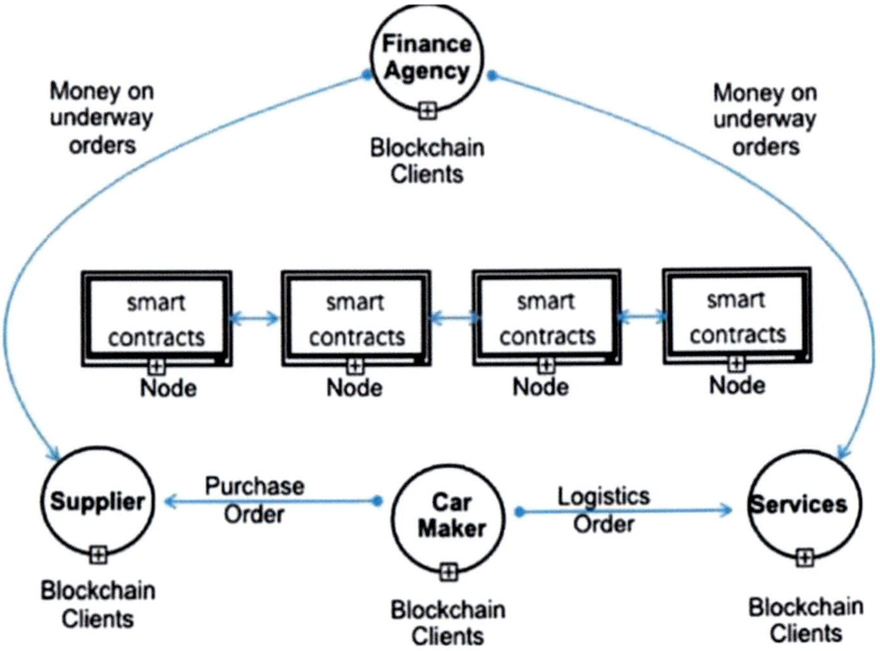

Fig. (1). A blockchain ecosystem with Smart Contracts for car supply chain.

Blockchains, with smart contracts, have the ability to designate more secure and trustable exchanges or coordinated business across a supply chain, according to Foster. Smart contracts can be used to automate the entire transaction development process while remaining cost-effective, transparent, and secure. For example, to regularise cross-enterprise relationships among mixed industrial capitals, a blockchain-based production credit mechanism (PCM) for industrial services is put in service to its customers [11].

SECURITY ATTACKS ON SMART CONTRACTS

Despite the fact that smart contracts employ external resources such as the current library, other smart contract functions, API calls, and third-party services, they are vulnerable to programming faults, human mistakes, and malicious hacking. Several smart contract vulnerabilities have been discovered and rated as critical by researchers. Among the most critical are destroyable smart contracts, unrestricted write operations, unrestricted fund transfers, integer overflow, integer underflow, re-entry, and external call issues. In recent years, these flaws have resulted in real hacks on smart contracts, with attackers profiting from massive amounts of stolen data.

Given that smart contracts are digital programmes written by humans, mistakes in programming and human error pose serious risks. The Ethereum blockchain's immutability prevents malicious modification and manipulation of smart contracts that have been deployed. However, this feature prevents smart contract owners or real developers from editing their code once it has been deployed. While running on the Blockchain, their active Ethereum smart contracts cannot be fixed if they have any errors. To ensure that smart contracts are precise and error-free, developers must carefully implement and test them.

Numerous open-source tools are accessible to analyse smart contract solidity source code or bytecode or contract address at Blockchain. Researchers submit the bytecode of smart contract applications to the selected analysis tools because all smart contract applications do not disclose their certified solidity code. Before any tools could be used to scan smart contracts with certified solidity source code, many compilation issues had to be fixed. Oyente is a security analysis tool that detects a parity multi-sig issue. Osiris, in particular, discovers a variety of arithmetic flaws, which are critical to verify in all smart contract applications. Mythril is a strong tool that scans for 14 different vulnerabilities related to solidity programming difficulties.

MULTI-CHAIN AND SMART CONTRACTS

Multichain technology [12] is a step that enables users to create secure private Blockchains that can be utilised for financial transactions by businesses. Multichain provides us with a simple API and command-line interface. This aids in the ambit and chain setup.

A smart contract is not artificial intelligence; rather, it is a series of codes developed using the sturdiness programming language, which operates on the IF/THEN concept. But it has the ability to automate a set of operations involving the movement of value (value, in this case, is a little hazy, but it's largely monetary) from one party/individual to the next. We can use Multichain to structure any nodes and develop a backend that defines the processes, which we can then use to interact with the smart contract blockchain.

Multiple “smart contracts” or “chain codes” can be written on the Blockchain with Multi Chains [13], each with its own database and code. The database of a contract can only be changed by its code, rather than directly by blockchain transactions.

The Objectives of Multichain

To minimise misperceptions and provide stability and control over which transactions exist, the Blockchain's perceptibility should constantly be actively kept within the chosen participants. With the help of proof of work and the expense associated with it, the mining process may be done more carefully. This Blockchain architecture, on the other hand, merely distributes the verified accounts to the chain's participants.

The Hand-Shaking Process

When the nodes in a blockchain communicate with each other, the process of handshaking in Multichain takes place. When two Blockchain nodes connect, the term "multichain" is used. Each node's uniqueness is represented by an address with a list of rights. As a result, each node it identifies sends a message to the other users. If they do not obtain any sustained results from the procedure, the P2P connection will be terminated.

The Process of Mining in Multichain Technology

Multichain is a term that refers to a group of miners that can be identified. It introduces a criterion called mining diversity, which has the value 0 = mining diversity = 1.

The efficacy of block is verifiable by performing the following:

- Pertain the changes in permissions set by transactions and the block, respectively.
- Sum the total approved miners set after these variations in the block.
- Reproduce the number of miners by mining diversity and round up to attain left spacing.

The round-robin schedule was activated as a result of this. To build an accurate Blockchain, the miners generate blocks in a rotation according to this timetable. The rigidity of the system is determined by the mining assortment criterion. The "one" value indicates that every permitted miner is included in the rotation. However, a zero result indicates that there are no constraints at all.

In Multichain, the transaction fees and the Block incentive is null by default. Nevertheless, you can name these values in the **params.dat** file. ***This file encloses the whole configuration like:***

- The protocol of the chain.
- The target time for the block.
- Active permission type.
- Mining diversity.
- Mining incentive.
- An Appropriate type of transaction.
- Maximum block size.
- Maximum metadata per transaction.

How Smart Contracts in Multichain Redefine Value Exchange

Smart Contracts [14] are self-executing code on a blockchain that automatically implements the conditions of an agreement between parties, thereby expediting procedures that are presently dispersed across multiple databases and ERP systems.

They are lines of software programmes, not contracts in the legal sense, that extend the utility of blockchains beyond just keeping track of financial transaction entries to automatically enforcing multiparty agreements. This is accomplished through Consensus protocols, which allow users to agree on the highlighted lines of action in response to an event.

The following are some of the advantages of smart contracts:

- **Speed:** As smart contracts automate manual procedures, they increase the speed with which various business processes are completed.
- **Accuracy:** They assist in the automation of manual developments as well as the reduction of errors.
- **Lower Execution Risk:** Decentralized and immutable processes eliminate the possibility of manipulation, and the possibility of erroneous execution is too remote.
- **Lower cost:** When compared to traditional business procedures, contract implementation costs are lower since there is less human participation and fewer intermediaries.
- **New business models:** The development of novel business models, ranging from trustworthy peer-to-peer sharing to trading in a safe environment, is aided by new means of transactions and contract execution.
- **Avoiding the use of third-party intermediaries:** Smart contracts eliminate or reduce the use of third-party intermediaries and provide an alternative technological trust factor.

Smart contracts may be used for a variety of purposes, from determining loan eligibility to completing trade agreements and transfer agreements, thanks to the aforementioned advantages. Due to the need to maintain separate databases, all of these sorts of smart contracts were previously unfeasible. All of the parties involved can now validate the results in real-time, without the need for a third party to intervene.

Smart contracts make the most sense when a network of participants conducts frequent transactions and the counterparties undertake manual or redundant processes or duties for each transaction. Smart contracts, in a nutshell, automate the exchange of values between parties without the need for an intermediary or human intervention in the event of a contract.

Agents were heavily reliant on **traditional contracts** and agreements to complete paperwork and other legal requirements. The primary trust criteria for transferring money or other valuable assets were agents and go-betweens. Smart contracts, which are coded into the system to automatically execute activities based on a predetermined set of discussions between the parties, have replaced agents with the help of Blockchain. The trust is built up through the use of secure blockchain technology. The expense of managing the flow of value is dramatically reduced, as is the time it takes to complete the agreement. Similarly, when 'value' is exchanged using the Blockchain's distributed ledger technology, new blockchain chains are formed and kept permanently without the possibility of manipulation.

Some of the example that shows the value exchanges due to Smart contracts are given below:

a). Freelance Work Exchanges

When a customer decides to increase the scope of a project or delays payment for an unknown reason, many freelancers are helpless. Companies who hire freelancers, on the other hand, may feel misled if they realise that someone's professional experience is false and that they are unable to execute the job for which they were engaged. Smart contracts encourage more open and honest communication between freelancers and clients, resulting in a better experience for both.

The contract's conditions include the project's scope, deadlines, and payment arrangements. At the outset of an assignment, payments are kept in escrow in a smart contract, to be released upon successful completion of work milestones. This helps freelancers prevent the scope creeps, ensuring that any new job does not hold up payments, and enabling them to get paid pretty for additional work.

b). Digital Rights and Intellectual Property

Smart contracts provide a framework for intellectual property creators to obtain payment for their labour. Smart contracts provide copyright and creator/owner credit, allowing for a traceable history of IPs used. When someone utilises their licensed work, content owners, creators, and, most importantly, artists are compensated very instantly.

MULTIPLE BLOCKCHAIN AND SMART CONTRACTS TRANSFORMING CONTRACT MANAGEMENT IN RECENT TIMES

The phrase "programmable economy" was coined by the research firm Gartner Inc. in 2014 to describe the rapid changes that are occurring in the global economy as a result of technological advancements. Disruptive technologies such as distributed ledgers, blockchains, and smart contracts will drive the programmable economy in 2018.

These technologies will fundamentally alter how businesses interact with vendors, partners, and customers. They will also have an impact on how businesses approach, execute, and enforce business contracts.

Blockchain and Distributed Ledger Technology

Although most businesses associate blockchain technology with the financial services industry, it has applications in manufacturing, government, healthcare, and education. This refers to the manner in which certain industries carry out and enforce contracts. Self-verifying, self-executing, and autonomous contracts are possible with blockchains that use distributed ledger technology. Companies can change terms, events, and information without relying on brokers or middlemen during the lifecycle of a contract. Contracting parties, for example, can automate payments owing to the contract's lifespan. As these contract milestones are met and payments are paid, they are recorded in such a way that neither side can repudiate or modify the record, thanks to distributed ledgers and blockchains.

Blockchains are also useful for controlling supply chains and ensuring compliance with standards. Because materials flow up the supply chain, each level can record its compliance data on a blockchain. Because Blockchain is immutable, this compliance data cannot be changed and may be used as a system of record.

Simultaneously, the technology can keep information safe: a consortium can be set up to only send relevant information to a buyer, giving suppliers' peace of mind that they are not exposing important commercial information while demonstrating compliance.

Smart contracts, which are really self-directed, reduce risk by eliminating the need for human administration. Contracts may now be written to interact with one another, exchange critical information, reproduce what impacts them, and stay current with the latest information, thanks to technological advancements.

Through the use of smart contracts, a business will become faster and more flexible in 2020 and beyond by:

- Offering the ability to learn from older contracts.
- Affording an understanding of the risk-taking ability of the organization.
- Forming adjustable contracts that change with underlying assets.

EtherCore:

A Multi-Chain Decentralized Application and Smart Contract Platform

EtherCore [15] is a multi-chain decentralised application and smart contract platform that hosts a variety of real-world apps. EtherCore is a network foundation for your blockchain business that is highly distributed, fault-tolerant, and mission-critical. To tackle the paradox issue for a public blockchain platform, EtherCore includes ProgPoW, Proof-of-Authority, and a Programmatic Proof-o--Work consensus method. Users and developers may enjoy the decentralised internet without any network capacity constraints by using secure, stable, and scalable consensus rules. Thousands to millions of transactions per second can be processed on the EtherCore Mainnet [15].

EtherCore Features:

Secure – ProgPoW, a Programmatic Proof-of-Work consensus method that is considered the most ASIC-resistant and GPU-friendly algorithm, is EtherCore's mainnet consensus algorithm. EtherCore is a secure and irreversible platform thanks to its strong decentralisation, which is powered by GPU miners at the grassroots.

Fast

EtherCore is a fast blockchain technology, with a 14-second transaction confirmation time on the mainnet and a 1-second average confirmation time on the sidechain, allowing for real-time blockchain explanation. It is feasible to have dynamic block capacity for both the Mainnet and the Sidechain, ensuring that DApp developers and users have ample network capacity on demand. EtherCore offers faster storage options for storing data in real-time, and the sidechain will be able to serve as a cache for Mainnet because it has 1000 times the processing power of the original Ethereum blockchain.

Stable

EtherCore is designed to withstand any type of third-party intervention, specifically a 51 percent attack or DoS transaction deployment to conquer the network or illegitimately exploit any DApp transactions. Any promise to Mainnet will be secured indefinitely by the ProgPoW algorithm, and the sidechain will be capable of handling any updates required for certain types of decentralised applications, such as network capability and real-time contract changes.

How Contract Vendors Benefit Forward-Thinking Organizations:

The many contract vendors platform gives businesses the insight, speed, and agility they need to manage and take advantage of the difficulties they'll confront in 2020.

This technology allows businesses to create contracts governed by business and compliance rules that intelligently and dynamically determine the terms, metadata, and templates used to create the contract. It also has a simple, straightforward user interface that makes it easy for any front-line employee to utilise. It will also allow businesses to construct and operate consortium blockchains for the management of their smart contracts. Companies may transform their commercial foundation using smart contracts as a major enabler to assure compliance, minimise risk, increase user productivity, and improve their bottom line.

Furthermore, advancements in Blockchain and distributed ledger will only increase the value of having a company-wide contract administration platform.

Tools for Smart Contract Deployment in Multichain Environment

a) Remix: Remix is a suite of tools to interrelate with the Ethereum blockchain to debug transactions (directly quoted from here). There is an IDE version (Remix IDE) and an online version, which we will practice here.

There are numerous tools inside Remix, but the following tools are of our interest,

- Solidity Compiler: This engenders a lot of useful information that we will use in another environment.
- Runtime Environment. Remix provides three:

o Injected Web3: to providers such as Mist or Metamask

o Web3 Provider: to local host throughout IPC

o JavaScript VM: a simulated environment

Amongst the runtime environments, we are exercising JavaScript VM. In the JavaScript VM, Remix derives five Ethereum accounts, each of which is credited with 100 ethers. This is decent enough for analysing our smart contract. Likewise, mining is not required as it is done automatically.

b). eb3 on TestRPC

TestRPC is a model of an Ethereum blockchain, which originates with ten pre-defined Ethereum accounts and provisions mnemonics (that is, one can generate the same set of accounts with the same set of mnemonics). It does not derive with a User Interface as Remix, and we requisite node console plus the web3 library to intermingle with this Blockchain.

CONCLUSION AND FUTURE SCOPE

Blockchain is the future of technology. It has the potential to transform the economy as well as reinvent the way we see operations. Of course, we have yet to fully comprehend this technology, which is why more Indian state governments are collaborating with start-ups from around the world, such as Chroma Way, to conduct proof-of-concept tests within their jurisdictions. Our understanding of Blockchain has greatly benefited from Chroma Way's expertise and previous implementation in countries such as Sweden.

As you can see, there are a lot more blockchain applications than simply cryptocurrency, and they can affect a lot more industries than just finance. We purposefully avoided depicting the impact of Blockchain on the banking sector in order to keep the list as non-fintech as feasible.

A smart contract can declare an almost limitless number of business use cases involving the immutability of data in multi-organizational decision-making. A smart contract developer's job is to convert a current business process, such as one that governs financial prices or delivery conditions, into a smart contract using a programming language like JavaScript, GOLANG, or Java. Smart contract auditors are gradually practising the legal and technological skills required to adapt decades of legal language into the programming language.

In a non-trustable distributed ecosystem, the primary use of blockchains is to establish a creditworthy ecosystem among independent members. The peer-peer nodes, consensus-based ledger mechanisms, chained blocks, anonymous accounts, self-regulated data ownership, and programmable smart contracts make up a blockchain system that is secure and autonomous. Only a few blockchain projects are necessary, viable, efficient, and long-lasting. Furthermore, whereas blockchains provide a creditworthy framework for data-level storage and activities, rigorous credit procedures are required to develop creditworthy blockchain systems.

CONSENT FOR PUBLICATION

Not applicable.

CONFLICT OF INTEREST

The author declares no conflict of interest, financial or otherwise.

ACKNOWLEDGEMENT

Declared none.

REFERENCES

[1] N. Gupta, A Deep Dive Into Security and Privacy Issues of Blockchain Technologies.*Handbook of Research on Blockchain Technology*. Academic Press, 2020, pp. 95-112. [http://dx.doi.org/10.1016/B978-0-12-819816-2.00004-6]

[2] N. Gupta, *Security and privacy issues of blockchain technology*. Springer: Singapore, 2020, pp. 207-226. [http://dx.doi.org/10.1007/978-981-13-8775-3_10]

[3] K. Lauslahti, J. Mattila, and T. Seppala, "Smart contracts–How will blockchain technology affect contractual practices?", *Etla Reports,* vol. 68, 2017. [http://dx.doi.org/10.2139/ssrn.3154043]

[4] D. Macrinici, C. Cartofeanu, and S. Gao, "Smart contract applications within blockchain technology: A systematic mapping study", *Telemat. Inform.,* vol. 35, no. 8, pp. 2337-2354, 2018. [http://dx.doi.org/10.1016/j.tele.2018.10.004]

[5] J. Liu, P. Jiang, and J. Leng, "A framework of credit assurance mechanism for manufacturing services under social manufacturing context", *2017 13th IEEE Conference on Automation Science and Engineering (CASE),* 2017pp. 36-40 [http://dx.doi.org/10.1109/COASE.2017.8256072]

[6] Eric Wall, and Gustaf Malm, "Using blockchain technology and smart contracts to create a distributed securities depository" 2016.

[7] Jonatan Bergquist, "Blockchain technology and smart contracts: Privacy-preserving tools" 2017.

[8] A. Barišić, E. Zhu, and F. Mallet, "Model-driven approach for the design of multi-chain smart contracts", In: *2021 3rd Conference on Blockchain Research & Applications for Innovative Networks and Services (BRAINS)*, 2021, pp. 37-38. [http://dx.doi.org/10.1109/BRAINS52497.2021.9569809]

[9] Y. Li, "Emerging blockchain-based applications and techniques", *Serv. Oriented Comput. Appl.,* vol. 13, no. 4, pp. 279-285, 2019. [http://dx.doi.org/10.1007/s11761-019-00281-x]

[10] R. Agrawal, N. Gupta, Ed., *Transforming Cybersecurity Solutions Using Blockchain.* Springer

Singapore, 2021.
[http://dx.doi.org/10.1007/978-981-33-6858-3]

[11] S. Chawla, and N. Gupta, "An analytical view of revocable attribute based encryption schemes", *2021 Second International Conference on Electronics and Sustainable Communication Systems (ICESC),* 2021pp. 1-8
[http://dx.doi.org/10.1109/ICESC51422.2021.9532873]

[12] G-H. Hwang, "InfiniteChain: A multi-chain architecture with distributed auditing of sidechains for public blockchains", In: *International Conference on Blockchain* Springer: Cham, 2018.
[http://dx.doi.org/10.1007/978-3-319-94478-4_4]

[13] X. Fan, Q. Chai, and Z. Zhong, "Multav: A multi-chain token backed voting framework for decentralized blockchain governance", In: *International Conference on Blockchain* Springer: Cham, 2020, pp. 33-47.
[http://dx.doi.org/10.1007/978-3-030-59638-5_3]

[14] A. Ismailisufi, T. Popović, N. Gligorić, S. Radonjic, and S. Šandi, "A private blockchain implementation using multichain open source platform", In: *2020 24th International Conference on Information Technology (IT)* IEEE, 2020, pp. 1-4.
[http://dx.doi.org/10.1109/IT48810.2020.9070689]

[15] J. Ladleif, C. Friedow, and M. Weske, "An architecture for multi-chain business process choreographies", In: *International Conference on Business Information Systems* Springer: Cham, 2020, pp. 184-196.
[http://dx.doi.org/10.1007/978-3-030-53337-3_14]

CHAPTER 9

Blockchain for Decentralized Services: On Improving Security and Performance of Distributed IPFS-based Web Applications

V. Le[1], R. Moazeni[1], M. Moh[1], R. Agrawal[2,*] and N. Gupta[2]

[1] *San Jose State University, San Jose, CA 95192-0249, USA*

[2] *Manav Rachna International Institute of Research and Studies, Faridabad, India*

Abstract: While cloud computing is gaining widespread adoption these days, some challenges are emerging around the security, performance, and reliability of centralized cloud resources. Decentralized services are introduced as an effective way to overcome the limitations of cloud services. Blockchain technology, with its associated decentralization, is used to develop decentralized application platforms. The Interplanetary File System (IPFS) is built on top of a distributed system consisting of a group of nodes that shares the data and takes advantage of blockchain to permanently store the data. The IPFS is very useful in transferring remote data. This work focuses on applying blockchain technology to the IPFS to improve its security and performance. It illustrates different types of blockchain and their advantages and challenges; it also describes the proposed design and its detailed implementation. For performance evaluation, we show the performance gains, analyze security enhancements, and discuss the tradeoffs between security and performance. The presented work is significant towards more secure, efficient web applications utilizing emerging blockchain technologies.

Keywords: Blockchain technology, Distributed system, Decentralized service, Interplanetary file system (IPFS).

INTRODUCTION

Blockchain is a progressive innovation set to change the eventual fate of processing and disturb a few businesses with additional inventive arrangements. It is open, changeless and appropriate for all means and purposes relevant to a variety of scenarios. The innovation increased enormous intrigue from the ascent of digital forms of money; however, it sees applications in numerous different divisions other than funds. Businesses and government organizations are using

* **Corresponding author R. Agrawal:** Manav Rachna International Institute of Research and Studies, Faridabad, India; E-mail: rashmi.fca@mriu.edu.in

Rashmi Agrawal and Neha Gupta (Eds.)

centralized cloud resources increasingly these days. Amazon AWS, Google Cloud, and other popular services provide a high level of security and reliability [1]. Using centralized cloud resources, however, has some limitations since the centralized cloud can be a single point of failure, as many examples in the past have shown. Take, for example, a careless mistake committed by a cloud operator that can cause the cloud, and all the companies and organizations relying on the cloud resource, essentially half of a country, to shut down for up to an entire day. Similarly, a power outage, a data loss, or a network attack on these services can potentially disrupt operations, causing huge damage to user data and business activities [2]. A survey was conducted by Right Scale in 2018; it asked 997 technical professionals about the challenges of adopting cloud technology. The survey showed some interesting findings. Security was the top concern mentioned by 77% of them, and 55% of them faced performance challenges while using cloud technology [3].

In the paper, Hassanzadeh-Nazarabadi *et al.* (2019), the author used the distributed hash table concept to design a blockchain architecture called LightChain. LightChain is a permissionless blockchain where any node can join the network. Any new transaction or block addition to this blockchain will be recorded in the distributed hash table of a peer in an on-demand manner, so each peer does not have to store the entire blockchain locally [4]. Although distributed hash tables provide efficient data lookup, they may take a noticeable amount of time when a lot of table searches are required to retrieve data.

The security and performance challenges of distributed systems are discussed in this chapter. The drawbacks of centralized cloud resources can be mitigated by blockchain-based solutions. As blockchains are stored on ledgers that are shared between all participating nodes on a network, they have the right characteristics and functionalities to handle these kinds of computations decentrally and by multiple parties. In addition, any transaction that takes place on the blockchain requires the consensus of all the nodes, so it is also very secure. Blockchain technologies, therefore, have been recommended to be used for achieving distributed, fault-tolerant consensus and for building efficient public-key-based secure infrastructures. It is important that there is no single entity that controls the blockchain, so it does not have the single point of failure issue as in other regular cloud storages [4].

A new file system called the interplanetary file system (IPFS) is designed to process large files decentralized and effectively [5]. The IPFS network operates on a peer-to-peer basis, with each peer providing its own storage. It helps prevent data losses since the same data is available on multiple peer nodes [6]. Based on the above reasons, IPFS combined with blockchain technology can serve as a great solution to address the security and performance concerns of cloud technology.

An approach to securing distributed web apps using blockchain and smart contracts is described in this article, which includes smart contracts to control access to IPFS [7]. The detailed implementation is depicted, including encryption/decryption schemes, smart contracts, remote application migration, and memory cache for key values. Performance and security analyses are presented, with a discussion of tradeoffs between the two.

This chapter is a substantial extension of earlier work. The rest of the chapter is organized as follows. Section II goes over preliminary background information and related work about blockchain technology, smart contracts, IPFS, distributed hash table, and memory cache [8]. Section III demonstrates the high-level architectural design of the web application as well as how each component is designed. Section IV talks about the implementation of each improvement method in our application. In Section V, we detail our experiments and analyze the performance and security aspects of our application. Finally, Section VI presents the conclusion and future work.

BACKGROUND AND RELATED WORK

Background of Blockchain Technology

Blockchain is a decentralized, public ledger that tracks online transactions. A decentralized blockchain ledger maintains a shared record of all the transactions distributed over a large user network. This is a completely decentralized network, which does not require any intermediary mechanism for exchanging services. A blockchain is a series of data blocks, in which a small patch of user-made transactions is stored in each row. Both these data blocks are clustered together electronically, using a top-tier level of cryptography [9]. Both of the blocks together then form a permanent and malicious public record of each and every transaction that occurs on the network. The user is connected to a blockchain in such a way that his / her data is made accessible without revealing their identity to any other user in that blockchain. Blockchain offers users complete transparency to make things simpler [10]. Through encrypting and validating, Blockchain guarantees the confidentiality, authenticity and privacy of transactions. By adding a new block to a blockchain, a cryptographic hash generated from the previous block's content is used to link it to the preceding block. It means the chain never breaks, and each block is registered forever [11]. Consequently, this is deliberately difficult to alter past blockchain transactions, as all subsequent blocks must be modified first. Blockchain databases are made up of many nodes, and decentralized. Administration includes the node: all nodes review recent blockchain additions and can add new data to the database. Consensus on the majority of nodes must be achieved for an addition to the blockchain. This consensus process guarantees network stability and makes it impossible to exploit. They enable a blockchain ecosystem to become self-governing, open, consent-based, and credible. Blockchains can run without human involvement thanks to a collection of smart contracts. The smart contracts are set up to run on predefined blockchain nodes [12]. They can be prompted by callbacks from the blockchain system, other smart contracts, or the information systems of the participants. As smart contracts, both blockchain processes and application-related rules can typically be predetermined. The use cases and real-world tasks vary, but the benefits of employing the technology stay consistent: immutability, transparency, redundancy, and security.

Dragon chain illustrates how blockchain technology facilitates transactions between two parties in a safe, verifiable, and trustworthy manner, demonstrating the benefits of the technology [13]. The underlying system behind blockchain is a distributed peer-to-peer network. There is no centralized authority that controls the network. Each node in the network performs its work independently. A new node needs to be verified by existing nodes before it joins the blockchain network [14]. All the nodes are required to reach a consensus on a transaction before the transaction is recorded on a ledger that is shared among all the participating nodes [15]. In order to reach consensus, each participant must solve a complex puzzle and provide a proof of stake or proof of work to a server. The server checks the proof from each participant and rewards the ones with the correct proofs [16]. Once the proof has been approved by the server, the transaction is confirmed, and a new block which contains the hash code and the transaction is added to the ledger, as illustrated by Tar [17]. The new block creation process is called mining. A node gets rewarded with money for successfully mining a block first, so all the completing nodes race to process a transaction and create a new block; refer to Salman *et al.* (2019) [18]. Data on the blockchain is immutable, so it will never change after it is written into the ledger. One limitation of blockchain is that it relies on continuous communications between nodes in the network, so its performance will be largely impacted in areas with low bandwidth or slow connection, as explained by Zheng *et al.* [19].

Even though blockchain is a great solution for decentralized computing resources, data storage on a blockchain is still expensive, since the data needs to be pushed to other blockchain nodes and processed there as well. A blockchain node will need a more powerful CPU, higher bus speed, more bandwidth, and bigger storage to process all the data since there is a lot of data on the Internet now, and it is expected to get larger in the future, which will increase the cost to operate.

Types of Blockchain

Blockchains can be classified as Public Blockchain, Consortium Blockchain, or Private Blockchain based on how clients participate, and they can also be classified as primary chains or side chains based on the relationship of chains. In addition, a few blockchains can shape a system. The system's chains are linked together to form the Interchain.

Open

Public blockchains have ledgers accessible to anyone on the internet, and the blockchain can be checked and modified by everyone. The pace is slower in public open, read/write access to the database, security is proof-of-work / proof-stake, identity is anonymous or pseudonymous, and assets are native assets. So, *et al.*, Bitcoin, Dash, Thatum, and Factom.

Private

All access to an agency is kept centralized. Private blockchains only allow unique individuals inside the company to validate and attach transaction blocks, but basically, anyone on the internet is able to access them. Entry to the database is allowed by read and/or write. Velocity is higher. Safety participants are pre-approved. All properties are established identities and properties only, *et al.*, Blockstack Multichain.

Smart Contracts

A Smart Contract is essentially a computer protocol that enforces negotiations between the two exchanging parties. This forms, more precisely, a contractual agreement between two parties. This immediately verifies the deal, which meets the conditions agreed. Ethereum is the largest decentralized network producing infinite Smart Contracts using a command line. When an application incorporates the following components would be called Decentralized: The program must be completely open-source, run autonomously and without managing any of its tokens. To prevent any central failure points, the application data and operating records must be stored cryptographically in a transparent, decentralized blockchain.

Clearly, the program must use a proper cryptographic token to access the code. The application will produce tokens based on a standard cryptographic algorithm, which serves as evidence of the value nodes' contribution to the application.

Blockchain transactions are executed by smart contracts, which are computer programs. Solidify is used to write executable code for smart contracts. There are variables, functions, and structures in Solidity, a statically typed language. Codes are based on agreements between two parties involved in the transaction. When a transaction is completed, compiled contracts are deployed into an environment that is capable of running them. As an example, for the Ethereum blockchain, smart contracts are deployed and executed in the Ethereum virtual machine (EVM) [20]. The code in a smart contract is publicly available on the ledger in a blockchain, so a new node that joins the blockchain later will receive a copy of the smart contract. There is no centralized authority controlling smart contracts; instead, they are distributed across multiple nodes on the network. It ensures the trust and anonymity of any smart contract-triggered operations. Before a smart contract executes a transaction, a transaction fee is required, and, in the Ethereum case, the fee is paid in ether, also known as gas. The transaction fee is higher for smart contracts with more complex logic.

Interplanetary File System

Interplanetary file system is a distributed file system where we can store any computer file or data for later access. Unlike a file system on a computer, IPFS divides a file into multiple chunks of data and distributes the chunks across different nodes on IPFS. While other file systems use a location-based address to look up a file, IPFS uses a content-based address where a file's address is based on the hash of the file's content. A single unit of data on IPFS is a block. IPFS constructs a directed acyclic graph to link all the blocks in a file, which facilitates data retrieval. IPFS maintains a distributed hash table to know where to find the data or the path which leads closer to the data [21].

Data downloaded from IPFS can be stored on the node and accessed as a new data provider. This way, the node can send the data to its nearby computer when it requests the data, like other IPFS nodes.

Distributed Hash Table

Distributed hash tables allow IPFS to locate a peer node with certain data or to identify a path leading to that node by storing key-value mappings. IPFS nodes maintain their own distributed hash tables and use these when requesting a key. Keys are individual identifiers for data, Interplanetary Name System (IPNS) keys, or peer IDs.

RELATED WORK

In order to protect the privacy of users' data on the network, Rahulamathavan *et al.* (2017) proposed an attribute-based encryption method. The data owner creates user groups and assigns an access policy that consists of certain user attributes to each group. A user must possess all the specified attributes that satisfy the policy to access the data [22]. This encryption technology does not look at users' identities and does not work in a decentralized network as it requires a centralized access policy server. With smart contracts, this problem can be solved by using a decentralized network and customizing their implementation logic for user verification with every transaction.

The usage of smart contracts has been previously proposed for access control between smart devices in the Internet of Things (IoT). Song *et al.* (2019) developed an attribute-based access control scheme that checks device attribute information and decides whether to allow a device to join an IoT network. This scheme uses blockchain and smart contracts to store and manage access control policies [23]. In addition, Nakamura *et al.* (2020) [24] proposed a capability-based access control using smart contracts in the IoT. In this scheme, the author suggests having smart contracts manage capability tokens. Every capability or action has a token, and smart contracts that grant or deny the access requestor based on the token ownership and validation.

The paper by Shen *et al.* (2019) [25] analyzes the I/O performance of IPFS and notices a bottleneck in IPFS data retrieval because of the resolving and downloading operations. When a node in IPFS receives a data retrieval request, if the data is not local on the node, it needs to perform a lookup to find the storage node of the data. If the data size to download is larger than 256KB, IPFS will break it into multiple blocks of 256KB each. When all the blocks arrive at the requesting node, they will be re-aggregated to a file of the original size, so the block size also affects the I/O performance of IPFS [26].

APPLICATION DESIGN

The application consists of the following components, as shown in (Fig. **1**):

- Web client: the user interface that runs on a browser where the user can interact with and perform operations in the application.
- Web server: the web server has all the implementations to support file upload and download
- IPFS data storage: a distributed data storage that stores and manages the data.
- Blockchain: a local Ethereum blockchain to host smart contracts and record user activities from the application

By using smart contracts, users' identities are verified, and transactions' hash codes are written to the blockchain. (Fig. **2**) illustrates how the blockchain contracts are deployed on and running on the network.

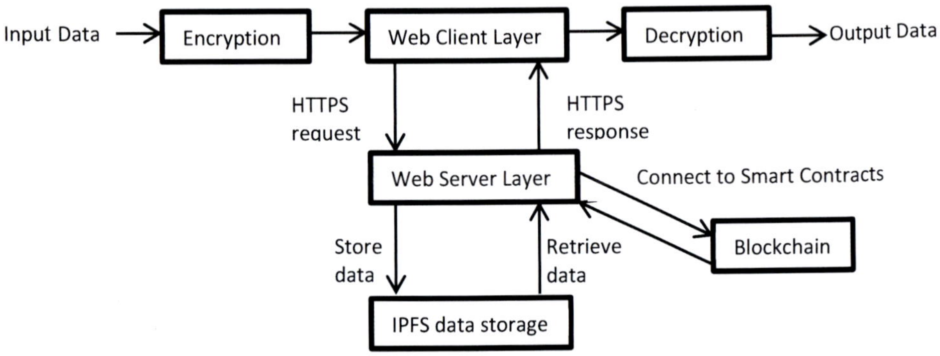

Fig. (1). High level architecture diagram.

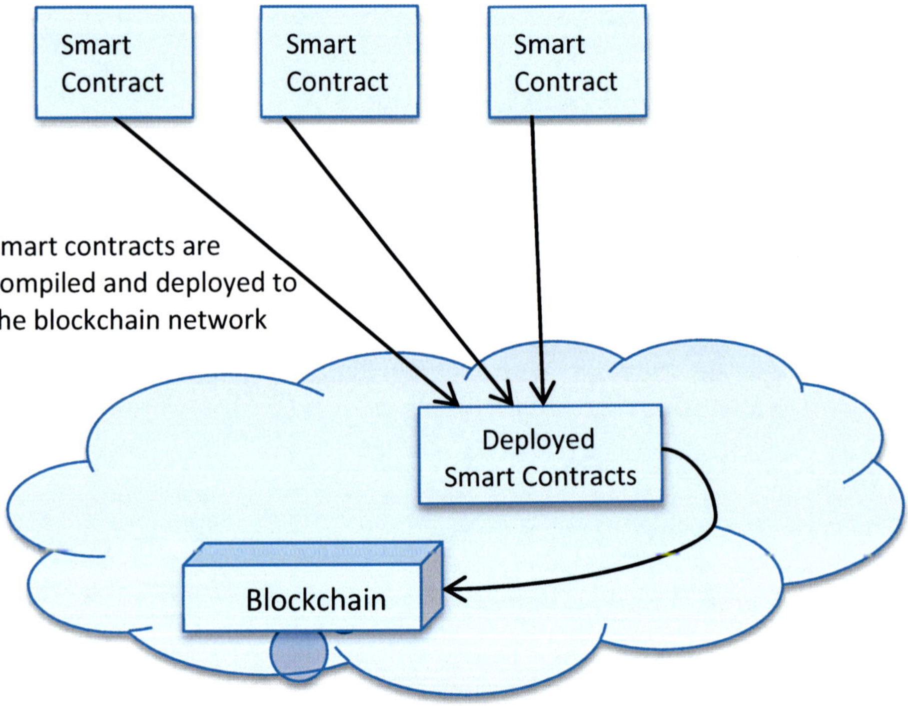

Fig. (2). Smart contracts in the Ethereum blockchain.

Fig. (**3**) shows the sequence diagram of data retrieval in IPFS: The web application server uses an IPFS client to talk to a remote IPFS network of nodes or the local IPFS daemon. To test the differences made in code to improve IPFS data retrieval, we run the IPFS daemon locally in our experiments. A key-value cache is added to two APIs in IPFS. In one API, a root file node is found by generating a hash of the file, and in the other API, the provider nodes are identified by generating a key. An identifier for a file's content is called a key. In addition to querying data, the web application also adds new data to IPFS by utilizing the Add API of the IPFS client.

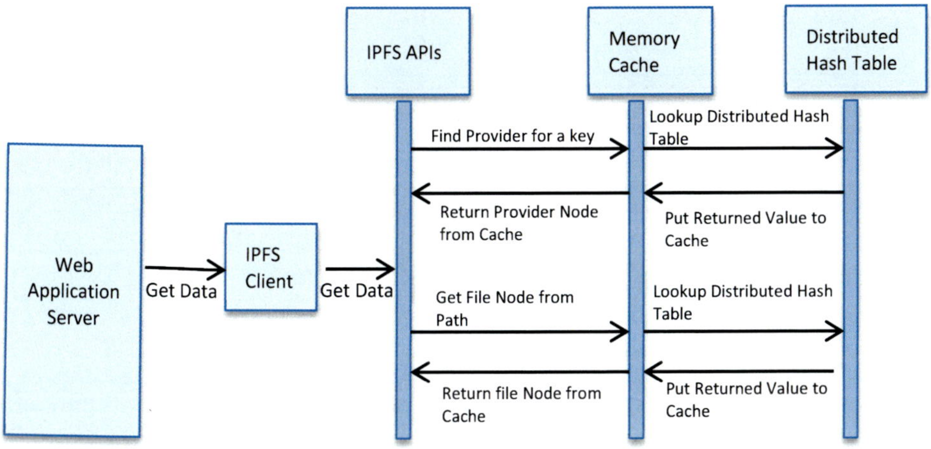

Fig. (3). Sequence diagram of data retrieval in IPFS.

IMPLEMENTATION

This section describes the detailed implementation, including encryption and decryption, access control using Smart Contracts, migration of the application to Remote IPFS, and the key-value memory cache.

a. Encryption and Decryption

To protect the privacy of our IPFS data, we use encryption and decryption. To generate public-private key pair, we first used OpenSSL commands. A file was encrypted and uploaded to IPFS using the public key. The hash code we received for the file was used to retrieve the file from IPFS after it had been successfully added to IPFS. Ultimately, we decrypted the file with the private key obtained from the pair of keys previously generated. It is expected that the downloaded file will contain the same contents as the original.

b. Access Control using Smart Contracts

We have integrated smart contracts into our application to implement access control of the data on IPFS. For our experiment, we have written the logic in a smart contract to check the user's email address. The smart contract is compiled and deployed to our local blockchain. When a user tries to download a file from IPFS, they are prompted to enter their email address. This email address is sent to the application server, and the server calls a method on the smart contract for email verification. If the verification succeeds, the server proceeds with fetching the requested data from IPFS. Otherwise, we show an error message to the user that they do not have access to the requested data.

c. Migration of the Application to Remote IPFS

In case one or a few nodes fail, the application can still be accessed using IPFS, which allows decentralization of application hosting. As opposed to internet applications accessible through HTTP, IPFS applications are accessed *via* IPFS peer-to-peer or IPFS Gateway API. It is even better since once the application is on IPFS, it can be pinned to the local node using the hash output generated by IPFS [27].

We have used a tool on fleek.co to deploy our application to a distributed IPFS network. Once deployed, we create a domain name on GoDaddy and change the CNAME record in our domain's DNS to have a better URL to access the application.

Key-Value Memory Cache

Method Get File Node from Path

This method takes an IPFS hash path to a file and resolves to a file root node that points to the start of the file. The method queries the directed acyclic graph (DAG), which is the underlying data structure of IPFS and returns a node pointer to the file. Since the hash path is based on the file content and is the same for the same content, we can put the hash path and the resolved file node in the cache. Future requests with the same hash path will hit the cache and immediately return the file node.

As a first step, the given path is resolved to the last resolvable path. This method queries the DAG using the content identifier in the last resolvable path. Data is typically returned as nodes in a DAG as links to nodes within the graph. A Unix file system-based file node is created when the method receives the root node. There are different hierarchies of the file system represented by this node, including files, directories, and symbolic links (Fig. **4**).

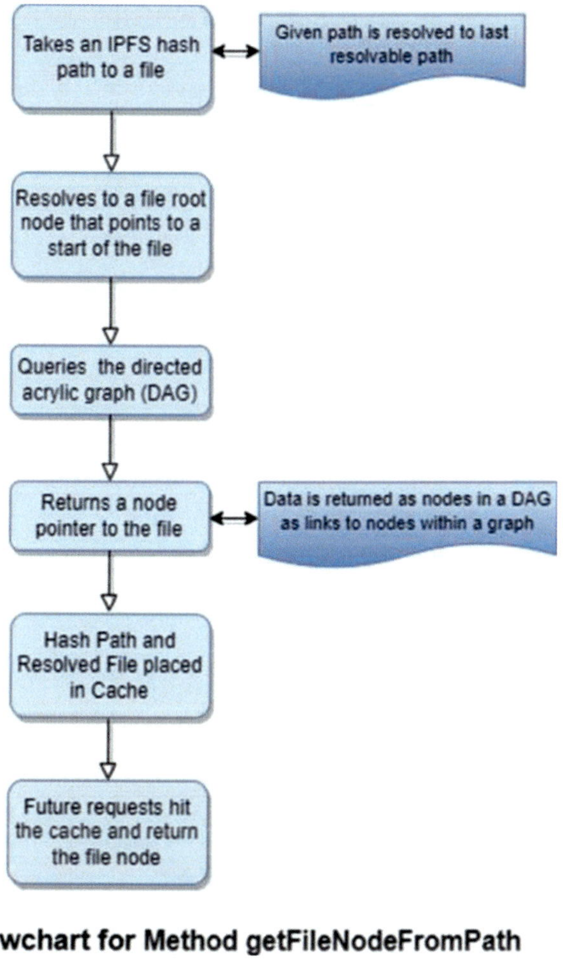

Fig (4). Flowchart 1.

Method find ProvidersAsync

While get File Node FromPath returns the file root node to a specific given hash path, this findProvidersAsync method searches for peers that are close to the current node and can provide a given key. The method takes a content-addressed identifier and a count and then returns a set of peers that have or know where to get the requested content. A content-addressed identifier is formed by a version, a content type, and the hash of the content. The count specifies how many peers we want to get. If the count is zero, the method returns an unbounded number of peers. Because the content identifier is unique for the same content, we cache the content identifier and the set of peer providers. Therefore, future calls to this method with the same identifier will be able to directly get the providers from the cache.

This method internally tries to find providers from the local network as well as the wide area network. In each network, it creates a channel that is responsible for sending back a peer's address when it is found. Since a peer can be found again and again, the method keeps a local map that stores a newly found peer. We just ignore the peer that has already been found and is on the map. If, at the end of the method, we cannot find any new peers, we publish a query event to the query event channel. The query event has the context of the initial data request (Fig. **5**).

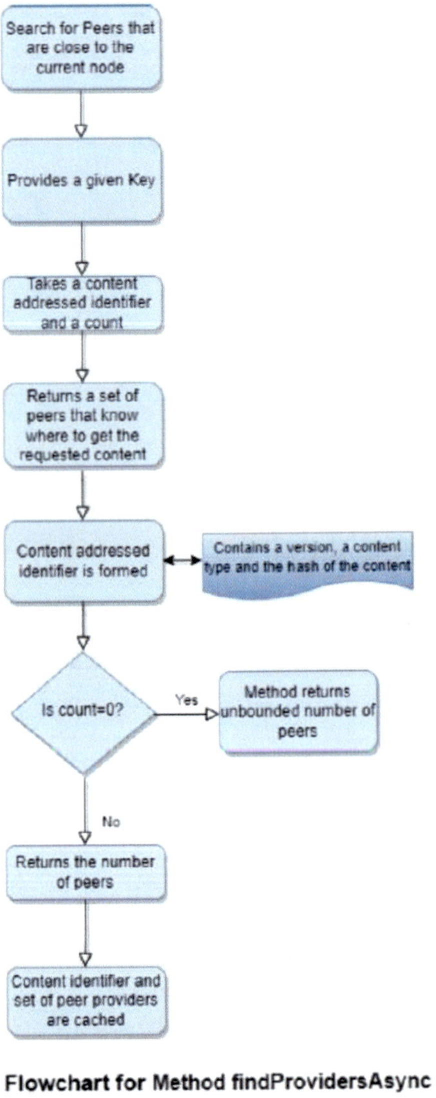

Fig. (5). Flowchart 2.

PERFORMANCE AND SECURITY ANALYSIS

Security Analysis

With the encryption mechanism, we are able to get rid of the privacy risks caused by the traditional IPFS implementation. By querying the blacklist, only the data that is protected from the users we blacklisted is able to be downloaded from IPFS. This IPFS implementation will be able to serve as the backbone for the new DDoS mitigation solution.

In the second experiment, we used smart contract-based access control to verify the user's identity before giving them permission to download a file on IPFS. When we downloaded a file from IPFS, we were required to enter an email address for the smart contract to validate. For experimental purposes, we created a blacklist of email addresses, which should be blocked from accessing our data on IPFS. When the entered email address passed the verification, we showed a success message to the user and started downloading the file from IPFS. When we deliberately put an email address, which is in the email blacklist, it would fail the verification by the smart contract. We showed a failure message to the user and did not allow them to download the file.

We have migrated the web application from the local host to a remote IPFS network, so the web application can be accessed even though the local server is not running. We also set up an SSL connection and a custom URL https://sjsu-cs298.on.fleek.co for secure and easy access to the application.

Performance Analysis

Our tests included uploading and downloading files of various sizes, to see how long it takes to get data from IPFS without the cache and with it. Every file was run ten times, and the average latency was calculated. The results are shown in Fig. (**6**).

We can see that without the cache, the average latency fluctuates from 300 ms to 400 ms. In our experiment, sometimes it can take up to a few seconds to get the root file node because it depends on when the lookup algorithm finds the node.

We also measure the download latency for different file sizes, shown in Fig. (**7**). With the cache, it only takes about 10 ms to get the root file node, and the latency is pretty consistent. The latency the user observes when downloading a file from the application will be higher due to the Internet latency to transfer the data. With the Internet download speed of about 90 Mbps in our experiments, the Internet latency is insignificant and not noticeable for a 1Mb file, and it increases as the size of a file gets bigger.

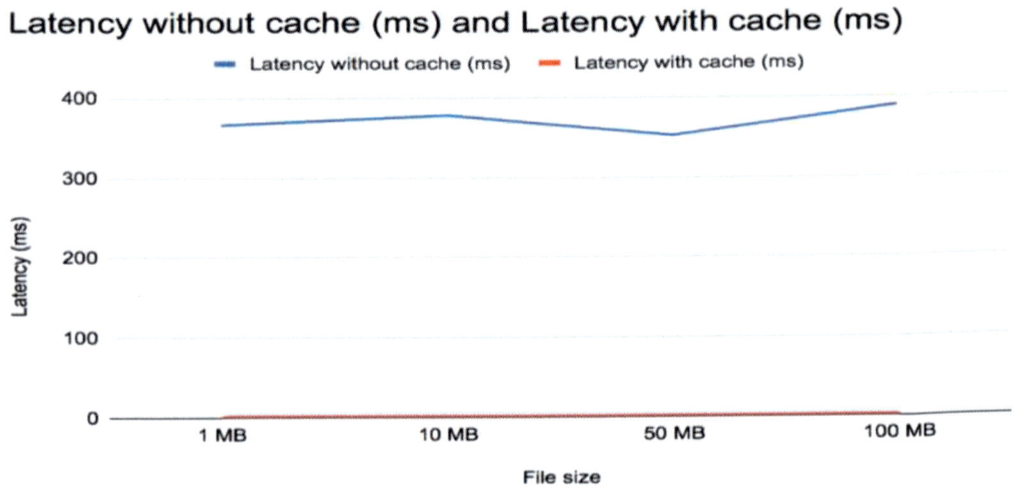

Fig. (6). Comparison between IPFS files retrieval latency with cache and without cache.

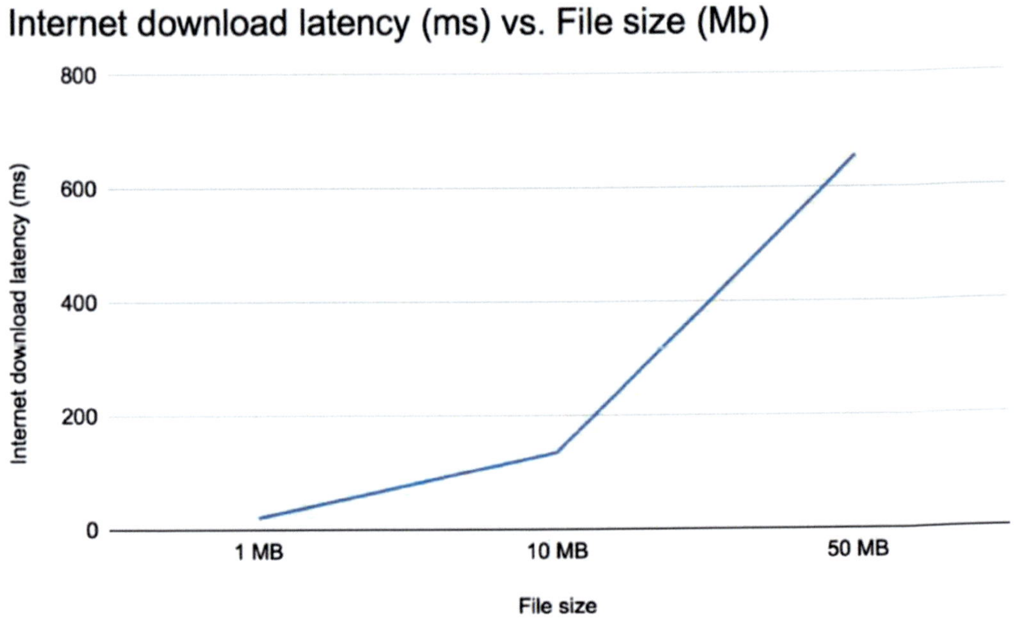

Fig. (7). Internet downloads latency for different file sizes.

We also tried varying the expiration time of the memory cache; the results are shown in Fig. (**8**). We pre-uploaded 100 different text files of about 1 Mb each to

IPFS. We tried setting the expiration time to 10 seconds, 30 seconds, 1 minute, and 5 minutes, and for each expiration time, we ran a script to continuously download random files from the pre-uploaded files on IPFS and measured the latency. The resulting latency is drawn in the chart below. As the chart illustrates, when the expiration time increases, the latency decreases because more entries are kept in the cache, and we get more cache hits in the download operation.

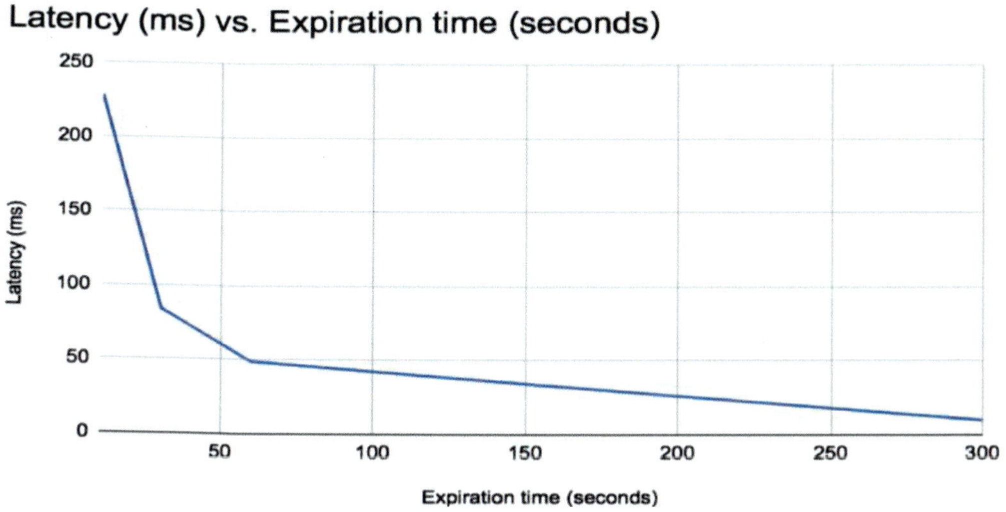

Fig. (8). Latency vs. expiration time of the memory cache.

However, we do not want to have a very large expiration time as the cache will maintain a lot of entries that are not frequently accessed. From our experiments, the reasonable expiration time should be at the minimum of 1 min to about 2-3 minutes because at 1 min, we can already get a significant latency reduction from more than 200 ms to about 50 ms. From 1 min and above, the latency is only gradually decreasing.

The memory cache is backed by a key-value map in the Go language. Since a map can have a dynamic size, when more data is added to the map, the map will get more slots internally. Therefore, the maximum amount of data in the cache will depend on the available heap size and the operating system where IPFS is running. For example, a map in a 32-bit operating system can have 2^{31} - 1 slots, and a map in a 64-bit operating system can have 2^{63} - 1 slots. Because of the above reason, initializing a map with a different size for our memory cache will not result in any difference in terms of the latency to get the data. However, the size of the cache is limited by the heap size and the memory available in the operating system.

It should be noted that using the memory cache can have some disadvantages. Data from IPFS cannot be cached when it is too large; it will result in a cache miss when the requested data comes in too big [27]. The performance of IPFS will be slowed down when many cache misses happen. If IPFS, with its integrated memory cache, does not seem to be a good fit for the application's intended use cases, it is possible to consider other alternative distributed file systems, such as Ceph, GlusterFS, and HDFS. Described as a distributed file system, Hadoop is an open-source system that can store and process huge amounts of unstructured data. It facilitates high throughput access to data. Ceph is a POSIX-compliant network file system that offers high performance and large data storage, and is highly compatible with legacy applications. GlusterFS is also a fast and scalable distributed file system that has caching of data and metadata. GlusterFS can be integrated with HDFS to process large data for data analysis purposes.

TRADEOFF BETWEEN PERFORMANCE AND SECURITY

There is a computing cost for each added security mechanism in the application, so it incurs a tradeoff between performance and security. When an additional layer of security is integrated, the application's server has to do more computing work in the security check, so the application can run a little slower. If security is more important, we need to sacrifice the performance of the application, and vice versa. Therefore, it is important to choose the right balance between performance and security to meet the requirements and use cases of the application.

We have measured the performance impact in our application for each security method. We upload and download files of 1 Mb in size. The encryption and decryption using OpenSSL each take about 50 ms. The call to the smart contract to verify the user's identity takes between 20 to 70 ms. Because the identity check by the smart contract is simple, assuming no network failures, the time it takes is small enough to be acceptable and very consistent in the aforementioned range of 20 and 70 ms. In short, the security implementation adds an additional 50 ms to the file upload flow and an extra 70 ms to 120 ms when downloading a file.

As we know from the experiments, IPFS with the memory cache only takes about 10 ms to resolve the root file node, so the additional latency from the security protection is about 7 to 12 times longer on average for a file download. From the user experience, the added latency of about 100 ms in a download should not be noticeable. However, if we want to upload a very large file, we may need to split it into chunks and encrypt each chunk at a time because there is a size limit in OpenSSL encryption. This splitting and encrypting of a large file may add a significantly longer latency for uploading a file, which is something we need to consider.

CONCLUSION AND FUTURE WORK

Our research and experiments show that it is imperative to protect the security and privacy of data on a distributed network, and we have used several methods in our application to improve it. Data encryption ensures the data can only be seen by the authorized user who has the right key to decrypt the data. Access control by smart contracts provides another layer of security checks to verify the user's identity before giving the user permission to access the data. Combining the two methods can significantly improve security and lower the risk of data being stolen by malicious users. Future work in this area will focus on adding access control policies to smart contracts to verify the user's identity, for example, verifying the public key and the signature of the user. It is also possible to implement a blockchain-based service that manages the user's secret key and encrypts it, and if an application wants to access the data, it can call the service to get the key and decrypt it. This key management service can use smart contracts' access control to authenticate the user before sending them the key.

Besides the security concern, our experiments demonstrate performance improvement in IPFS by using key-value memory caching. The cache helps significantly reduce the time it takes to find a data provider or the root node of an underlying directed acyclic graph in IPFS, which in turn makes it faster to retrieve data from IPFS. In the future, another way we can try to add on top of caching is to use a recursive lookup instead of the current iterative lookup. When the iterative lookup asks a node for the associated value of a key, if the node does not have the value, it will return a list of other nodes closer to the requested value. The same process continues until it finds a node that actually has the value and can return it. With the recursive lookup, when we ask a node for a value, and the node does not have the value, it will ask another closer node which will ask another closer node. Once the value is found, it will be returned to the original requestor following the same chain of requests in the reversed order. The recursive lookup can reduce a lot of network traffic between nodes and the latency in processing requests and responses in each node, so it will certainly improve the performance of data retrieval in IPFS.

It is possible for the performance of the system to degrade when an extremely large file is transferred, since the entire file will not fit in the memory cache. The chances of caching misses will be greater. One of the future works that should be done is to help find a solution to handle such an occurrence and optimize, if possible, the performance of both IPFS with large data requests as well as the cache.

DISCLOSURE

"Part of this article has previously been published in Improving Security and Performance of Distributed IPFS-Based Web Applications with Blockchain in Advances in Cyber Security. Communications in Computer and Information Science, 2021, vol 1487, pp 114-127".

CONSENT FOR PUBLICATION

Not applicable.

CONFLICT OF INTEREST

The author declares no conflict of interest, financial or otherwise.

ACKNOWLEDGEMENT

Declared none.

REFERENCES

[1] S. Voshmgir, "Blockchains & distributed ledger technologies", Available from: https://blockchainhub.net/blockchains-and-distributed-ledgertechnologies-in-general/(visited on 2019-08-31)

[2] T. Koens, and E. Poll, What blockchain alternative do you need?*Data Privacy Management, Cryptocurrencies and Blockchain Technology*. Springer: Cham, 2018, pp. 113-129. [http://dx.doi.org/10.1007/978-3-030-00305-0_9]

[3] V. Le, R. Moazeni, and M. Moh, "Improving security and performance of distributed IPFS-based web applications with Blockchain", In: *International Conference on Advances in Cyber Security* Springer: Singapore, 2021, pp. 114-127. [http://dx.doi.org/10.1007/978-981-16-8059-5_8]

[4] Y. Hassanzadeh-Nazarabadi, A. Küpçü, and Ö. Özkasap, "Lightchain: A dht-based blockchain for resource constrained environments", *arXiv*, . Hassanzadeh-Nazarabadi, Yahya, Alptekin Küpçü, and Öznur Özkasap. "Lightchain: A dht-based blockchain for resource constrained environments." preprint arXiv:1904.00375 (2019).

[5] I. Zainab, "Privacy preservation in resource-constrained IoT devices using blockchain—A survey", *Electronics,* p. 1732, 2021. [http://dx.doi.org/10.3390/electronics10141732]

[6] B.K. John, V.S. Ceph, V.S. GlusterFS, and V.S. MooseFS, "Computing for Geeks", Available from: https://www.datapine.com/blog/cloud-computing-risks-and-challenges/Accessed on: Jun 4, 2021.

[7] N. Khudhur, and S. Siva, "The IPFS search engine", *2019 Seventh International Symposium on Computing and Networking (CANDAR),* 2019pp. 150-156.Nagasaki, Japan Available from: https://doi.ieeecomputersociety.org/10.1109/CANDAR.2019.00026 [http://dx.doi.org/10.1109/CANDAR.2019.00026]

[8] L. Kohorst, *Decentralizing your Website.,* 2020. Available from: https://towardsdatascience.com/decentralizing-your-website-f5bca765f9ed

[9] A. Lipton, and S. Levi, *An Introduction to Smart Contracts and Their Potential and Inherent Limitations.,* 2018. Available from: https://corpgov.law.harvard.edu/2018/05/26/an-introduction--o-smart-contracts-and-their-potential-and-inherent-limitations/

[10] Y. Nakamura, Y. Zhang, M. Sasabe, and S. Kasahara, "Exploiting smart contracts for capability-based access control in the internet of things", *Sensors,* vol. 20, no. 6, pp. 1793-1793, 2020. [http://dx.doi.org/10.3390/s20061793]

[11] M. Naz, F.A. Al-zahrani, R. Khalid, N. Javaid, A.M. Qamar, M.K. Afzal, and M. Shafiq, "A secure data sharing platform using blockchain and interplanetary file system", *Sustainability (Basel),* vol. 11, no. 24, p. 7054, 2019. [http://dx.doi.org/10.3390/su11247054]

[12] Y. Rahulamathavan, R.C. Phan, M. Rajarajan, S. Misra, and A. Kondoz, "Privacy-preserving blockchain based IoT ecosystem using attribute-based encryption", *Proc IEEE Int Conf Adv Netw Telecommun Syst,* 2017pp. 1-6 [http://dx.doi.org/10.1109/ANTS.2017.8384164]

[13] T. Salman, M. Zolanvari, A. Erbad, R. Jain, and M. Samaka, "Security services using Blockchains: A state of the art survey", *IEEE Communications Surveys & Tutorials,* vol. 21, no. 1, pp. 858-880, 2019. [http://dx.doi.org/10.1109/COMST.2018.2863956]

[14] J. Shen, Y. Li, Y. Zhou, and X. Wang, "Understanding I/O performance of IPFS storage: A client's perspective", *IEEE Access,* pp. 24-24, 2019.

[15] L. Song, M. Li, Z. Zhu, P. Yuan, and Y. He, *Attribute-Based Access Control Using Smart Contracts for the Internet of Things.* ScienceDirect, 2019, pp. 2019-2019.

[16] M. Steichen, B. Fiz, R. Norvill, W. Shbair, and R. State, "Blockchain-based, decentralized access control for IPFS", *IEEE Access,* pp. 15-15, 2019.

[17] A. Tar, Available from: https://cointelegraph.com/explained/proof-of-work-explained

[18] S. Wang, Y. Zhang, and Y. Zhang, "A Blockchain-based framework for data sharing with fine-grained access control in decentralized storage systems", *IEEE Access,* vol. 6, pp. 38437-38450, 2018. [http://dx.doi.org/10.1109/ACCESS.2018.2851611]

[19] W Zheng, Z Zheng, X Chen, K Dai, P Li, and R Chen, "NutBaaS: A Blockchain-as-a-service platform", *IEEE Access,* vol. 7, no. 10, pp. 134422-134433, 2019. [http://dx.doi.org/10.1109/ACCESS.2019.2941905]

[20] V. Le, R. Moazeni, and M. Moh, "Improving security and performance of distributed IPFS-based web applications with Blockchain", In: *Third International Conference on Advances in Cyber Security (ACeS2021)* Springer, 2021.

[21] M. Moh, D. Nguyen, T-S. Moh, and B. Khieu, Blockchain for Efficient Public Key Infrastructure and Fault-Tolerant Distributed Consensus *Blockchain Cybersecurity, Trust, and Privacy* Springer, 2020, pp. 69-97. [http://dx.doi.org/10.1007/978-3-030-38181-3_5]

[22] B. Khieu, and M. Moh, Cloud-Centric Blockchain Public Key Infrastructure for Big Data Applications.*Security, Privacy, and Forensics Issues in Big Data,* R.C. Joshi, B.B. Gupta, Eds., IGI Global, 2019, pp. 125-140.

[23] B. Khieu, and M. Moh, "CBPKI: Cloud Blockchain-based public key infrastructure", *Proc. of 2019 Annual ACM Southeast Conference,* 2019 Kennesaw, GA, USA [http://dx.doi.org/10.1145/3299815.3314433]

[24] N. Gupta, A Deep Dive Into Security and Privacy Issues of Blockchain Technologies.*Handbook of Research on Blockchain Technology.* Academic Press, 2020, pp. 95-112. [http://dx.doi.org/10.1016/B978-0-12-819816-2.00004-6]

[25] N. Gupta, Security and privacy issues of blockchain technology.*Advanced Applications of Blockchain Technology* Springer: Singapore, 2020, pp. 207-226.

[26] J. Shen, Y. Li, Y. Zhou, and X. Wang, "Understanding I/O performance of IPFS storage: A client's perspective", *2019 IEEE/ACM 27th International Symposium on Quality of Service (IWQoS),* 2019pp.

1-10
[http://dx.doi.org/10.1145/3326285.3329052]

[27] Y. Chen, H. Li, K. Li, and J. Zhang, "An improved P2P file system scheme based on IPFS and Blockchain", *2017 IEEE International Conference on Big Data (Big Data),* 2017pp. 2652-2657
[http://dx.doi.org/10.1109/BigData.2017.8258226]

SUBJECT INDEX

A

Accelerometers 99
Access control 44, 55, 72, 117, 118, 120, 121, 122, 123, 124, 148, 150, 158
  blockchain-based 121, 123
  policies 118, 121, 122, 148
  services 117, 121
  systems 117, 118, 121
Access management system 122
Access policies 121, 122, 147
  managing dynamic 122
Adoption 53, 82
  delayed 82
  growing 53
Algorithms 19, 44, 70, 71, 108, 109, 110, 111, 114, 122, 137, 146
  cryptographic 44, 70
  machine learning 109, 122
  standard cryptographic 146
  traditional security 114
Application(s) 6, 44, 45, 129, 131, 144, 150, 154
  programming interface (API) 6, 44, 45, 129, 131, 150
  web 144, 150, 154
Architecture, blockchain cryptographic 62
ASIC mining 9
Assault 34, 54, 55, 67, 74, 77, 88, 91
  blockchain rearrangement 74
Attacks 70, 73, 82, 88
  remote 70
  transaction verification mechanism 73, 82, 88
Attribute-based encryption method 147
Authentication 101, 105
  mechanism 101
  of IoT device 105
  process 105
Automated vehicles 38

B

Banking systems use blockchain in cybersecurity 37
Big data 52
Bitcoin 27, 64, 75, 87, 88, 89, 90, 119, 121, 130
  blockchain 64, 90, 119, 130
  network 27, 75, 87, 89
  platform 121
  transaction 64
  storing 88
Blockchain 10, 12, 19, 20, 29, 31, 32, 34, 37, 40, 41, 42, 43, 67, 69, 70, 73, 75, 82, 122, 123, 127, 128, 129, 130, 131, 133, 145
  and cybersecurity combination 41
  applying 31
  authenticate devices 34
  business-oriented 130
  community 67
  consensus system 75
  cybersecurity 29, 37
  development environments 130
  ecosystem 127, 128, 129, 130, 131, 145
  encryption 29, 37
  in cyber security 34
  networks 10, 12, 19, 20, 40, 41, 42, 43, 67, 69, 70, 73, 82, 129, 130
  nodes 82, 122, 123, 133, 145
  popular ledger technology 32
  processes 145
  records data 40
  for supply chains 130
Blockchain system 26, 28, 32, 42, 51, 77, 87, 127, 129, 140, 145
Blockchain-based 29, 32, 43, 84, 122
  architecture 122
  cybersecurity 43
  cyber threat intelligence 84
  system 29, 32
Blockchain-enabled 22

healthcare applications 22
industry 22
Blockchain technology 37, 40, 142
adopted 37, 40
applying 142
emerging 142
Blockchain transactions 49, 65, 73, 82, 119, 132, 144, 146
Brute force method 107
Byzantine general's problem 11

C

Chain split attacks 45
Cloud 30, 66, 30, 86, 109, 110, 121, 143, 144
storage 66
system 30
technology 143, 144
Cloud computing 98, 142
platforms 98
CNAME record 151
Cold wallet system 88
Computational complexity 109
Conduct proof-of-concept tests 139
Consensus 8, 10, 11, 12, 16, 69, 81, 145
mechanisms 8, 10, 11, 12, 16, 81
method 69
process 145
Consensus algorithms 22, 32, 82, 103, 104
blockchain's 32
Continuous-time Markov chain (CTMC) 90
COVID-19 pandemic 97
CPU mining 9
Credentials 12, 123
combined 12
Creditworthy ecosystem 139
Cryptocurrencies and financial transactions 118
Cryptographic 8, 67, 70, 77, 81, 84, 109, 119, 124
communication 84
designs 77
protocol 119
techniques 8, 70, 109
Cyber threat intelligence (CTI) 84, 92
Cybercriminals 30, 49, 62, 70, 74
Cybersecurity 31, 32, 33
blockchain-powered 33
of blockchain technology 31
tool 32

D

DAO attack 72
DApp 137, 138
developers 137
transactions 138
Data 39, 40, 41, 59, 101, 104, 129
recovery 41
redundancy 129
transfer 39, 59, 104
transmission 40, 101
Decentralized 6, 54, 56, 63, 64, 144, 148
arrangements 54, 56
Autonomous Organizations (DAOs) 6, 63, 64
network 144, 148
Defense 53, 62
advanced research projects agency (DARPA) 53
research activity 62
Delegated proof of stake (DPoS) 8, 10
Design 38, 56, 59, 82, 90, 121, 128, 130, 142, 143
ecosystem 128
insecure security 59
Devices 27, 31, 33, 38, 50, 51, 58, 59, 86, 88, 98, 99, 101, 109, 123
cold 88
communication 101
Digital security business 52, 53
Distributed 34, 36, 49, 63, 127, 135, 136, 158
ledger technology (DLT) 34, 36, 49, 135, 136
network 63, 127, 158
Double spending 73, 84
attack 73
security measures 84

E

ECDSA cryptographic technique 70
Encryption 36, 108, 109
blockchain's technology 36
homomorphic 108, 109
Energy consumption 20
Environment, software programme 67
ERP systems 134
Ethereum 63, 72, 123, 130, 138, 139, 147, 149
accounts 139

based smart contract platforms 63
blockchain 72, 123, 130, 138, 139, 147, 149
virtual machine (EVM) 72, 147

F

FAW attack problem 92
Fee, bitcoin mining 64
Fork after withholding (FAW) 75, 92, 93

H

Hand-shaking process 133
Hardware wallet information 87
Hashed health's system 36
Hashing techniques 103
Healthcare companies 35, 36
Human-only solvable puzzles (HOSPs) 86, 93
Hyperledger 102, 130
blockchain 130
project 102
HYPR corp 52

I

Information 52, 53, 59
security 52, 59
storage 53
transmission 59
Infrastructure, cyber-physical 38
Internet security infrastructures 94
Interplanetary file system (IPFS) 142, 143, 144, 147, 148, 150, 151, 154, 156, 157, 158
IoT 49, 104, 148
gadgets 49
networks 104, 148
IoT device 104, 117
data management and data transfer 104
management 117
IPFS 143, 148, 154
data storage 148
implementation 154
network 143

M

Management information systems 129
Mechanisms 5, 8, 10, 30, 88, 89, 121, 124, 131, 139
blockchain-based production credit 131
consensus-based ledger 139
Miners decrypt 9
Mining 9, 16, 18, 19, 31, 111, 113, 133
machine system 31
process 9, 16, 18, 19, 111, 113, 133
Money 35, 49, 50, 56, 58, 67, 73, 74, 77, 130, 132, 133, 135, 142, 145
digital 56
transferring 135
virtual foreign 67
Multichain technology 132, 133

N

Nature 1, 11, 51, 119
communicated 51
NEO platforms 71
Network 5, 8, 10, 11, 12, 20, 33, 64, 65, 67, 68, 69, 73, 74, 81, 85, 86, 89, 93, 98, 102, 145
communication threats 67
cryptocurrency 64
devices 98
edge 86

O

Office of the comptroller of the currency (OCC) 37
OpenSSL encryption 157

P

Peer-to-peer 63, 85, 93, 106, 119
communication 93
network 63, 85, 106, 119
PoW 9, 90
based security technique 90
consensus mechanism 9

R

Reducing human safety adversity by cyber-attacks 38
Reinforcement learning (RL) 122

S

Safety, software program 67
Secured transactions 42
Security 27, 30, 31, 34, 51, 55, 59, 64, 70, 76, 81, 94, 97, 103, 109, 114, 117, 142, 143, 144, 157, 158
  arrangements, transmitting blockchain cyber 51
  blockchain's 70
  contemporary 59
  measures 76, 94
Servers 109, 122, 123, 148
  proxy 122, 123
  third-party 109
  web 148
Service(s) 32, 39, 40, 55, 64, 65, 66, 67, 70, 82, 88, 89, 92, 118, 121, 128, 131, 158
  attacks 55, 65, 82
  blockchain-based 158
  duplicating brokerage 66
Smart 38, 97, 150
  agriculture systems 97
  contracts, integrated 150
  health care systems 97
  homes 97
  security home systems 97
  switches option 38
  watches 97
Smart home 99, 114
  application 99
  devices 114
Software 44, 66, 76, 86, 121
  antivirus 76
Supply chain 32, 33
  activities 33
  management 32

T

Target network communications 65
Taxonomy of attack surfaces 66
Techniques 69, 90, 92, 108, 109
  security protection 90
Technological 134, 139
  skills 139
  trust factor 134
Technology 27, 30, 34, 35, 36, 45, 49, 99, 100, 122, 124, 135, 136,
  blockchain cybersecurity 27, 36
  cryptocurrency wallet 35
  distributed access management 122
  distributed ledger 34, 36, 49, 135, 136
  recordkeeping 124
  secure 35
  traditional security 45
  transformative 30
  wearable 99, 100
Threats, cyber 41, 45
Traditional banking application 8
Transactional data 105
Transactions 5, 8, 10, 19, 42, 43, 44, 63, 64, 67, 73, 82, 87, 88, 89, 102, 104, 107, 108, 117, 119, 120, 121, 131, 133, 145, 147
  automatic 108
  development process 131
  fee 10, 133, 147
  legitimate 64
  policy creation 117, 121
  public address's 63

V

Validating gadgets 50
Validation process 5, 7, 8, 16, 44, 120
Value-generating assets 58
Vehicular Ad-hoc networks (VANET) 63
Violating government laws 43
Virtual 67, 71, 72, 93, 118, 147
  footprint 67
  machines 71, 72, 93, 118, 147
Visual monitoring, real-time 130
Voting system 10
Vulnerabilities 45, 62, 66, 67, 71, 76, 81, 82, 102, 128, 132

W

Wasted resources 21
Web 86, 93, 149
  application firewall (WAF) 86, 93
  application server 149

Z

Zone-based wallet encrypts data 87

Made in the USA
Las Vegas, NV
21 August 2025

735e5fb1-ff1a-4f6a-97e8-e68598e6901bR04